DOODLEBUGS, GAS MASKS & GUM

CHILDREN'S VOICES FROM THE SECOND WORLD WAR

CHRISTINA REX

AMBERLEY PUBLISHING

To
PETER REX and ANNE GIESSER
with thanks for these years of love, friendship, trust and laughter.

First published 2008

Amberley Publishing Plc
Cirencester Road, Chalford,
Stroud, Gloucestershire, GL6 8PE

www.amberley-books.com

British Library Cataloguing in Publication Data.
A catalogue record for this book is available from the British Library.

ISBN 978 1 84868 085 2

Typesetting and Origination by diagrafmedia
Printed in Great Britain

CONTENTS

ABOUT THE AUTHOR

Christina Rex was two years old when war broke out and eight when VE Day was celebrated. She has interviewed childhood friends and collected their reminiscences about the war, as well as researching published memoirs and contemporary newspapers in preparation for the writing of this book. She lives in Ely with her husband, Peter Rex, the author of five history books. Her son, Dr Richard Rex, is Director of Studies in History at Queens' College, Cambridge. She is currently writing a new history of British women's experience of the Second World War, also for Amberley Publishing.

INTRODUCTION

This book came about thanks to a wish to leave for my grandsons a true account of what life was like for children during the Second World War, from which grew the idea of compiling it from a sample of "those who were there", to represent several different ages of 'child' that would also present a view of what childhood was like then in countries other than Britain. Largely, the recollections presented have not been published elsewhere, save for those of Louise Milbourn, who published privately a book based on the correspondence from her American foster family, her sister and herself and her parents back in Plymouth, and Leslie Oakey and Marie Jordan, who both wrote short volumes of memories of the Ely area which were printed by the Ely Museum. All other material comes from my school contemporaries, relatives, friends and friends-of-friends, and from research into six years of back copies of the Ely Standard newspaper.

The main title of this book reflects three things that affected the lives of all of us during the war. Doodlebugs were the nightmare revenge weapon of the last months of it, gas masks we were all issued with, and "gum" came into the language with the arrival of the American G.Is in this country after the entry of the U.S. to the war, post Pearl Harbor. "Got any gum, chum?" became a catch-phrase of the children, and the wrappers of the sticks of gum handed out by the Americans were often avidly collected - they were considerably less dangerous than shrapnel!

My thanks for their efficient assistance go to the staff of the Ely Library, who were extremely helpful in my tussles with the microfiche reader; to the current editor of the Ely Standard for permission to quote from those back numbers; to Dr. Anne Hudson, Head Teacher of the Central Foundation Girls School; Tower Hamlets, for her ready permission to use the material in their Evacuation Chronicle (and to Margaret Haq of the same school for her assistance); to David Lerner of Alumni, the journal of the Jews Free School, Kenton, for his generous help with detail and especially photographs of the school's evacuation stay in Ely; to the Trustees of the Ely Museum for permission to quote from Marie Jordan's work; to Leslie Oakey for permission to use his work; to Muriel Gent for her enthusiasm and assistance with detail of the C.F.G.S. in Ely and to Louise Milbourn, for permission to quote from her book. Then thanks are due to my friend and neighbour

Nancy Voak, who skilfully translated into visual terms the sketch and verbal description of Monette Meulet's expeditionary vehicle! Above all, though, I must thank those 37 girls from my school, Beckenham County Grammar School for Girls, most, but not all, of them in my actual year, who sent me their wartime recollections and photographs, with ready permission to use them, and Jill Jones, Adremians secretary, for permission to use material from wartime school magazines. Then, those marvellous friends along with my sister Wendy Walton and my husband Peter, who have been so supportive and encouraging in this whole project, have to be thanked. I am indebted to you all, and just hope the end result of all your efforts justifies them!

This book is not, I hope, a glorification of war, nor any kind of "them and us" account of a conflict that happened nearly seventy years ago, just a telling of our story while we are still able to do so and before the social historians turn it into yet another academic study of the effects of conflict. We lived our childhood during a war; we were bombed, shot at, some of us suffered occupation; we lost our homes to high explosive; sometimes, horrifyingly, we lost family members or neighbours to fighting or to bombing; we were participants in the huge social upheaval of mass evacuation; but above all we were children and those included in these pages were happy despite everything. We played, went to school, made our own entertainment and had adventures unimaginable to the children of today. I know there were many children desperately unhappy and exploited due to the evacuation; I just did not encounter any of them as contributors so could not include that aspect in this text.

Contributors told their stories straightforwardly, as a matter of record. I hope this is how I in turn have presented them here, as a matter of record of the general ordinariness of childhood in a time of unparalleled upheaval and conflict. The research and writing have been a challenge; I hope you enjoy reading the results.

The voices contained within this book are written as quoted and in their own words.

There are a few sets of initials used throughout the book:
C.F.S is the Central Foundation School
G.T.C. is the Girls' Training Corps
J.F.S. is the Jews Free School
W.V.S. is the Womens Voluntary Service.

Christina Rex.
Ely, May 2008.

CHAPTER 1

DECLARATION AND PREPARATION

From 1933 onwards, after Hitler had become Chancellor of Germany, another major war became almost inevitable as his lust for the restoration of the Germany he had known prior to the First World War and his resentment of the "humiliation" of the terms of the Treaty of Versailles which ended it appeared to grow in parallel and without restraint, as the country left the League of Nations in 1933. Most European powers, not wanting to repeat the conflict of 25 years earlier, appeased the monster in his territorial demands, serving only to increase them and permitting him to get away with the creation, in 1934/35, of a new German air force and the expansion of the army and navy.

Military expansion continued over the next two years, with troops marching into the Rhineland (demilitarised since Versailles, 1919), the encouragement of German nationalism in the Sudetenland (then part of Czechoslovakia) and the increasing hounding and harassing of Jews throughout the country.

Hitler annexed Austria in 1938 and invaded the Sudetenland; then came Kristallnacht, the smashing of the windows of Jewish-owned shops and businesses and the despoiling of synagogues throughout German-controlled territories. Chamberlain, the perpetual appeaser, flew to Munich, where the agreement reached divided up the territory of Czechoslovakia, returning with the infamous piece of paper that was supposed to have brought peace in our time.

1939 came and with it ever more demands, now centring on the Danzig Corridor, which allowed Poland access to ports on the Baltic. German domestic legislation forbade Jews to drive cars and Heydrich was detailed to speed up the evacuation of all Jews from the country. Remaining Jews were ordered to surrender all precious metals and stones, and anti-Nazi ministers were dismissed from the government. By July 1939, Jewish emigration from Germany had peaked at 78,000 as mass deportations to Poland had started. Attacks on Polish property in Danzig commenced. Earlier, Britain and France had pledged aid to Poland in the event of aggression, all three countries signing a mutual assistance agreement. Border troubles escalated and the Polish Army was mobilised. Hitler issued an ultimatum on Danzig and the Polish Corridor, followed the next day by Britain initiating the evacuation of vulnerable civilians from London and major cities.

The same day, early in the morning, Germany invaded Poland, while Ireland, Italy, Norway, Finland and Switzerland declared their neutrality. Britain issued an ultimatum to Germany requiring an affirmative response by 11.00am on Sunday September 3, 1939 which was ignored. This is where this book commences.

At the appointed hour on Sunday 3 September, most of the nation huddled round its radio sets to hear what the response had been, hoping that sense would prevail whilst knowing that it would not.

Jean Parrott (b.1933. West Wickham)

Certainly at the start I have only an impression of the atmosphere around, first of pending problems and finally - well it has happened! We were spending our annual holiday at Shanklin when my father had a telegram recalling him and we had to travel back on trains with no lights, change at stations with no lights and it was all rather frightening and confusing to a 6 year old.

Diana Scott (b.1933. Beckenham).

My mother and I were staying with relatives in Hove for the week leading up to 3rd September. I remember being very shaken on Friday 1st September when we came back from the beach to find my Aunt (a most controlled lady) in floods of tears. She said to my mother "Hitler has walked into Poland". My first reaction was that it was strange that my Aunt should be so upset about someone going for a walk! For the next two days, we listened to the radio constantly but we still missed the broadcast about the declaration of war.

John Taylor (b.1930. Coventry)

As a nine year old, I realised that something unusual was afoot in the months leading up to the war. In early August 1939 I was taken to Bournemouth with my family for a week's holiday. On the beach I remember making friends with another boy about my own age. I still recall being told quite distinctly that he was Jewish, from Austria.

Joyce Kitching (b.1935. Doncaster)

We were on holiday at Bridlington when war was declared. We were staying in a converted bus called "Ling-a-Longa". The warden came and told my dad we would have to black out all the windows.

Christina Watt (b.1937. Hull, E. Yorkshire)

My parents sat listening to the radio, with mum sniffing and muttering "oh no, not again". I sat on the sofa, clad in my best brown velvet dress, playing with dad's 'smoker's companion', a circular wooden ashtray on a longish spindle with a larger circular base. This was my steering wheel. "Vroom vroom" I said revelling in not being stopped. (Generally the game provoked the response "Stop that, you Tina. You'll break it".) "Och dammit" said dad as he stood up and turned the radio off. Mum stopped my game...things were back to normal. Later I asked if I could watch a TV programme (we had one of the earliest sets, very small, which took ages to warm up and on Sunday afternoon there was something for children). She said no and, asked why not, replied that Hitler might appear on it. Asked who Hitler was, she replied "A nasty man".

Anna Piper (Anne Giesser, b.1937. Winnenden, Stuttgart)
Early memories - a Sunday lunchtime - listening to Hitler making a speech on the radio, the voice never since being forgotten - Vati (daddy) lying on the settee with me sitting on him - everybody being very grave. It must have been the Sunday Britain declared war on Germany. Shortly after this, Vati volunteered, despite being in a reserved occupation.

Valerie Bragg (b.1929. Barking)
My younger sister and I were evacuated to Cirencester on September 1st 1939. Our father was a Conscientious Objector. He committed suicide on 3rd September 1939.

The British Government, as the inevitability of war drew ever closer during the later 1930s and mindful of the devastation caused by it during the First World War, became convinced that some kind of gas would be Hitler's primary weapon of choice against this country. Display advertisements appeared in newspapers advising how to protect house and life in the event of gas attack and radio talks were given on the subject. One method of gas-proofing a house, they advised, was to hang a wet blanket (but which had been wrung out after wetting so that it did not drip!) inside the front hall in such a way that it formed a barrier against anything getting through to any part of the house. Betty Yates' family in Wimbledon did this, but after a few days decided to dry off the blanket and restore it to normal use, as the clammy dampness it caused throughout the house made the place very cold.

Another manifestation of governmental concern was the issue of gas masks to the entire civil population. This was started well before the declaration of war so that by 3 September most of the population had their gas mask and those that had missed out soon acquired them during the rest of that month. Adult masks were of black rubber, fitting closely round the face, with the fitting adjustable by straps, a visor at the front and the snout - this contained the filter at its base through which all air was drawn and filtered to make it safely breathable. Children's masks were called Mickey Mouse as they were of bright pinkish-red rubber with protrusions on either side of the head representing ears, presumably to persuade the children to wear them without too much trauma. From vivid recollection the writer states that these subterfuges were not completely successful; the masks stank of rubber, the visor tended to mist up and there was a feeling of fright at being so enclosed. However, not everyone felt the same!

Jennifer Bedford (b.1941. Norwich)
The issue of gas masks is still vivid. I remember being most indignant when we were issued with them that some children in our road had Mickey Mouse ones and mine for some reason was a basic model, probably because I had a big head and they didn't do Mickey Mouse ones in my size!

Jean Runciman (b.1937. Beckenham)
I loved my pink Mickey Mouse gas mask, which we had collected from the Town Hall and, as instructed, carried it everywhere with me. My mother's two brothers had been gassed in the trenches in World War I and never fully recovered, so the family were under no illusions as to what gas masks were for.

Diana Scott (b.1932. Beckenham)
In 1938 our local air-raid warden had arrived at our house to fit us up with gas masks. I was 6 years old and found the whole thing most intriguing. I was taught how to make sure the mask was working by putting a piece of cardboard at the bottom of it, (while I was wearing it,) and if the cardboard remained sticking there, the mask was in working order. This drill was carried out at school at various times throughout the war - we had to take our gas masks with us everywhere. They were issued in square cardboard boxes but most people bought cases to put them in - they became a necessary part of one's wardrobe like a handbag.

Richard Ellison (b.1935. Liverpool)
During the "Phoney War" I went off from home at Waterloo to the station for a train to my Kindergarten with my gas mask in a yellow tin slung over my shoulder.

Peter Rex (b.1930. Bristol)
Gas masks were issued in their little cardboard boxes and I remember that we had to test them by putting them on then entering a green van which was then filled with some sort of gas to test the mask. Fortunately there were no problems!

Gwen Pritchitt (b.1937. Hayes. Kent)
Other memories are of going into the gas mask testing van which was parked in the road and being warned about picking anything up - however attractive they looked - in case they were 'butterfly' bombs.

There were also respirators for babies. These were extraordinary devices that the baby was placed inside (the top was clear so the child was not too greatly panicked) and there was a hand operated pump so the mother could operate it while the baby slumbered. How mothers managed with being supposed to have these masks with them at all times one cannot guess. As the war progressed and the dreaded gas did not appear, then carrying the masks became a thing of the past - certainly outside of the big cities. The writer has no recollection of gas masks in the country village where she lived, no-one took them to school and they were not taken on visits to any of the nearby towns. They were just left in a safe place for handing back at the end of the war.

Perhaps as a result of the heavy bombing of Guernica by the German Air Force during the Spanish Civil War (1937) the government also acknowledged that high explosive posed a considerable threat to the country. Initially trenches were dug in parks and playgrounds so that people could shelter, but these were a temporary measure. For households with gardens, the Anderson shelter was issued. This was a corrugated iron "shed" with a curved roof. A large hole was dug by the householder and the shed half buried. The earth removed to make the hole was put over the roof to reinforce it and many people grew vegetables of some kind there. The shelter had a door and frequently had bunks built inside. The only snag was that, in most towns, the things were likely to flood so that they were not the best idea for protection.

Various authorities developed ways of coping, but the best method was the Morrison shelter. This was for use indoors, a metal structure with solid roof, cage-like walls of crossed metal mesh, and a solid base, about table height and in many households it did replace the family dining table. A mattress was placed inside it and the family would shelter there. However, there were all sorts of solutions to the shelter problem, public and private.

Brenda Booker (b.1937. West Wickham, Kent)
At Farncombe, the siren was near the end of our garden, and when it went off my mother, brother and I would hide in the coal cellar under the stairs.

Frank Bunce (b.1938. Battersea)
We lived in a terraced house in Battersea. Brick air-raid shelters had been built in the street outside and at the first alternating wail of the siren we would rush out to these.

Sylvia Bunce (b.1937. Anerley)
An early memory is being dragged out of bed when a raid began. Mother would run down our long garden, carrying me all wrapped up in her arms and shrapnel would be falling from the sky. She would leap into the Anderson shelter and we only emerged when the 'All Clear' sounded.

Richard Ellison
In the first air-raids over Liverpool, we went down to the cellar with my mother and grandfather who taught me the symbols on a pack of cards while we ate biscuits and my father, out on ARP patrol, would call down to us through the grille.

John Gamêt (b.1933. West Wickham)
The Anderson shelter was a major construction project by a group of amateurs, very entertaining. The first time the air-raid warning sounded we rushed out to the shelter only to find it two feet deep in water so we rushed back indoors. Following these problems a makeshift shelter was constructed of 2 armchairs and a settee against the central load-bearing wall of the house. We huddled there for several nights until the Morrison arrived, much more robust.

Sheila Kelly (b.1932. Derbyshire)
We lived at a hospital and when the sirens went, my parents would wake us, get us dressed and we walked uphill to the underground communal shelter shared by the medical staff. This walk became dangerous when the guns began to fire from the emplacements on Derby race course. We cowered against a wall.

Joy King (b.1937. Penge)
Although we had an Anderson on which my father grew marrows we sometimes just sat under our dining table - not a Morrison, just an ordinary oak table - during an air-raid and I have an abiding memory of mother sitting with her eyes closed and her fingers in her ears!

Joyce Kitching

There was a shelter in the school playground. We went down some steps and sat in rows with our gas masks on and our feet in puddles of water as it was always getting flooded.

Glenda Lindsay (b.1937. Beckenham)

We often slept in bunks in the reinforced brick built shelter next to the front door. I remember the condensation dripping on us at night. If during the night my aunt wanted to use the outside (only) toilet at the end of the yard she would put a saucepan on her head as protection from the shrapnel!

Margaret Mould (b.1937. West Wickham)

At the start of the war we used to scramble into the cupboard under the stairs with the smelly gas meter! We progressed to a concrete undergound shelter in the garden which was usually flooded so when the siren went first thing on was 'wellies'. I had a shelf bunk, the adults sat on slatted benches. We had heat - an electric bowl fire! How did we escape electrocution?

Marlene Newson (b.1938. Ely)

I recall when the siren sounded my mother bundling me in a blanket and hurrying to the shelter, which was in a small lane close by, belonging to the Brewery, I think, some sort of underground store turned into a shelter.

Molly Oakley (b.1937. Anerley)

We did seem to spend quite a lot of time in the air-raid shelter and if the raid took place during the day my mother would open the front door and invite passers by to share our shelter and a cup of tea.

Corinne Older (b.1937. West Wickham)

I never remembered the sitting room before it was reinforced with large wooden uprights, the windows covered in brown paper and the French doors all hidden by sandbags. We slept there - my brother, sister, Granny and me.

Jean Parrott

We began to sleep regularly in the Anderson my father had erected. I remember it being built and a plank left in the hole that was dug in order to allow a hedgehog to escape. Dad had dug a central well with concrete surround on which we could sit. There was a full length bunk one side and shelves the other over seating, made more comfortable with slatted wooden seating and cushions. Candles were used for lighting.

Gwen Pritchitt

I remember dad dug out a huge hole under the apple tree near the back door and built a shelter for us. We used to play 'house' in there. At first, when the siren sounded, we used to dive into the coat cupboard under the stairs until the 'All Clear'. Later I remember my mum coming into my bedroom and carrying me out to the shelter in the garden, during the night. Later, we had a Morrison as I had had pneumonia and mum considered it damaging for me to be in a damp, cold shelter outside.

Peter Rex
My father built an air-raid shelter, about 12 or 14 feet square, in the back basement under the concreted yard. He piled earth over about one third of the yard, several feet thick, for extra protection and installed bunk beds in the cellar. It was only rarely used, probably during daylight raids, and when the Blitz proper began, we used the local community shelter as the cellar was not really safe. The only exit was up the basement stairs into the house and if that had been hit there would have been no way out.

Jean Runciman
We were eligible for an Anderson, a corrugated iron monstrosity erected in the back garden. However, after a shower of rain it filled with water and became unfit for use. The authorities were forced to line it with a very thick concrete shell. This kept the water out and made an excellent fishpond after the war when the shelter was removed.

John Taylor
My parents had cleaned out the outside coalhouse with its static water tank roof, to act as a shelter. There were sleeping areas for my 3-year-old brother and me and chairs for my parents. While it would not have stood up to a direct hit it did provide shelter from the flying glass and falling shrapnel which I used to collect.

Jill Thomas (b.1937. Beckenham)
We had a shelter in the garden at first but I do not remember ever going into it as it always seemed to have water in it. Then we had an indoor one, so my brother and I slept in it while my parents had their mattress on top of it and slept there. Mother had friends opposite without a shelter so when the siren went the mother and her three children joined us in ours. It was pretty crowded, as you can imagine.

Linda Zerk (b.1937. Beckenham)
We had a Morrison shelter in a room at the back of the kitchen. We slept there when the raids were bad. I can't remember Father ever sleeping there. Mother did, but always with her head well and truly out from under the table as she suffered with claustrophobia. One can't help but wonder what would have happened if a bomb had actually hit us. One night the cupboard above my bed (in the room close by the shelter) burst open and I was hit on the head by a can of baked beans - my only war wound!

Ruth Hixson (b.1937. Anerley)
We didn't have a proper shelter but my father fixed a wide shelf in the alcoves beside the living room fireplace making hopefully safe places to shelter during an air-raid. He made another larger construction under the window, more suitable for adults.

Louise Milbourn (b.1931. Plymouth) records that Plymouth was very heavily bombed. The shelter the family used had been placed so that it could be shared with their grandparents, who lived next door. It had been dug into the Devon hedge (where the hedge is grown on a bank separating two properties) between the houses, taking advantage of the difference in height between the two gardens to lessen the digging load. It was a dark, dank place with the smell of damp earth, containing narrow bunks for the children to sleep on and another where the adults sat. For her elder sister, Blanche, with her fear of spiders, it was a decidedly inhospitable place. There everyone stayed until the 'All Clear' sounded, although the aerial hunt between searchlight and bombers was fascinating. They were not permitted to watch.

In addition to trying to ensure that all suitable properties had their own shelter, the authorities also built communal shelters in the crowded streets, while in the towns and cities, basements of commercial and municipal buildings became shelters, with sandbag barricades at the entrance. In London, after a short while, during the Blitz, the Underground stations became the shelter of choice for many thousands of Londoners.

There were problems arising – a report from Norwich said that some surface street shelters had to be kept locked because of wilful damage done inside them by irresponsible people and gangs of youths. People were asked to watch out for street shelter smashers. The need to find the key to a shelter had cost lives in a German raid on the city in April 1942.

The last "preparation" measure by the government was the imposition of the blackout, which was signalled well before the declaration so that people would have suitable provisions in place when necessary. The blackout meant exactly what it said - from dusk, there should be no light visible in any part of the country, urban or rural, to betray the presence of buildings or to act as a means of guidance to enemy aircraft. All windows had to be covered in something which would not allow light through. Generally that meant that special curtains were made, of heavy black fabric, the householder frequently also lining these to make doubly sure. They were normally much wider than the window they were covering and a lot longer, so that no stray flicker of light might penetrate to the outside. Shutters were used by many households but had the drawback of not being swift to close. The order also applied to all glass panels in external doors and the writer recalls her father painting them in thick black paint. Others screwed wooden panels over them. Roof lights also had to be covered which must have caused quite a problem for those whose properties boasted them. The portrayal in "Dad's Army" of the A.R.P. Warden on his nightly inspection of the effectiveness of blackout measures, and his cry of "Put out that light!" was very true to life; that is how it happened. Offences against blackout regulations were punishable by fines.

There were considerable drawbacks outside the home, because the night was pitch black and very dangerous in the absence of all street lighting. Pedestrians fell off pavements because they could not see the kerb, or walked into trees, or walls, or even into vehicles. Something had to be done, so white paint came into its own - as bands round trees or on walls or marking out the kerb, and it was permissible to carry a really small pocket torch with only a minimal strip of light (masking out the main beam, as with car lights) to be pointed at the path in front of the pedestrian, not pointing upwards at all. The casualty figures from blackout accidents reduced considerably after these measures were introduced.

Blackout regulations were strictly enforced during the long months of the Phoney War so that when the Blitz finally arrived, the ritual of "the blackout" was well entrenched.

CHAPTER 2

EVACUATION I, HESITATION AND CONFLAGRATION

The government, during the 1930s, although hoping to appease Hitler, nevertheless was very concerned for the safety of the civil population in the event of war. Towards the end of the First World War there had been air-raids on Britain and, after the recent example of Guernica, (where in 1937 the city was bombed to total desolation by the Condor Squadron of the Luftwaffe, "assisting" Franco's Nationalists in the Spanish Civil War) people were worried about the danger. Official plans for the evacuation of those who could not adequately care for themselves, children, the elderly and the disabled, were drawn up. After Munich, the plans divided the country into three "areas" - Evacuation, Neutral and Reception, Evacuation designating those areas at greatest risk, like London and the industrialised cities and ports, and Reception those areas which would take the people, evacuees, like East Anglia, Kent and Wales.

Schools were evacuated as a unit, pupils and teachers alike moving to the same area all on the same day. Siblings were supposed to go together, with the younger ones accompanying the school of the eldest. Under-fives were evacuated with their mothers. As the declaration of war became inevitable, the evacuation plans were put into action on the morning of 31 August. Over the next four days nearly two million people were evacuated, 1.5 million of them children, more than half of whom were in school blocs. There are many excellent studies of the logistics of this incredible mass movement of people so it is not proposed to rehearse them all over again here, but to consider both private evacuations from the Beckenham area of Kent and the evacuation from the East End of London of two schools, the Jews Free School and the Central Foundation School for Girls, which both spent the war years in Ely, Cambridgeshire. Other stories include two young girls who respectively were evacuated to America and South Africa.

The local paper, the Ely Standard, on Friday 1 September 1939, reported that arrangements to receive evacuees were in place - and it also reported, which must have been a source of great comfort to the citizens in those troubled times, that all poisonous snakes and most of the others in London Zoo would be destroyed at once on the outbreak of war, but that the twenty-eight-foot python had been reprieved and would be kept in a specially guarded tank.

The following week's paper, 8 September, reported that although just under 18,000 evacuees were expected, only 8,443 had so far been billeted in the county (the Isle of Ely was then a separate county from Cambridgeshire), and that the reception had gone off very well. There were many Jewish children, numbers of whom had only been in the country for a very short time prior to evacuation and did not speak English, so it had been decided to open a Jewish home in St. Mary's Street, where they would be looked after by their teachers; the home being run on similar lines to hostels where they had lived in London. Most of these children were Polish and had not adapted yet to English food and customs, these problems would be overcome by the new home. Education would be provided when the home was organised. Not all Jewish children in Ely were accommodated there, but all those with the language problem were. All the food would be prepared following Jewish dietary laws as there had been problems over this with families who were unaware of the existence of these rules.

Leslie Oakey (b.1928. Ely)
When school resumed that autumn (1939), among the pupils were some very unfamiliar faces. Refugees from Austria, Poland and Czechoslovakia had arrived in Ely and had now appeared at the local schools. They were a strange and pathetic sight to we insular boys. They wore weird and non-English clothes, with trousers which reached below the knee, unlike our own. I remember only two names, the brothers Pinkosovitch, Jewish boys who could not speak a word of English and who clung together in the playground as we taunted them unmercifully. In class they sat silent as the bustle of the school day unfolded around them. Occasionally they would be seen to have tears coursing down their cheeks, eliciting more scorn from their classmates. Later they went to their own Jewish school which was housed in Hereward Hall, courtesy of the King's School. The Jewish Free School had been evacuated from Bethnal Green and soon became an integral part of the life of the city. Along with the Central Foundation School for Girls, which was housed in Archer House, the two schools remained in Ely for some considerable time and many lasting friendships were forged.

"Mig" (b.1926. Pupil of Central Foundation School evacuated to Ely)
I was going to be evacuated with my sister who was 18 and soon to start at Teachers' Training College. With our new rucksacks we went with the school to Liverpool Street Station. Packed into carriages, luggage piled onto the racks, we chattered and chattered, wondering where we were going. It was hot and the carriage very crowded. The journey was a nightmare. It got hotter and hotter. We ate sweets, sandwiches and chocolate - there was nothing else to do - and we got thirstier and thirstier. At the end, apart from the heat, the memorable part was stopping at Bishops Stortford where helpers walked along the platform with buckets and ladled out water into mugs for us, just like watering animals on market day! What humiliation, but how welcome was the water and after all, the buckets did look brand new!
Suddenly, over the flat countryside Ely Cathedral came into sight, with its tall tower at one end and beautiful octagonal tower in the middle. Our destination was the City of Ely, which, although a city by virtue of having a Cathedral was really a market town set on a hill. We pulled into the station, collected our rations and were then transported to a small village called Littleport, outside Ely, to stay until school arrangements had been sorted out.

Muriel Gent (b.1928. Stepney)

I was 11 and my sister Phyllis, 7. We lived in Brick Lane. Noise and bustle went on night and day. We walked to school through Spitalfields Market and on that day in 1939 all the traders shouted out goodbyes and good luck. The day was hot and long, but exciting.

We spent the first week in Littleport. The cottage was tiny, our bedroom miniscule and we slept together in a single bed. It was warm, cosy and welcoming but during the night we both woke and looked out of the window. I can remember the moonlight and we could see endless fields with no sign of life - no houses, trees, lights or sounds - and we cried. After a week we were moved to Ely where we spent the next four years in the same billet, before returning to London in 1943.

Leslie Oakey

The culture shock for evacuees and "new" families alike was profound. Some of the children had never seen the countryside before and were quite unprepared for what was to come. Many of the children were verminous which was a great surprise to the mothers of the local children. Mistakes were made, for instance Jewish children billeted on Catholic families, but eventually things were sorted out and the children found homes where they were welcome.

Pam Blakeman (b.1929. Ely)

One of the excitements of my life, as an only child, was the arrival of evacuees and I can remember being most disappointed when we were not allocated any until about 2 weeks after most other people. Then it was three sisters from the Central Foundation School who stayed with us for a year or two. The two younger girls both had their hair in ringlets and after a while we all had nits. I was terrified one would drop out on a book at school and be seen by everyone! However with special soap, possibly Jeyes' Fluid and much hair washing and combing we all became clean again. This was not before the sisters' mother, at that time living in Ely, had been instructed by the Billeting Officer to wash her children's hair herself!

Marie Jordan (b.1933. Sutton nr. Ely)

We had two very different sets of evacuees. Firstly, two Jewish boys, one Austrian, who had seen his grandparents run over and killed by the Germans because the grandfather had refused to make the officer a pair of boots, the other, Polish, who spent most of the time in his bedroom. They only stayed until the Jewish home was opened in Ely. Then mother had a pair of teenage girls from the East End of London to stay with us. They came with just the clothes they stood up in. Much to mum's disgust, they hadn't any proper undies to wear, just a ladies slip tied at the shoulder straps to make it fit their size then a safety pin held it together between their legs to form a sort of cami-knickers. They also had fleas and mum soon had them combing and brushing their hair. She soon had this pair as she thought they should be. They eventually went to Bury St. Edmunds.

Pat Manning (b.1929. Lower Sydenham)

We were evacuees from Haseltine Road School, Lower Sydenham and had been in the Poundfield Hall, Jarvis Brook, Sussex since dinner time on 1st September 1939. The ladies were clearing up. Edna Ely and I had watched all the other children leave for their foster homes and no one wanted us so we hoped we were going back home. Now it was five o'clock and as we piled into the back of a car and headed back along the lane we couldn't wait to catch the train home to London. On the way, we stopped at what seemed to be a church and were told to knock on the door. We were being billeted at the Rest House of Lady Trevor! We were taken up the centre staircase to a room immediately above the front door and told that we were NEVER to go into the West wing of the house which was Lady Trevor's. Lady Trevor died after Christmas and I was rebilleted with a rose grower and his family, which suited me far more, but I have never forgotten the mysterious Lady who lived in the West wing.

June Thomsitt (b.1937. Beckenham)
My father worked as an engineer at Croydon Airport. Early on in the war it was bombed. My father was lucky to escape injury. He was ineligible for the armed forces having heart problems. The engineering company relocated to Snowdonia and we all went off with him, my mother, two sisters, brother and myself. We rented a very small cottage in the village of Llanrug. It was very primitive.

Jill Moxon (b.1937. Hayes, Kent)
My father served in the 1914–18 war and, although eligible for military service in the Second World War, was given the job of bringing evacuees out of London. Along with my mother and brother I remember meeting at a London mainline station and boarding a train for a secret destination - Dover! From there, this train loaded with London children was sent to different parts of the South and West Country. I recall sitting on a pile of mattresses in a large hall, waiting to be claimed. We had arrived in Dolton, N. Devon. After several overnight stays with different people our family rented a small cottage near the village school where my father was to teach.

Within a few days of the declaration of war, many precautions for the protection of civilians were in place; they had gas masks and shelters, with public shelters being built as rapidly as was feasible, and a million and a half children had been shunted off from home to safer foster homes around the country. Many of the major boarding schools had removed their pupils to safer areas of the country where they had been able to rent a large country house, for example, the boys of Malvern went to Blenheim Palace and Roedean was evacuated to Keswick. The precautions were in place, all it needed now was for the action to start.

Everyone expected immediate bombardment of some kind or other. The sirens sounded shortly after the declaration and had the populace scurrying to the shelters, only to emerge again at the 'All Clear' to find absolutely nothing had happened. Nor did it, in the sense of visible or audible conflict, for several months to come.

Military historians agree that Hitler had not expected Britain to go to war and he was unprepared to wage a campaign of such magnitude at that stage. He simply did not have immediately available the men or matériel for it. Even less did Britain and France. Both sides needed time to raise the forces and their arms, transport, heavy artillery and ammunition. So the stage known as the Phoney War came about, which lasted until 9 April 1940, when Germany invaded Norway and Denmark. A British military expedition to assist Norway was disastrously unsuccessful. Then in May, Hitler invaded Belgium, Luxembourg and the Netherlands. Chamberlain resigned and Churchill formed the National Government. Up until that time, from September 1939, men were called up, some ministries and commercial companies relocated from major conurbations to safer places and life, for children, seemed much as normal.

The British Expeditionary Force was stationed in northern France with all its equipment as were many R.A.F. squadrons with their aircraft and all handling equipment for them. And they waited…

Back home, the call up of those eligible for military service continued. Seeing military personnel in training became part of daily life; the children just accepted it.

Pat Fulmer (b.1937. Catford)
My father, having been with the TA before the war, was called up just before it started. He was away for six and a quarter years.

Ruth Stobart (b.1937. SE London)
My father volunteered to serve. He wanted to do his bit to help, but felt in conscience that he could not fight, so he became an ambulance driver in the RAMC.

Janet Ellison (b.1937. Worthing)
There is a shadowy memory of feeling like tears as I told some sympathetic person that "my daddy is going away to the war". He served in the Royal Marines as a musician and stretcher bearer mainly on battleships in the North Atlantic and Arctic.

Gwen Pritchitt
Dad was not called up for a while because of his age - over 30. Strangely, I don't remember saying goodbye when he eventually went away. He was home fairly regularly at first but I have no recollection of the big goodbye when he was posted abroad.

Anna Piper
Within a week or two of the declaration, Vati and his brother, having volunteered, were called to the colours. We accompanied Vati to the Induction unit at Balingen and stayed the weekend. It all seemed very exciting. I just remember being made a great fuss of, riding on shoulders and going for walks. That was the last time I saw my father.

Life continued. In all newspapers and magazines, official adverts appeared urging parents to leave their evacuated children where they were, for seeing that nothing was happening and wanting to see their children, many parents were taking them home again.

Hannah Langley (b.1929. East London)
We were evacuated with the Jews Free School and ended up, my sister and I, in Pymoor, a village eight miles from Ely, and our two brothers were close by. After a few weeks my parents visited us; they had caught a special coach from London but had to walk the last eight miles as there were no

buses running from Ely to Pymoor that day. We were not happy in our billet; the family had one son who bullied us and made our lives a misery, although his parents were alright, so after a few months, with no proper lessons, just makeshift classes in some kind of hall, my parents took us back to London. I don't think I ever went back to school in London, everything was upside down.

It was officially estimated that by January 1940 around 600,000 evacuated children had returned home. Because of the evacuation of schools en bloc, teachers remained in reception areas with their charges so there was no school in the evacuation areas for these children. It was calculated that 430,000 children were receiving no education at all with a further million receiving scant and patchy schooling.

In Ely, mammoth efforts to sort out the educational needs of the Central Foundation School were made. A large house in the centre of town, Archer House, was requisitioned from its owner for the school to use and the Ely High School for Girls agreed to share premises, their girls having lessons there in the morning and the C.F.S. taking over in the afternoon, when the High School girls had extra homework. The London girls made the most of every opportunity that came along to sample life in the country. The Ely Standard of 6 October 1939 reported that the girls had enjoyed a novel experience on the morning of Monday 2 October when one of their lessons had comprised of potato picking. The part they had enjoyed the most was the ride back on the horse and cart when work was over!

Through the months of waiting, there was Christmas to look forward to and huge efforts were made to keep things as normal as possible, or, where there were schools evacuated, to do as much as possible to give the evacuated children a good time and to keep them occupied during the holidays when their foster families might need some time without them. The Jews Free School laid on games, sports, a special matinee at the cinema and an entertainment put on in a local hall. This was a Pierrot Show, written and produced by Mr. Joseph and performed by about a dozen boys which was greatly appreciated by the Ely foster families invited to this 'thank you' show.

That first wartime Christmas, despite the disruption, was kept traditionally by the parents and the foster families, as much "business as usual" as they could make it.

Christina Watt.

The first Christmas I remember is that one of 1939. I could not (or would not) get to sleep in excitement as Father Christmas was coming. We lived in a flat above the pharmacy my father managed; all the rooms were on the same floor, so through my bedroom door, (left ajar) I could hear and sometimes see, my parents putting up the decorations in the hall and living room. I kept calling to see if Father Christmas was there yet, the "No" in reply becoming steadily more exasperated...I must have fallen asleep eventually as I woke in the morning to find my heart's desire had arrived, a fairy cycle. From then on, this spent every minute with me but eventually it was incinerated in the conflagration which engulfed the warehouse where our furniture was stored during our evacuation. I hadn't even had time to learn to ride it!

The New Year saw the introduction of Food Rationing on 8 January, initially of ham and bacon, sugar and butter, to be followed in March by meat. Rationing was imposed largely because so much food was imported and merchant shipping was a target for the German navy virtually from the declaration. This way, everyone would receive an entitlement and there would be a saving in merchant shipping tonnage. There was with this a parallel campaign to make the population aware of how they could increase their basic rations by the cultivation of vegetables and the keeping of poultry and rabbits.

Hitler's invasion of Norway in April, then of Holland, Luxembourg and Belgium in May made apprehension rise. On the day of the latter invasion, Chamberlain resigned, Churchill formed his National Government, and a call went out for men to become Local Defence Volunteers (later the Home Guard).

Reports of the evacuation from Dunkirk are still very clear, the worry in the tones of the voices of parents discussing what was happening and even pictures in the newspapers, but it did not seem to impinge personally.

However, it did impinge on the Beckenham and Penge Grammar School for Boys. On the morning of Tuesday 4 June, a long train was held at the signal gantry for Kent House station, at the bottom of the school playing field. The boys started going to the tuck shop for cakes and biscuits and taking them, along with jugs of water, up the embankment to the French and Belgian soldiers packing the train. These generous boys were able to give the soldiers a welcome to England that they had not expected.

Dunkirk was both magnificent and a catastrophe. The army was home, along with 120,000 or so French and Belgian soldiers, but all the equipment, from revolvers to tanks, was scattered across northern France, most of it rendered useless to either side. What was not there had been left on the beaches of Dunkirk. Now the fear of invasion really took hold. It is chilling to realise, from studying military histories of the time, that the only weapon Britain held ready to repel an invasion was Gas (phosgene gas), which would have been deployed had it been necessary. No wonder we had all been issued with gas masks!

All the matériel being in France meant that Britain had to find a considerable quantity of suitable metal for armaments as quickly as possible. Lord Beaverbrook, Minister of Aircraft Production, appealed for scrap metal and the children rose to the occasion, scavenging every item of scrap they found and frequently removing good saucepans from the kitchen, to help build a Spitfire. The aircraft industry was working ten hours a day, seven days a week.

In Germany, Hitler took a short breathing space. The only way he was going to subdue Britain was by invading, but his Generals would not countenance such an idea without control of the skies to avoid the army being cut to ribbons on the beaches or else sunk while at sea. So came about the Battle of Britain, which began on 13 August with an all out air attack on south east England.

CHAPTER 3

THE BATTLE OF BRITAIN
AND THE BLITZ

There were air attacks all over south east England on 13 August 1940, the date from which the action known as the Battle of Britain, an action against Fighter Command, is generally dated, but these were not the first air attacks experienced.

Leslie Oakey

On the night of 19th June 1940, Ely was woken from its complacency with a bang. German aircraft appeared over the city at 12.10am and dropped eight high explosive bombs in the vicinity of West End Road where there was a large hutted camp occupied by the military. One person was killed and one hut destroyed; further into the area, stray bombs killed 13 head of cattle.

This was not an isolated example, there were many exploratory raids in those breathing space weeks, but the main onslaught was to come after the Luftwaffe had destroyed the Royal Air Force. Battle of Britain raids were on airfields and radar installations, or any installation which assisted the R.A.F, particularly Fighter Command. It was during this sustained daytime attack that the people of the South East would forget about taking shelter and watch the spectacular aerial dogfights, aeroplanes chasing and wheeling at high altitude with vapour trails, ammunition whizzing about, often a hit and a plane would come spiralling down, or would sink lower and lower belching smoke and flame, to crash into the ground. There was also the thrill of watching crew parachuting to safety. The excitement was huge. And when the fight was over and the skies cleared again, the boys would be out seeking shrapnel, the currency of wartime childhood.

Janet Ellison

I can remember sitting on my mother's lap at a window after dark. The red flashes and noises in the distant sky were a thunder storm, according to her and I can remember thinking that it was a peculiar thunder storm. The Warden in the street outside shouted to us to "get back from that window". Of course it was one of the dogfights that used to go on along the south coast above the South Downs.

(Heath) Robin Hazelton (b.1938. Bromley)

I spent the war in a house above Coney Hall with great views over to Biggin Hill, and we watched the dogfights there with great excitement (no fear when we were young!)

Jill Thomas

It was while staying in Acton in Suffolk that I remember being in an upstairs bedroom watching a dogfight between a British plane and a German one, the battle taking place over farm fields. Then suddenly the German plane fell to the ground, with the blast from the impact coming through the open windows and we were all thrown to the ground. Everyone was very frightened.

John Gamêt

We were close to the airfields of Croydon, Biggin Hill and Kenley. On a bright summer's day I was playing in a wood in Shirley, Croydon at a friend's birthday party when we became aware of the ground shaking and loud thumps and bangs occurring. We were swiftly ushered back into the house. Clearly something major had happened. Mother was summoned by telephone to come and fetch me. Half an hour later we were hurrying back up our road and saw a squadron of twelve Spitfires returning to their base at Croydon from which issued a great plume of black smoke, this was clearly a surprise attack.

The destruction of the R.A.F. was a long time coming about, largely because the British fighter planes, Spitfire and Hurricane, were superior to the German Messerschmitt. It is reported, (whether or not apocryphally one cannot say) that Goering asked his Luftwaffe pilots why they had not been able to defeat the R.A.F and was told that if he would give them squadrons of Spitfires, they would do so. British pilots flew beyond the point of exhaustion day after day until on September 17th these raids on the airfields ceased. R.A.F. Fighter Command had won the Battle.

From these days, the collection of shrapnel became almost the holy grail of children. Shrapnel was a collective name applied to pieces of shell casing, ammunition cases, pieces of bombs, pieces of wrecked aircraft, indeed anything connected with battle that was lying around to be picked up and treasured. The larger and more varied the collection, the higher the status of its owner became among the children of the locality. And this was mainly a town thing - children in the countryside were largely excluded from the fellowship.

David Elcome (b.1938. Sanderstead)

After the siren had sounded the 'All Clear' most air-raids brought a rich harvest of exciting additions to my ever-increasing collection of shrapnel (I'm told I called it 'shraknel'): jagged slivers of steel; the polished nose cone from an anti-aircraft shell; fragments of painted metal, wood or fabric from damaged aircraft (green or brown for British, slate-grey for German); shards of a copper-coloured metal; strips of silver paper dropped to confuse the radar, and (my pride and joy) the twisted fin off an incendiary bomb!

John Gamêt

As the war progressed I was able to collect spent rocket cases, fins and other pieces of detritus from the raids and on one occasion actually got caught in a raid as I returned from school. I was aware of shell bursts in the sky almost directly overhead. Then pieces of shrapnel rained down some yards from me. It did not occur to me that this was potentially lethal and I took great delight in thinking I could add to my collection of war trophies. This did not last long as the jagged shrapnel pieces were red hot!

Sheila Kelly

After the night in the shelter, we would search for jagged lumps of shrapnel on the ground, gleeful of sharing it with friends at school.

Peter Rex

A major activity was collecting shrapnel; a mistake on my part. I scratched my left thumb on one piece and it became infected, so much so that I lost most of the thumb nail and bore the scar where it grew back for many years afterwards. It was exciting when my father brought back (from his Home Guard activities) two defused and empty incendiary bombs. He kept them on a shelf in the cellar for years.

Linda Zerk (b.1937. Beckenham)

I remember playing on bombed sites, exploring crumbling buildings, swinging on door frames, going down into cellars and breathing in all sorts of dust! Of course the biggest thrill was shrapnel. Collecting pieces was fun and having a bigger and better bit than anyone else was the ultimate thrill.

John Buckingham (b.1930s. Forest Hill, SE London)

My father was a Master Mariner - he said he felt more in danger at home than at sea! We were watching a raid when I commented to him that the bees were about late that night. He replied that those were not bees, that was shrapnel. I never did find any shrapnel, though.

On 6/7 September 1940, the main force of the German attack changed from daytime raids to night bombing, the Blitz. "Blitz" was British shorthand for 'blitzkrieg', (lightning war), the devastating campaign used so successfully by the German military in Poland, Holland, Belgium and France earlier in the year. The tactic consisted of surprise, speed and overwhelming power delivered in those countries by motorised artillery, tanks and aircraft, so perhaps it was not quite the right term to apply to the campaign against Britain as only air power was going to be usable and so far, Hitler's air power had not appeared as overwhelmingly superior!

Blitzkrieg was going to do what the air battles had failed to do - open the way for the invasion of Britain. The blitz began on 7 September 1940, a warm September day. The sirens wailed around 5.00pm to a drone of approaching planes which grew to a thunderous roar. Then came the thuds and crashes of exploding bombs. In that opening raid, 600 heavy bombers were escorted by 600 fighters. The raids continued well into the night as the population fled for the shelters. Targets were first, Woolwich Arsenal, then the London Docks. With these, the houses of the East End were inextricably mixed and therefore under attack. Wave after wave of bombers came that night. By the morning 430 East Enders were dead in their streets and gardens and the whole area was ablaze, a furnace of highly combustible commodities, flames and billowing smoke pouring poisonous fumes into the heavy atmosphere. Rum, rubber, paint, sugar, timber, newsprint, all stored in the dockside warehouses, made an unimaginable bonfire. The London fire brigade battled non-stop for two days to bring it under control.

Pam Blakeman
I remember one evening going with my father to the top of the leather factory (four storeys) to look towards London to see the red glow in the sky which was London burning in the heavy bombing. [Ely is some 70 miles from London.]

John Buckingham
I remember that first night and day of the blitz. We saw the vast flames of the docks from the top of Duncombe Hill, some 6 or 7 miles away.

From September to November London was bombed every night. This really was Total War, where civilians were as much legitimate targets as the military. For fifty-seven consecutive nights high explosive rained down on the population as thousands of tons of assorted bombs and incendiaries cascaded from the heavens. Nothing was sacrosanct - Wren churches were destroyed or damaged almost beyond repair, the Houses of Parliament and Buckingham Palace were severely damaged, but the spirit of the people could not be broken. They got up and went to work, often in makeshift premises or even the open air, the shared hardship uniting everyone with a determination not to give in. Only one house in ten, in central London, escaped damage, but the damage "to London" included certain suburbs that became Bomb Alley because of being near the flight path to the targets, being near to famous Fighter Command bases and being near to strategically important rail/road routes.

Linda Zerk
My earliest war recollection is eating cornflakes at the side of the road near Ravensbourne station. Early in the morning, father was shaving when he saw what he thought was a tent in the garden next door and thought it an odd time of the year to be camping! Then the Home Guard came to the door with orders for us to get out quick - there was a bomb next door. Landmines always came in pairs, and one had exploded near by, this was the second. Landmines were carried one either side of the bomber, colossal bombs attached to parachutes so they would descend gently, explode on impact with anything and cause huge collateral damage. (Conventional bombs made a big hole in the ground on impact, thereby causing less damage.) Luckily for us, "our" bomb was swinging from a tree as the parachute harness had got caught in the branches. Having to get out, mother grabbed my sister and I, the cat and canary, cornflakes, bowls, spoons and milk, then bundled us into the car and down the road for a breakfast picnic, which even I, as a 3 year old, thought an odd thing to be doing. After that, we went to a friend's house for the rest of the day. Later, we were allowed home after the heroic bomb disposal experts had dealt with the bomb.

Frank Bunce

The first thing I remember is being carried downstairs by my mother and her stepping onto a wooden door which had been blown off its hinges. It wobbled and it transpired that one of my sisters was under it, thankfully uninjured. Once out into the street I remember being struck by the fact that the whole area was covered with slates and dust. It seemed very dark and foggy. A young man who was a neighbour took me from my mother and carried me into the nearest air-raid shelter. Mother went back into the house to find the rest of the family. None of them were injured, thankfully. While in the shelter, I remember thinking my face was all wet and that it was running into my eyes. I was told that this was blood from a head wound, but I didn't feel any pain. When we were all together again we were taken to a nearby school where all the neighbours who had been bombed out were assembled. I saw a row of ragged people with torn and dusty clothes, suffering from various injuries, sitting on the floor with their backs to the wall. I couldn't understand why they were so scruffy, not realising that I probably looked the same. I recognised one young girl in her teens who was crying out in great distress, asking where her brother was, then I realised what had happened and was frightened and sad for her.

The next thing I remember is being in an ambulance and eventually arriving at a hospital. My mother was in the ambulance as well. We both spent two weeks in hospital at Virginia Water in Surrey, being treated for head injuries. Mother told me there had been no warning siren; somehow the bombers must have slipped through, attempting to bomb the railway line. She heard the whistling of the first bombs falling and threw herself across me. The front room windows blew out, showering us both with broken slates and glass. She suffered serious cuts to the back of her head, saving me from being disfigured or blinded for life. I had a two inch cut on my forehead, the blue scar of which I have to this day.

John Gamêt

The nightly air-raids were evidenced by the local anti-aircraft barrages trying to shoot down the raiders. There was one gun in particular which we called Big Bertha, whose noise started softly, rose to a crescendo and then diminished in sound - it was possibly a mobile Bofors gun which moved along the main road. This was accompanied by the crash of other guns going off; the occasional whistle of a bomb; the crump and percussion of the exploding bomb followed by the sound of falling masonry. Sometimes, if the blast was near, windows cracked. I can still hear that throb of German bombers as they made their way to London.

Ruth Hixson

Our road ran along the bottom of the railway embankment. The enemy, planning apparently to destroy the railway, sent planes which dropped flares to identify the target for the following bombers. Immediately, the more agile residents scrambled up the bank to extinguish them before the bombers arrived. The railway was unscathed but there were many instances of nearby buildings being hit leaving expanses of bomb sites. In one raid our house was damaged by the blast from a bomb that fell at the top of the road. My last memory as we left the house for the reception centre was of the remains of a glass lampshade swinging crazily on the flex from the ceiling - and the carpet had been sucked into the chimney!

At the reception centre we all sat on the floor, in family groups around the walls. The matriarch of a family well known as petty criminals complained loudly that she had lost all her silverware in the raid. This was possibly rough justice as it was unlikely to have been hers in the first place.

Kathy Jackson (b.1937. Anerley)
I remember a landmine demolished all the houses on the opposite side of the road from us and made our house unsafe so we moved into my grandparents' house in Sydenham. Their garden onto the London-bound platform and I would go to wave to daddy waiting for his train to go to work.

Bob Jackson (b.1932. Greenwich)
We lived by the Thames in Greenwich. When the docks were bombed, the burning barges were towed down river to be sunk opposite where the Cutty Sark is now. A wreck light would be put on them to warn other shipping.

Maureen Jordan (b.1937. Beckenham)
I recall the constant tension to be alert for the sirens which signified an impending air attack and deciding which communal shelter to rush to, where we would spend the entire night all huddled together, wrapped in blankets in bleak surroundings. Before reaching sanctuary we would often see the searchlights criss-crossing the sky and hear the heavy drone of the approaching bombers. Fires from bomb hits would be seen blazing in the distance and we would try to work out the location.

Corinne Older
I can remember knowing the difference between the sound of a German plane and one of ours - and if one returned in the night, as they often did, I can remember calling out "Mummy, one of our boys is back" - we copied the sayings of our elders!

In the daytime I can remember rushing out into the garden to wave to the squadrons of 12 as they passed overhead and waiting for their return. We lived near Biggin Hill and counting them back and feeling sad when few returned and elated when odd ones returned with damaged wings was a normal part of life. We would wave to the pilots, some of whom would wave back - it all seems so incredible now.

Gwen Pritchitt
Being near to Biggin Hill we used to watch the planes. It really did not dawn on me that anyone would get hurt until the whole family of one of my class-mates was killed by a direct hit while we were at school one day.

Jean Runciman
My earliest recollection is of planes flying overhead, day and night, during the Battle of Britain, followed by the Blitz. To facilitate evacuation during a raid, my parents made me sleep downstairs in a cot. During the night of 3rd October 1940 a bomb did indeed fall

opposite our house in Dunbar Avenue, causing much damage and confusion. My shocked parents rushed into the room where I slept to see what had happened to me. They were appalled to find that, due to the blast, all the wire netting that had been placed over the windows had piled up on top of the cot, and much of the furniture and broken glass had settled on top of the netting. It seemed certain that I must be dead. While they stood, horror-struck, in the doorway, a calm little voice from deep under all that said "Mum, I can't find my jelly-babies", showing an excellent sense of the importance of getting one's priorities right even in wartime!

Diana Scott

One August evening in 1940 my friend and I were playing in her garden when we saw lots of aeroplanes circling overhead and then saw bombs falling from them. We were witnessing the bombing of Croydon Airport at the start of the blitz. One Saturday afternoon in early September mother and I walked down to the shops - I had my new dolls' pram which was a very prized possession - when the siren went. We spent the next few hours sitting in the air-raid shelter built under Elmers End Green - my main worry being the dolls' pram which I had had to leave outside at the top of the shelter. When we came out of the shelter, the pram was fine. The sky over London was bright red; this was the start of the bombing of the docks. After this we had raids every night and often during the day - on one occasion I was going to Marian Vian School, which I now attended, and did not get further than the Elmers End Green shelter again. I and my friends were luckier than the rest of the people there as we had our packed lunches with us! We spent many long hours in that shelter.

But the Blitz was not confined exclusively to London, the whole country faced it, with London being the first target and continuing to be the main target, of course.

The Luftwaffe was seeking out other objectives as early as October 1940, going for the industrial jugular of Coventry and Birmingham several times that month.

Marie Jordan

Our village was spared from bombing as when the German raiders lined up to Ely Cathedral and Sutton Church they knew that if they kept going straight they were on course to bomb the factories of the Midlands.

John Taylor

Air-raids began in Coventry at the end of June 1940 and ended in August 1942. The heaviest raids were 14th November 1940 and April 1941, by which time we had become somewhat inured to bombing! The November blitz (from memory) was on a Thursday. I was in the kitchen around 6.30 when my father came home from work - early for him in those days. His first words to mum were to make some sandwiches and a flask of tea for we were in for a hard night. The ARP post at his factory had been warned to expect a heavy raid. It is claimed that no prior warning was given to the civil authorities but my father knew somehow and I'm sure he wasn't clairvoyant. The fury of around 450 German aircraft bombing the city was unleashed in waves until about 5.00a.m. the next day. During lulls we used to come out for air and I remember the skyline being a wall of flame with the Cathedral - one of England's finest - at the centre of the inferno. If I close my eyes, I can still see that skyline today! My home was on the edge of the city and we had a hard frost but the heat in the City Centre meant there was no frost there. It was the night of the full moon, which had guided the pilots of the first wave in, but once they had dropped their 30,000 incendiary bombs they needed no moon. (I learned later that the leader was the leader of the German aircraft that destroyed Guernica.) In this November raid, some 550 people died and over 1,000 were injured. Some of the rubble was dumped at the bottom of the field behind our house. Playing there one day we saw an arm and a leg sticking out of the rubble.

On the 8th & 10th April 1941 raiders made fierce attacks comparable with the November raid but shorter. There were many shorter raids, some in daytime! One plane machine-gunned the Holyhead Road as I walked along it delivering the evening papers. I dived into the ditch as I'd seen this done in the pictures.

Virginia Watkinson (b.1941. Basingstoke)
Although born in Basingstoke I am a Coventrian, my mother returning to the city fairly soon after my birth. I recall life in Coventry after the blitz, when town centre shopping involved a visit to the much bombed market and the fishmonger who always seemed to be surrounded by rubble. I'm sure I remember the remains of a plane with a wing protruding from the roof of the Co-op. I certainly remember lots of rubble and bomb damage, holes in the ground, corrugated iron everywhere and acres of emptiness where there should have been shops and offices, houses and libraries. I don't think any of this worried me!

The flames and glow of Coventry ablaze were seen for miles around. From attic windows in Witney, Oxfordshire, a town approximately forty miles south of Coventry, it was possible to see when Coventry was being bombed. The sky was red with the glow. Similarly, in the town of Coalville, Leicestershire, approximately twenty miles to the north, from the bedroom windows of the houses, people saw the sky lit up with the flames on the night of 14th November.

Bristol, with its docks and considerable important industrial and commercial centres, was another major target. The city suffered very badly and large areas were devastated. The first full weight of attack came on the night of Sunday 24th November 1940, with a savage fury of bombardment that saw whole city centre streets, big stores and shops, offices and well-known buildings crash to blazing ruin, the flames from which were seen in the towns and villages for miles around. The official German News Agency reported that Bristol had been wiped out, but then contradicted itself as two more big raids, on 2nd December and 6th December, were mounted by the Luftwaffe, "to conclude a work of destruction similar to Coventry." Then on 3rd January 1941 there was a twelve-hour onslaught from dusk almost until dawn, a night so cold that water froze in the hoses used by the fire brigade. There were several prolonged raids of up to ten hours' duration at frequent intervals with many shorter ones - a total of thirty up until 11th April (Good Friday).

The raids destroyed 2,500 houses and seriously damaged a further 46,000. 1,159 men, women and children were killed and an unknown number seriously injured.

Peter Rex

My memories of the Blitz are quite scattered; vivid mental pictures of striking events recalled in no particular order. Our elderly next door neighbour put out an incendiary which had come through the roof by smothering it with a bucket of sand, then scooped it up on a shovel to dump it in her back garden. Gas, electricity and water supplies were disrupted. I remember being sent out with buckets to fetch water from the Fire Tenders. Pumped from the River Avon it could be used for washing and cooking, or even drinking if first strained then boiled. At one point all water in the city was cut off and the only continuous supply of fresh water which was never interrupted was the spring in the wall behind my grandparents' house, in Hotwell Road. The closest the war came to me directly was when the area adjacent to Park Place, (near where I lived) called The Triangle, was destroyed. There were four large buildings making up one side of The Triangle; Lennard's Building, built by the eponymous shoe-maker but used by the Ministry of Aircraft Production to store extensive files; then came The Triangle cinema; next, a furniture warehouse and lastly a cavernous garage full of sugar. The Luftwaffe managed to drop a stick of incendiaries neatly from one end of the row to the other without hitting any houses in Park Place. But the whole row of industrial premises went up in flames and burnt for days. Jacob's Well Road ran with molten sugar, like molasses. This was at the height of the Blitz, coinciding with the failure of the water supplies.

Strangely, much of this had little real impact on me or, as far as I could tell, any of my contemporaries. It all seemed like some sort of odd adult activity over which we had no control. We all later enjoyed playing in the ruins of The Triangle cinema, where a large metal box, possibly part of the air-conditioning, came in useful as a tank, a battleship or submarine, or later, a bomber!

After the Blitz had ended, I was allowed into the centre to visit the News Theatre. After the show I walked further into the heart of the city and was astonished at the extent of the devastation. As far as the eye could see everything had been destroyed and all there was, was acres and acres of rubble.

Plymouth with its harbour, and the neighbouring Devonport dockyard were soon the target of the Luftwaffe, seeking to destroy them. The city was heavily bombed in late 1940 then again in March and April 1941, raids involving more than fifty bombers per wave, as a result of which, like Bristol, churches (40), civic buildings, theatres and complete shopping areas, were flattened so that there were just endless acres of rubble interspersed with less devastated areas where simply a few houses were missing from a row. But the bombing was not confined just to these dates; these were the major, blitz-style attacks by vast numbers of aircraft. Each town and city was also subject to ongoing smaller raids. Port cities, such as Hull, Southampton and Liverpool, were subject to constant heavy bombardment. Then there were the Baedeker raids, turning the fury against historic towns such as Canterbury or Exeter.

The Blitz as experienced in Britain might best be described as a continuous wave of powerful bombing raids involving fleets of bombers and their escorting fighters, interspersed with "normal"-size attacks. Targets of this were all major industrial cities and ports but primarily London. Provincial cities had fewer of the juggernaut-size attacks, but as these cities were lower in area than London, the effects were more immediately spectacular; city centres were reduced to rubble in one or two raids.

The end of the Blitz came on 10 May 1941, the final and most devastating night of it for London. Unfortunately for poor London, this was the night of a full moon coinciding with a low tide, so that it would be difficult for the Fire Brigade to extract water from the Thames. There had not been a big raid in London for some time making this one almost unexpected. The Luftwaffe started 2,500 fires all over London; 1,500 people died, 5,000 houses were destroyed in that one night. The House of Commons almost burnt to the ground (they met for the remainder of the war in the House of Lords - one does wonder where their Lordships gathered!) and the British Museum lost 250,000 books. Almost every major building in the capital suffered damage that night.

But when the 'All Clear' sounded on the morning of 11 May, it sounded the end of Blitzkrieg. In Britain this had not been short, sudden and overwhelming, resulting in the surrender of a now-subject nation, nor had it provoked the intended clamour by a demoralised and terrified populace for peace at any price. No, it had united all classes of the nation into a unity determined to resist no matter what the price, stirring the nation's notorious bloody-mindedness when "written off", to "show them"! With the start of the Blitz, the Luftwaffe had launched a different campaign of attack, targeting the civilian population. For virtually eight months, with no discernible respite, industrial cities and seaports had been relentlessly bombed in a deliberate attempt to smash the British war effort and economy and destroy civilian morale. It was the first time in any war that a civil population had been subject to mass attack, night after night after night.

The invasion never happened. Hitler's advisers must have realised they could never do it, for their military ambitions turned towards Russia. The launching of Operation Barbarossa, invading Russia, happened six weeks after the end of the Blitz - and arguably Hitler thereby launched his own defeat as fighting a major war on two massive fronts could never be a good military idea.

CHAPTER 4

EVACUATION II

The onslaught of the Battle of Britain and the Blitz, while not breaking the British spirit of defiance one jot, did raise an immediate fear, in parental minds, for the safety of their children, leading to a second wave of evacuation, this time more "private" than official. Small children were sent to relatives in safer areas, frequently with the mother accompanying them. However, many of the city children evacuated to the coast in September 1939 now found themselves re-evacuated as the coastal areas had become At Risk - of the anticipated Invasion Forces - rather than Safe, so this re-location became the "official" aspect of the second wave. These children were moved to Wales, into the shires of central England such as Northamptonshire, to Yorkshire, anywhere which was seen to be beyond the comfortable range of the bomber fleets.

The most remarkable aspect of the second evacuation was the removal of numbers of children not within the country, but right away, to America, Canada, South Africa or Australia. Parents had assumed it would "only" be a parting of a year or so, but for most it became a four, five or even six-year separation, with considerable problems of re-adjustment for the children when they came home. Overseas evacuation was an option for those who could afford it up until the torpedoing of the City of Benares in September 1940.

That ship set sail from Liverpool on Friday 13 September 1940 with a passenger list including ninety children being sent to Canada to safety under the provisions of the CORB (Children's Overseas Reception Board) scheme and ten children whose parents had made private arrangements for them. Four days out, the naval escort to the convoy was called away leaving the convoy to continue unguarded. In a Force 8 gale, one of the predatory North Atlantic U-boats fired a torpedo which holed the ship just below the cabins where the CORB children slept. Two children died immediately and the order to abandon ship was given shortly afterwards. Half an hour after being hit, the ship sank. In a dreadful storm it seemed there were no survivors, but after eight days one lifeboat was found with six CORB boys and two escorts, rowing vigorously. Just a few survivors; eighty-one children died, five from one family. A few more survivors had also been picked up by a Royal Navy vessel that had answered the distress call.

That terrible incident saw the end of evacuation overseas. Government and parents alike seem to have realised that the risks far outweighed the promise of safety.

John Taylor

My family debated whether to send me to relatives in Canada and I believe that I was due to sail on the evacuee ship (City of Benares) which was torpedoed but my mother would not have the family split up - luckily for me!

Margaret Wood (b.1929. Beckenham)

Aged 11, I lived with my family on the outskirts of London, in Beckenham, Kent. There was a chance to send me, the younger sister, abroad, so arrangements were made for me to be evacuated to South Africa. On 19th August 1940 I left; we thought it would only be for a year or so but that was the last time I saw my family for 6 years. We sailed quickly from Liverpool due to the risk of being bombed. It felt at first as if we were going on a lovely holiday but after 2 days we realised we were sailing away from home and we all became homesick. The journey to Cape Town took 4 weeks, twice as long as normal. We were well looked after with games, lessons about South Africa, exploring the ship, and concerts, BUT all the time we had to wear life jackets as we were sailing in dangerous waters where there was the perpetual risk of being torpedoed by a U-boat. We had lifeboat drill every day. As we travelled south towards the equator, the days became hotter and the crew rigged up a swimming pool for us from a large tarpaulin - we did have fun! On 20th September 1940 at 7.30am, we spotted land and the shape of Table Mountain. We all crowded on deck and cheered.

Louise Milbourn remembers that her parents, Quakers who had been active in assisting Jewish refugees in the immediate pre-war years, were concerned over the potential repercussions of those activities in the light of the possible invasion by Germany.

After a great deal of heart-searching and discussion, the decision was taken that the two sisters should be sent to North America. The Central Offices of the Society of Friends were linked with the American Committee for the Evacuation of Children, who would make arrangements for Quaker children to be placed with Quaker families. So, nearly a year after the outbreak of war, mid-August 1940, they sailed, with new clothes into which name tapes had been sewn. Everyone assembled at the Grosvenor House Hotel in London, where farewells were said to parents, then were escorted by train to Liverpool, the train being badly delayed by an air-raid which was passed sitting on the floor of Euston Station. They joined the Duchess of Atholl for the Transatlantic crossing in a convoy of 28 ships. In the early stages the convoy travelled far faster than usual, zigzagging and gaining 2 days as it was chased by U-boats. The destroyer escort had dropped several depth charges to protect the convoy. One night, 11 ships had been lost from it.

As they moved north to enter the mouth of the St. Lawrence, icebergs were seen, and then came the notorious fog of the Grand Banks, so slowing the speed that they were only one day ahead of schedule in arrival at Montreal. There was a concert for the dignitaries of the city when they arrived. They all had to sing "The Maple Leaf Forever", the Canadian national anthem, in the words of several verses of which they had been drilled as they sailed the St. Lawrence. From Montreal they travelled by train to New York for 5 nights (where all immigration details were completed) then on to Philadelphia where they were claimed by the Wood family, with whom they stayed for the next 5 years.

Margaret Mould

I was not evacuated but, living so close to Biggin Hill - Spitfires and Hurricanes (and I still get damp eyes and spine shivers when I see/hear a Spit!) - when Adolf let rip on London in 1940 my mother and I moved down to Grandma at Fareham, near Portsmouth. Three months later Hitler turned his attentions to Portsmouth, so we headed back to West Wickham. Mum decided she'd prefer to die in her own bed!

Richard Ellison

In 1941, aged 6, I wrote a 3-line report for our school magazine about the serious damage to our house in Waterloo (Liverpool) inflicted by a bomb dropped by a "Donr" (i.e. Dornier). Mother and I then went to live in Windermere.

Pat Fulmer

As soon as war began my mother and I left Shirley, Croydon, to stay near relatives in Oxford. For the next few years we moved between Oxford and Minehead living in one room in someone else's house, but it was not all doom and gloom! In 1941 we went to Northern Ireland to join my father in army camp there, beside the glorious Dundrum Bay, within sight of the Mourne Mountains and for a few months we were able to be a family again. My mother had little to do as my father's batman seemed to do all the heavy work. It stands out as being a really happy time.

Ann Gamêt (b.1937. Beckenham)

Dad was called up fairly early and was posted to Leeds. We followed him some months later, after my brother had been born, living in a lovely old house near where dad was stationed. Life there was great! No signs of fighting. You only went to school if the coach arrived to take you. No loss there then! I was a free spirit, running wild in the fields and woods, catching minnows and tadpoles, having a whale of a time. No-one worried in those days about children out alone in the countryside, we went where we liked.

Joan Hardy (b.1937. Beckenham)

I remember a lot of moving around from place to place and three different places in Cornwall. My father was in the forces and as my mother and I appeared to be staying with family in various places it would seem we were not part of the official evacuation programme. We were staying in a large house (possibly my great-aunt's) in St. Austell, where the only signs of being at war were the occasional bomb off-course, landing in the field opposite, and later, the Italian P.o.Ws who waited on the corner for the truck to pick them up for work then, much

DOODLEBUGS, GAS MASKS & GUM

later, the American officers who were billeted on us and who introduced me to striped, hard candy. A different experience was on a farm at a place called Trevanion, paradise for a city child. I roamed freely through the orchards and was trotted round the yard on horses. The third location was the seaside village of Gorran Haven where we lived in a fisherman's cottage overlooking the harbour. The only sign of war (if I recognised it as such) was the barbed wire barricade around the harbour!

Joy King

Being the youngest of 6 children, my mother was loath to let me go on an official evacuation with the school but we went instead to Worcester where my elder sister was on 'war work' making munitions, and we stayed with her. I attended the local school where I was the only evacuee (an alien species). Whenever there was a visitor to the school (local councillors, etc) they always came into our classroom to 'see the evacuee'. I always had to stand up and was usually asked what it was like to be an evacuee.

Jean Parrott

It was arranged through friends that mother and I should evacuate to Colyton, in Devon, where we finally arrived in the household of Mr and Mrs White. I felt very nervous passing through Waterloo station which was milling with people in all manner of uniforms. When the Blitz really got under way, either my mother or my grandmother would be with me in Devon while the other stayed in Wickham, housekeeping for the men folk of the family who were all doing "warwork" of various kinds as well as their 'day jobs'. It was not until Plymouth and Exeter were bombed that the local people accepted we might not be cowardly to want to get away from London.

Pam Wellsted (b.1930. Beckenham)

Right at the beginning of the war I was evacuated to Tavistock in Devon to stay with one of my grandmother's sisters. The two daughters of the family were much older than me. I was always referred to as 'the child'. Although with family, I was very unhappy there but had no way to tell my parents as my weekly letter home was read by my aunt who would then put it in the envelope, seal it then send me to post it. My letters from home were always read by Auntie. After two and a half years, grandmother came down to stay with another sister and met me from school one day and on the walk home I was able to tell her. She was very sad and wrote to tell my parents who fetched me home the following weekend.

Christina Watt

As the blitz really got under way, we were living in the flat over the pharmacy in Mottingham, SE London, which my father then managed. My sister had been born in April that year. Every night was noisy, and being close to Woolwich Arsenal probably did not help things when the Ack-Ack guns started up. My parents decided that mother and the girls would leave London. Somehow or other we got to Kilbirnie in Ayrshire to stay with my father's mother, even taking Wendy's pram with us. We did not stay long. The weather was very cold; I remember always grumbling about the wind biting my cheeks and mother never did get on all that well with

Grandma. We went to stay in Glasgow prior to moving to Yorkshire. Mother had a heavy cold, so rested on the bed. Aunt Janey brought her a hot toddy. Then mother was called away to see to Wendy. When she got back, the toddy glass was empty and her three-and-a-half year old elder daughter was standing on her head, kicking her feet up the wall and singing Popeye the Sailor-man. I recall the consternation clearly! Nevertheless, we caught our train to Doncaster. I sang the whole way, Popeye the Sailor-man alternating occasionally with Jesus Wants me for a Sunbeam, my entire repertoire. Mother kept 'shushing' me and the other passengers seemed to laugh a lot! We spent the rest of the war in a small village some 8 miles from Doncaster and I was never allowed near whisky again in my childhood!

So it was that towards the end of 1940, there was a criss-crossing of the country with children and mothers moving to places of safety and a parallel movement of those initially evacuated to the depths of the country returning to the cities, preferring to take their chance with the bombs rather than to continue with the dullness of rural life. Observers estimated that there were as many children returning to the towns as were leaving; of those mothers and children who had returned, almost seventy percent flatly refused to be evacuated again. It was at this time that the Underground stations became the shelter of choice for many thousands of Londoners; a semi-official estimate thought as many as sixty percent of the capital's people were sleeping in unsafe houses. As the ferocity of the blitz waned, so the evacuees drifted back home again, many leaving yet again when the bombing worsened in 1944.

As the war progressed, private evacuations from provincial target areas also increased, so that at times there could be a to-ing and fro-ing of young children and parents from all points of the compass to all points of the compass. The big wonder is that the railways coped so well. They were, understandably, a prime target. Stations, not necessarily all of them major termini, were hit, rolling stock was hit, tracks were sometimes hit (but often people nearby would put in heroic efforts to clear tracks of marker flares [see Ruth Hixson's memory] to save their homes and the lines) yet civilian passengers, military personnel, goods, armaments were delivered at their destinations as near on time as was humanly possible and generally in remarkably good order. The spirit of defiance which made the nation stand up to Hitler must have permeated the railway companies, too, the good old "we'll show you" rising to the fore again.

The town of Beckenham, Kent, was not deemed to be sufficiently dangerous enough when war first started, for the children to be officially evacuated. However, the Fighter Command bases of Biggin Hill, Kenley and Croydon were very close by and a strategically important railway line and long tunnel ran through part of the Borough. The tunnel was a key target of German bombers and efforts were concentrated on knocking it out of commission. A small area of Penge therefore received extraordinarily heavy bombardment and children from that area attending schools nearby were offered evacuation. The Beckenham County School for Girls was one of those involved.

Pam Daymond (b.1928. Penge)

On 2nd January 1941, 18 of us from Beckenham County School boarded a London bus for an unknown destination, which turned out to be Paddington station. We then took a long train journey during which we were served with a cup of greasy soup and a pasty. We arrived at Exeter and were taken to the local Children's Home overnight, where we had a medical examination and slept 2 in a 2' 6" bed with a dip in the middle! The next day we were taken to our billets by the W.V.S.. My friend and I arrived in a large house in a private crescent by accident. Our original hostess was unable to take us as she had already taken evacuees from Plymouth so we returned to the Home. Miss Every, our hostess, was there and decided she would take us. We were made very welcome in this household of elderly mother, middle-aged daughter and two maids (pre-war there had been four!). We had our own room with single beds. All the Beckenham girls had very reasonable billets and were well looked after, but we were only there for sixteen months as the Baedeker raid caused most of us to return home because of damage to billets.

However, it was not only in Britain that evacuation and air-raid precautions were introduced. Similar events were happening on the Continent.

Geseke Clark (Geseke Brandis, b.1935. Hamburg)

In 1940 we three older children were evacuated for the first time, to relatives. Air-raids started to bring dangers to big cities like Hamburg. Here, the important bridge over the Alster River, the Lombardsbruecke, was camouflaged. The inner part of the Alster was covered up so it looked like one of the fleets and another, dummy, bridge was constructed further out, which was in fact later bombed. The public air-raid shelter was above ground. Our shelter was like a round tower with a pointed, hard roof designed to deflect bombs. Inside, a wide corridor spiralled upwards with benches against the wall.

Helmi Spitze (Wilhelmine Neumaier, b.1938. Munich)

In 1942 my sister and I were sent to live with our grandmother in the town of Moosburg, about 50 kilometres north of Munich. The town was safe from Allied air-raids because it was the site of an International Prison camp. I remember that often as we walked to school the air-raid sirens would sound (a sound I still recall) and looking up, we would see the sky full of planes on their way to a bombing raid on Munich. All of us would run to the nearest building with a basement and seek shelter. School interruptions because of bombing became almost normal!

Rita Blackie (b.1935. Amsterdam)

My youngest sister was born in October 1940, five months into the war. (Holland was a neutral, so the war there dates from the date of invasion, May 1940). The hospital my mother was in was bombed the same night so my baby sister spent her first night in the basement. We had air-raid alarms a few times a day and if possible we had to go into the shelters. These were few and far between. When the alarm went and we were at school, we had to sit under our tables.

Near our home was a large open common where we would go for Sunday picnics and to play. It was popular and we went there regularly. The first Sunday we went in 1941, we saw that the Germans had installed seven huge cannon to shoot the English planes down on their flight to Germany. The common was full of families when the Germans started their game; they levelled the cannon to ground level and moved them from left to right as if threatening the people. Panic broke out and everyone rushed for safety.

From the beginning of the war, we had to black out the windows. It brought anxiety, first the hanging of the (black) paper and then preventing it from tearing. Every night the Germans inspected the streets and if they saw any light they were at the door, threatening and fully aware of the impact of their uniforms and brass plates with skulls around their necks. (S.S.). Daily, we heard the planes going to England to drop their bombs, and the English planes coming to Germany for the same reason. We prayed for cloudy weather as then neither side could fly!

Since the blitz, then, Europe and Britain had evacuated children, where possible, had constructed shelters or made extensive use of the basements of buildings, and were blacked out at night. Anti-aircraft precautions were in force. The children just took this as normal and carried on being children. Under wildly abnormal circumstances they had a 'normal' childhood and enjoyed it.

CHAPTER 5

ADAPTATION

Prodigious feats of adaptation occurred as a consequence of the war, perhaps epitomised by the way in which inner city children adapted to the challenge of rural surroundings and their host families shouldered the burden of caring for them. Many other young people had to cope with being in another country, thousands of miles from home, after a dangerous sea voyage, while in Ely, Orthodox Jewish children, many of them Kindertransport refugees, were faced with being in a town where the very existence of the Mosaic dietary laws was largely unknown and their original family upbringing had taught them to reject everything that was not kosher. It took patience and good will to sort all this out, but it was done.

Margaret Wood

In Cape Town, my new home was a very very large house standing in its own grounds. There were 6 bedrooms. Oh, what a change from my house in England which was a little terraced one. This house was 7 miles from the centre of Cape Town, in a suburb called Kenilworth. There were three children in the family, a girl my age, a boy of 8 and another girl, 5. We soon became friends.

My new school was called Wynberg High School and we were taught English, Afrikaans, Maths, South African history, Geography of the southern hemisphere, Science, and Biology which included South African insects and animals. We played netball, hockey and tennis. Our swimming lessons were in open-air pools next to the sea and so were washed out twice a day with the tides. Sometimes the tide brought in jellyfish with long blue stinging tentacles! We certainly swam much faster when they were about.

Melvyn Zerk (b.1935. Balaklava, South Australia)

The German Lutheran community in South Australia were keen to demonstrate their allegiance to "King & Country" by joining the armed forces and generally helping with the war effort. People changed their names...i.e. cousin Johannes Heinrich Hoffman became Jack Hoffman when he joined up, understandably. Parents and grandparents with their distinct German accents tried hard to lose them. Place names like Hahndorf were changed during WW1

(Hahndorf became Ambleside) and those which had been changed back after that war were 'anglicized' again during WW2. There was a certain mistrust of the people of German descent by the rest of the community and there was a story about a family who used to spy on their Lutheran neighbours by climbing onto their own roof to watch through binoculars for any subversive activities!

In school all the children, including the Lutherans, were fiercely Australian; in the morning we saluted the Union Jack and recited a patriotic piece, before school. I remember being asked by a teacher where my forebears came from, and the taunts of the other children when I replied "Germany".

K. Tribble (Central Foundation School Chronicle of the Wartime Evacuation)

As soon as I had left the town behind me, as I was being evacuated into the country, I began to feel a new interest in watching the changing scenery. Instead of the factory chimneys and grey slate roofs, I saw fields of wheat or I watched cows lazily lift their heads to gaze after the train, no more disturbed than if a bee had buzzed by them, and I felt that I wanted to get out and walk alone among the fields.

When I had settled into the small country town to which I was brought, I often set out for long tramps into the flat, open country. How different it all was from the town! I felt so much freer in being able to see a far horizon, in feeling the wind blowing my hair back from my face and in not being hemmed in by houses.

In London we had to rely on some of the girls to bring in flowers for the art class to draw and paint, and they were sometimes faded, but now it is infinitely more delightful to draw the plants just as they are growing. Altogether a thousand new interests have come into my life since I have been evacuated into the country.

D.H. Senior (Central Foundation School Chronicle of the Wartime Evacuation)

We lacked many accustomed things in our School in Ely, but music was not one of them. One of our first discoveries was the beauty of the Cathedral organ, and of the music of the services. Early in our stay, Dr. Conway, the organist, generously offered to give us a short recital after Evensong, so one winter afternoon we assembled in the Octagon, where Dr. Conway talked to us for a while of the music he would play. Then he departed to the organ loft and while we waited for the feast of sound to begin we enjoyed another feast - the sight of the vast cathedral, unlit except for the candles on the choir stalls, and the glorious colours of the east window fading slowly as twilight merged into darkness. Then, into that vastness stole the music of the organ, and for a short time we forgot our troubles, our exile from our homes, and even the war, and were entirely happy. We shall not soon forget that experience, that organ recital which was our very own occasion, and as such we will remember it.

The Jews Free School, from Spitalfields, was evacuated to the Ely area. There were more than 500 boys and 325 girls with this large school, so they could not all be accommodated in the same town. Where possible, pupils from the same division of the school were placed in the same area so that disruption of teaching could be kept to a minimum, for instance the boys' Central School was located in the villages of Isleham, Fordham and Soham; girls were in Littleport and Ely and their satellite villages. (There were three "divisions" of the JFS; Junior School, Central School and Elementary School. A Central School was a mix of grammar and technical schools, as they became known after the 1944 Education Act, teaching secondary-age pupils: an Elementary school provided basic education to senior pupils up to the school leaving age of fourteen. The JFS had these schools, all organised on single-sex basis, all under the umbrella of their faith and on the same site in London.)

There were problems initially due to the dietary laws. One of the teachers with the school was also a Rabbi so he was able very quickly to minimize the difficulties by relaxing the laws so that the youngsters could eat whatever was being prepared, an action swiftly followed throughout the country by the Jewish authorities. The Orthodox refugee Jewish boys had their food prepared at the hostel where everything was strictly kosher.

The Ely Standard for 5 April 1940 reports a performance of Gilbert & Sullivan's Pirates of Penzance by pupils of the Jews Free School, presented by younger pupils. All work on the production had taken place in the pupils' own time, directed by Mr. B. Cousin, a teacher at the school who had 20 years' experience of music staging and dancing, having worked with many leading London amateur operatic societies. The show was put on for the benefit of the Red Cross and to express thanks to the foster families of Ely and district. Normally Mr. Cousin would have conducted the performances but at the last minute the cathedral sub-organist took over the baton as Mr. Cousin had to assume the role of Frederic as the voice of the young boy originally cast had broken.

Zena Yorke, of the Commercial VI form of CFS, reports:

> We were very interested in this performance because three people in it were connected with our school. Sylvia Kaplan was in the chorus, the leading lady was our own Seena Bernstock, who delighted Ely with the beauty of her voice, and those of us who remembered Gerald Fridman as a naughty little boy in the juniors, were pleasantly surprised to see his excellent performance as the Major General.

The same newspaper, in its edition for 5 July 1940 reports that Ely's Refugee Home for young foreign refugees who were with the Jews Free School had put on an exhibition of their work and excellent progress all round. Dr. Bernstein (Headmaster) said these 40 foreign boys had found kindness, happiness and a real home in this country. He also felt that no evacuated school in the country was more fortunate than they were in their destination.

Perhaps the best illustration of how well the pupils of the Jews Free School adapted to and integrated into the society of the Isle of Ely comes from an Ely Standard report on 27 December 1940. A group of boys from the school had, under the direction of Mr. H.H. Joseph, one of their teachers, on Christmas Eve, sung a programme of Christmas Carols to the residents of Tower House (then a Poor Law Institution).

At the first Prize Day of the Central Foundation School in Ely, rather than London, in May 1941, the report of the headmistress, Miss Menzies, was followed by a few short speeches given by members of the school about their war-time activities in their adopted town, illustrating the wide variety of new experiences into which they flung themselves with enthusiasm. The speeches were well received.

Extracts from the Evacuation chronicle Central Foundation Girls School, of those speeches:

Plum-Picking

I never expected, when I was evacuated to Ely, that I should one day become a professional plum-picker! But as one is always happy to get a day's escape from school for a change, I was one of the girls who eagerly put up their hands when volunteers for plum-picking were requested. Shortly afterwards we met at a farmer's orchard where we were shown several plum trees bending with the weight of ripe Victorias.

Each of us had a basket. The farmer allowed us to eat as many as we liked, but warned us not to eat too many because of the consequences! Eagerly we ate to our heart's content but after a while the novelty wore off and we all said we would never look another plum in the face again.

After a week of hard work, our pay was put very virtuously into National Savings.

Sugar-beet Singling

In Wellington boots, dark overalls and shady hats, fifteen of us set out on bikes to a ten-acre field of sugar-beet, to help single it.

The beets, like small parsnips, grow in groups of five or six. To single them, all but one of the clump has to be pulled up and thrown aside, enabling the one left to have plenty of room for maximum growth. Each of us was given a row of beet extending almost the length of the field. During the first half hour we worked hard and fast, full of enthusiasm, singling almost twenty beets a minute. After that first half hour, we still worked steadily but much more slowly as the sun was beating down on us, making us hot and sticky. Our backs felt as though they were at breaking point; our heads throbbed and we were parched with thirst. By lunch time we felt pretty sorry for ourselves.

After lunch we finished another row of beet then the farmer announced he would award a prize to the swiftest and most efficient workers. We each had to single a row of beet extending the whole length of the field and two lucky members of our party were awarded boxes of Black Magic chocolates!

The after effects of our labours I shall never forget: an aching back, painful legs which would not straighten out and a splitting headache, all of which decided for me that I never wanted to see sugar beet again except in its final stage - in the sugar basin!

Pillow Stuffing

Since being in Ely I have occupied myself in many unusual ways. Perhaps the most novel was pillow-stuffing. Soon after the blitz began in London, Ely was filled with evacuees. Bedding was desperately needed and one day during our summer holiday a teacher asked for volunteers to fill pillow cases for those unfortunate people driven from London.

About ten of us were directed to a shed at the back of the WVS premises. There, confronting us, were two enormous bundles of kapok and a pile of empty pillow cases. We were given needles and strong thread and some overalls were brought from Archer House. Then we divided ourselves into groups and started work. Some undid the bales of kapok and broke it into smaller pieces; some filled the pillow cases, others sewed them up and two girls then carried them to the WVS depot, returning with a further supply of empty pillow cases. As the afternoon wore on, the kapok soon found its way into our mouths, throats and noses and the shed reverberated with sneezes. The atmosphere became thicker and thicker and we grew hotter and hotter but we had great fun and, with much coughing and spluttering, triumphantly finished our pile of pillows.

Potato Lifting

One September morning a teacher told us that when lessons were finished we were to go to a field in Downham Road to pick up potatoes. It does not sound a very inspiring occupation, but we were quite excited about it and set out in the highest of spirits.

On arrival at the field, we found that the potatoes had been brought to the surface by a spinner. Our task was to pick up the potatoes and put them in the large basket with which each of us was supplied. When full, the baskets were emptied into sacks. Experienced potato-lifters worked with us; they snatched up the potatoes like wildfire and our efforts seemed very ponderous compared with their lightning execution.

It was back-aching work, but when we felt really tired we would go to an old farm labourer and beg for a ride in his cart. He would usually refuse, but sometimes we were lucky and then we rode in triumph round the field. We were very sorry when the time came for us to stop, and we went home tired, hot, but happy, feeling elated at our first experience of working on the land.

The girls of the Central Foundation School, being of secondary school age, were more likely, perhaps, than younger children, to take advantage of the new experiences opened up to them by the circumstances of war translating them to this novel environment, but the locality must have been relieved to have such a source of willing volunteers. As the demands of mobilisation took more and more of the men away to the forces, the volunteer labour of older school pupils helped to keep "normal services" running. A vivid example is the Christmas mail. The *Ely Standard* for 27 December 1940 reported that despite many of the men of the Ely sorting office having been called up, the post was still delivered in time. Women were employed as sorters and deliverers, but a call had gone out for volunteers and the indefatigable girls of the CFS along with boys from Soham Grammar School had answered this call.

Helping at the Post Office

The bright red vans of the G.P.O. are familiar to all of us, but I never dreamed that one day I should ride in one as an employee of the Post Office.

As usual at Christmas time, extra help was required for delivering parcels. To our great surprise and delight we were given the opportunity of helping the country in this small way. A large hall in the district was converted into a sorting-room and, one morning, a week before Christmas Day, twelve of us presented ourselves at the hall in order to start work. Each of us was given an armlet, official proof that we were employees, and we were told the number of the van in which we would be travelling, each being allotted a certain district in Ely.

We then loaded the parcels into our vehicles before setting off. We sat in the back on top of very uncomfortable packages and hung on for dear life as we skidded round corners, trying all the time to sort the parcels into numerical order. We enjoyed jumping in and out of the van, delivering the parcels to their surprised but delighted recipients. Many were the comments about the "youthful postmen". Although frost lay everywhere, we were kept warm by chasing up and down garden paths and then frantically hastening to catch the van which was probably halfway up the road. Great was our joy if we could ride a little way with our feet dangling dangerously over the edge of the van.

But all good things come to an end and this pleasant task ended when we were paid at the end of the week and - to our great surprise - interviewed by a representative of the local newspaper [*Ely Standard*]

The girls were all members of the Commercial Sixth Form and their short spell of Post Office duty, which they saw as a great treat, had given them an opportunity to see into the inner workings of one of the nation's greatest commercial enterprises - and they had been paid for it as well!

Another new experience for the girls was carol-singing. For two consecutive Christmases, some of the CFS pupils formed a carol party with some girls from Ely High School. The first year, they raised £9 5s 0d which was divided between the Greek Relief Fund and Dr. Barnardo's.

Carol Singing

Twice we have spent Christmas here and twice a party of us has gone carol-singing. We started in daylight but soon the blackout was upon us. Luckily there was quite a bright moon and it was thrilling to sing in the frosty air. We imagined our top notes sounded even better out of doors than in!

Several people invited us to sing inside their houses and, at the Bell Hotel, one lady, who was ill, asked us into her bedroom. Somehow about thirty of us managed to crowd in and to sing softly enough to give her pleasure; anyway, she put a pound note into our box!

In 1939 we were regaled with chocolates and sweets at many of the houses: by 1940, alas! these were scarce, but we enjoyed biscuits and hot lemonade - though not the siren, which wailed once, just as we were counting our money.

In London our homes are too scattered for us to enjoy this adventure, so we were delighted to have the opportunity of singing and more than delighted with the £15 we raised in the two years! So, we hope, were the recipients, Greek Relief and Dr. Barnardo's and, in the second year, the Cambridgeshire Comforts for the Troops fund. And if we should be here for Christmas 1941, we shall sing again.

In the United States, Louise Milbourn and her sister Blanche were adapting to life at the other side of the Atlantic. Louise reported that there had been quite a melee on Philadelphia station with all the children, their prospective 'adopters' and the reporters all milling about. Out of a sea of faces they were finally put with a family called Wood who assured the girls they were going to look after them. Four Woods, Mr. and Mrs. Wood, Rebecca and Anne, had come to meet them and offered a really friendly welcome. The youngest, Richard, had stayed at home in Moorestown. Six passengers climbed into what seemed a very big car. In those days, three adults could sit on the broad bench seat in the front, and the rest in the back.

On the drive from Philadelphia to Moorestown, where the Woods lived, they established that Rebecca and Anne were older than Blanche, and Louise was just three months older than Richard.

So many things were different from England; the first, most notable, being the food they were given to eat. The girls' experience of food from other parts of the world was very limited and their recent meals in England even more so because of food rationing. At one of their first meals they were given corn on the cob, hot and dripping with butter and which was eaten with fingers - "lovely stuff" - Louise's description of it, becoming part of family folk-lore.

Moorestown, where they now lived, is about 20 miles from Philadelphia, in the state of New Jersey. The land is very suited to what the English call market gardening, which in America is "truck farming". The town was established by Quakers in the seventeenth century. The Woods lived on Main Street, a very pleasant area with open lawns, many trees and old clapboard houses, frequently with porches. Houses stood back from the road with no dividing hedges in the front and not many in the back.

The girls were introduced to many new words as we settled into their American home. Anne would say "Will thee go get those games from the closet, Louise?" "The what?" Louise would ask. "The closet is what thee calls a cupboard" Anne would explain. The use of "thee" and "thou" within the Wood family was new too, a practice common among Quakers in the past but no longer used by English Friends. Quakers believe that all men and women are equal before God so used the terms thee and thou as these were generally used for friends and equals, rather than the more formal "you". This "Plain" language was still being used in Moorestown, though dying out.

Laundry at 272 Main Street was done in an electric washing machine with an electric mangle, quite a new-fangled labour saving device, but not as labour saving as today's! This was a top-loader that needed standing over to be filled with water with hoses and emptied again, and then the clothes put through the electric mangle. A lot of the back-ache was removed! Drying was on a clothes line with a prop, and woe betide the person who knocked the pole down when rushing about the back yard who put the clean washing on the ground.

The ease with which Blanche and Louise adapted into their American family was quite remarkable. Apparently they talked of England and everyone left behind frequently, yet were content to become part of the new family with no qualms. Louise's school report for the end of that term reads (in part) "One has not been conscious that Louise has had to make any effort to adjust. The children appreciate her ability and she is very much one of the group".

Back in Ely there had been difficulties with some elements of society complaining about the number of "foreigners" (meaning Jews) brought to the town, the matter being aired at council meetings. Happily, a meeting between Dr. Bernstein and the Dean of Ely (who was also Chairman of the Urban District Council) managed to smooth out most of the problems, to the extent that in April 1940 the teachers of the JFS were able to arrange for the pupils to celebrate Passover in the traditional way. Host families were asked to provide crockery and cutlery for each child and the special meal was prepared at the St. Mary's Street hostel by a special cook who came from London.

The representatives of the Churches helped throughout the year; in Ely, Saturday synagogue services took place in the Countess of Huntingdon chapel, (non-Conformist) while in some of the villages, an aisle of the Parish Church had been allotted for the use of the evacuees and their Rabbi. The young people maintained the normality of routine and in this important respect, the host community adapted to their guests. Many of the older Jewish boys were allocated to help on the farms at harvest time, and, as with the girls of CFS, the farmers were doubtless relieved to have this source of seasonal assistance.

CHAPTER 6

PRIVATION

For most of us who were children during the War, especially those who were very young when it started, after the end of the Blitz childhood became "normal". There were still bombing raids, but not of the concentrated ferocity there had been during those of September 1940–May 1941; men were still being called up into the armed forces, women were being urged (or conscripted, depending upon marital status and age) into work or the forces, but for most children, the war retreated a bit. School, playing with our friends, going into the town shopping, collecting salvage, urging people to save - all these came to the forefront of our daily lives, especially if we lived well away from London or other major cities. The course of the war we encountered mainly in the newspapers, on the radio, or on the newsreel at the cinema, in this latter case, the Allies being lustily cheered on and the enemy heartily booed!

We did not know these years were an era of growing privation, this dawned on us much later on, or we were told so by our mothers well after the events. To us, all of the paraphernalia of life in a nation at war was ordinary, everyday, to be taken in our stride.

For our mothers, though, those years must have been appallingly difficult. Food was rationed very early, (starting in January 1940, with various items being added in March then July that year) with clothes rationing following in June 1941. This must have been the worst, with children growing out of clothes and there being only a limited number of Clothing Coupons per person per annum, which also had to cover footwear.

The Board of Trade issued a booklet about the Clothing Rationing scheme, designed to ensure Fair Shares when factories were producing war materials instead of textiles, footwear, yarn and made-up garments, and when supplies in one area ran out but goods were available elsewhere. Initially, the "Margarine" coupons in the standard Food Ration Book were to be used for clothing. 26 to the page, the coupons did not have to be used by any specific date, but when used up, the owner had to take the book to the Post Office to obtain a new Clothing Card with 40 coupons, making 66 coupons for the full year ending 31 May 1942. Unlike food, Clothing Rationing did not require people to register with any particular supplier, goods could be bought anywhere, but the retailer had to cut the coupons out of the book, the customer was not permitted to do this (there would obviously be a thriving black market in them build up quite quickly) unless ordering goods by mail order. There were so many caveats attached to this, though, it seems highly probable that few people would venture into mail order unless they were absolutely desperate and the item was not available anywhere else!

Examples of the numbers of coupons required for specific items of clothing for a child are interesting:

Lined overcoat	10 coupons
Raincoat	7 coupons
Trousers	6 coupons (boys wore short trousers winter & summer!)
Dress	8 coupons
Gym tunic	6 (4 if not woollen)
Shirt, woollen	6 coupons
Shirt, cotton	4 coupons
Blouse, woollen	4 coupons
Blouse, cotton	3 coupons
Pyjamas	6 coupons
Nightdress	5 coupons
Vest/pants/knickers	2 coupons per article
Socks	1 coupon per pair
Sports footwear	2 coupons per pair
Shoes	2 coupons per pair.

Scarves and gloves also needed coupons if they were bought in a shop; most mothers knitted them for their children, or had someone else knit them, as knitting yarn containing more than 16 per cent by weight of wool cost one coupon per two ounces, against two coupons per completed item in a shop.

Clothing Coupons, however, not only covered "clothing" but all other textile items normally found in a house. Blankets, bed linen, pillows, towels, tea towels, curtains, all needed coupons to buy new. Some things were coupon-free, though - hernia belts, ballet shoes, black-out material, bootlaces, jock straps, curtain net, emery cloth, mending yarn in quantities not more than a quarter ounce in weight, surgical stockings and several other unlikely-sounding categories which would be not often be relevant to children!

Selling children's clothes second-hand became widespread. If sold through a shop, prices were set centrally and Clothing Coupons were needed but at a lower rate than the "new" rate. However, if the price second-hand was above that specified, the Clothing Coupons needed were at the "new" rate. Many transactions were wholly private!

To discourage even further the acquisition of new items, there was a concentrated official propaganda campaign, throughout the war, in newspapers and magazines, of "Make-do-and-Mend", which seems to have been followed avidly by the parents, grandparents and relatives of almost every child in every country in the conflict! Consequently many of the generation that were the beneficiaries of the national ingenuity, have vivid and enduring memories of the fruits of the makeover game in clothing!

Gloria Morgan (b.1937. Upper Norwood)

Nothing was wasted. I can remember my mum unpicking old jumpers and steaming the crinkles out of the wool to re-knit it. Everybody passed things on and nobody was ashamed of hand-me-downs. There was very little available to buy, even if you had the clothing coupons ready. I was a bridesmaid to some family friends when I was five. My dress was the first I ever had from a shop. I can still remember the long, lacy silver gloves. They scratched!

Jennifer Bedford

Many of my clothes were "hand-me-downs" especially outer garments. Since my mother sewed and knitted much else was made by her. Fabric must have been in short supply also as some garments were made out of something else, for example, a bonnet made from scraps of woollen fabric carefully embroidered to disguise the many seams and a baby's blanket made from scraps of shirt material (patchwork fashion) and backed with flannelette. Then my mother was absolutely delighted to acquire some parachute silk from which she made petticoats and nighties. We children always wore Liberty Bodices over our vests - these were made of a kind of brushed cotton with tapes attached and older children could somehow or other attach stockings to these. I always had socks, which were hand knitted and when the heels wore thin that part could be unpicked and re-knitted; the same applied to the elbows of jumpers.

Brenda Booker

We wore more layers than children today (no central heating; and fuel shortages); vests, Liberty Bodices with suspenders and thick stockings. Pixie hats for girls and balaclava helmets for boys were normal - and I was fascinated when one cousin arrived wearing combinations.

Ruth Hixson

Waste not, want not was the watchword. Sewn garments could be altered, children's' clothes were handed down to the next child they would fit. I had a coat from someone mum knew and when I outgrew it, it was passed on again. The one thing mum insisted on was that I did not have second-hand shoes. Knitted garments were always unpicked and re-knitted into other things, eventually ending up as squares which, sewn together, made blankets. Mum made my dresses from remnants she could buy, always having enough to make me matching knickers, of which I was very proud!

Gwen Pritchitt

Neighbours passed on clothes as their children grew out of them and mum took note of the Make-do-and-Mend orders - lengthening skirts by inserting bands of ribbons and unravelling old woollens and knitting them up again. Unfortunately - so did my grandmother! Oh, how those knitted chocolate brown tights itched! We were also taken round to the local WVS 'shop' where clothes were sorted into sizes and displayed - I presume we had to pay for them? We usually looked through the clothes when mum took us to do a stint making camouflage nets, but despite this, I arrived at school one day with soaking wet feet - much to my teacher's concern - as the only shoes I had to wear were plimsolls.

Margaret Haynes (b.1939. High Wycombe)
My mother was very good at sewing. I can remember a very smart white coat with red smocking that she made from a pair of my father's cricket flannels. She used to unpick hand-knitted articles and make them into new things. She would wash the wool and then I would hold the skeins while she wound it into balls.

Barbara Langridge
My memories are fairly mundane. They include my mother making most of my clothes; she had a treadle sewing machine and made me a siren suit out of thick blue curtains - impossible on a modern machine. I put this on when the siren went at night and we rushed to the shelter. She was also brilliant at smocking and my dresses often drew admiration when compared to the more utility-looking ones.

Val Lines (b.1937. Exeter)
As all clothing and material required Coupons, there was a need to alter all manner of pre-war apparel etc for younger siblings and to ensure that no item of clothing or footwear remained unmended. The youngest child had to swallow all protests about the constant hand-me-downs. As the youngest of three sisters I endured most of my mother's attempts at the 'alteration game' when materials that had survived the Thirties in an assortment of her dresses were hastily appropriated. My big day came when my eldest sister decided to marry her pilot boyfriend who occasionally flew over our Exeter house. (This courtship entailed us standing in the garden waggling a large sheet and on one occasion my sister receiving a black eye for her trouble when a big apple in the orchard fell on her!).

My middle sister and I were required to act as bridesmaids and from the black market that operated then, mother acquired a length of rainbow net which was made into two frothy dresses and matching hair bows. Netting close to the skin is very scratchy and my sister and I spent large parts of the sunny day trying to stop the irritation.

The wedding was hailed a great success, so much so that my sister and I were marketed as 'instant bridesmaids' and for a small fee we were engaged as 'ready maids' (always in the dreaded rainbow net) by quite a few brides and there were many photographs of us handing the silver horseshoes to an assortment of newly-weds!

Hundreds of people made mittens or gloves from the rabbit skins that were left from the process of preparing the rabbit for a meal. I don't know how they 'cured' the skins, but the fur easily detached itself from the skin and one was left with gloves that looked as though the moths had been making whoopee and the smell of one's hands would have matched those of the local poacher!

At the end of the war, when the blackout curtains were removed from the school windows, each child was handed a hastily-torn length with the instruction 'Ask your Ma to make you a pair of gym shorts!'

Margaret Mould
My mum was an expert at Make-do-and-Mend! Her youngest sister got married in 1941. Somebody gave mum a dark purple boucle coat which she converted into a coat and bonnet for me to wear. It had matching wooden buttons.

I went briefly to Hawes Down Infants School where I sat behind a girl named Sylvia. One Friday afternoon, during sewing class, I remember cutting holes in her jumper. She came from a poor family and my mother had to use precious clothing coupons to buy wool to knit her a new one - I remember it well - pea green with coloured flecks in it!! And I had to deliver it to her home and apologise!

Wendy Walton (b.1940. Mottingham, SE London)

Clothing was just part of our life. My sister would have a dress, probably passed on from older cousins in Hull, and then it would go to cousin Mary who lived with us. (She, her mother and brother came north from West Wickham to escape the V1s and V2s). She was a year younger than me but a lot bigger, so after those two, the dress would come to me much the worse for wear. It still rankles! Clothing coupons were saved for the Winter Coat, this deemed very important by our mother, involving going to Leeds to be measured by the tailor then at least once more for fitting. The coat had to last! My father managed to send lengths of material back from Italy, which made identical summer dresses in two separate fabrics for all three girls, a cause of great excitement, but we were only allowed to wear these for best so we grew out of them fairly quickly. They were passed down the line, but I was the smallest and there was no other relative to receive my hardly-worn pride and joy - whoever got my dresses got something very good...I hope they were suitably grateful...but I spent years wearing the selfsame dresses that had belonged to the two bigger girls!

Ruth Stobart (b.1937. Anerley)

My aunt was a seamstress and managed to get hold of some parachute silk, making lots of clothes from it. Was I the only little girl with knickers that had large black numbers across the seat? Of course, the best part of the material was used for things that showed like blouses and hair ribbons. Photographs show me sporting enormous bows. Auntie also made coats from her skirts and she would cut down dresses to make things for us. She even made trousers for my brother. Old jumpers were unpicked and re-knitted so we were always well clothed.

June Thomsitt

My memories of clothing are not very vivid with one exception, the liberty bodice. My younger sister and I were required to wear this garment over our vests. It was a high-necked camisole of thick cotton reinforced with strips of tape up and over the shoulders. At the waist there were buttonholes at the ends of the tape, two at the front and two at the back. These were to enable a skirt to be attached. Our skirts were made by our mother in navy blue woollen fabric and pleated all the way round. There was no such thing in those days as permanent pleating so when the skirt had to be washed the pleats had to be tacked flat before pressing. Pressing and ironing was done with old flat irons that were heated on the range or the fire. No electricity...

Parachute "silk", as the war went on, became legitimately available in the many markets around the country and did not require Clothing Coupons. It appears to have been quite expensive and highly sought after. It was sold by the panel, not by the yard, so perhaps came either from discarded enemy 'chutes after a crew bale-out, or from surplus manufacture - although, given the circumstances, this latter seems rather improbable! It has always been assumed, probably due to War films where parachutes are always white, that white was the only colour, but Jean MacDonald, a War baby, recalled in an interview for a D-Day commemoration publication that she never went without new clothes, her mother being a seamstress, although they could be a little peculiar, particularly when her mother acquired some lime green parachute "silk" and made lime green underwear and summer dresses from it! There is also a photograph in a small booklet "Britain in The Blitz" which shows women in a factory sewing parachutes from fabric coloured red, green, yellow or blue. Not a panel of white to be seen anywhere! Another assumption is that parachutes of that epoch were actually made from silk, but not even the entire farmed silkworm population of Britain would have produced enough to make parachutes for all the airborne forces, quite apart from the appalling expense. No, nylon was used (it was available in the U.S.A.) for them. One of the Make-do-and-Mend leaflets is devoted entirely to the laundering of this fabric and to aspects of dressmaking with parachute nylon to avoid puckering at the seams! One wonders how hot the summer dresses were in this quite heavily woven nylon.

Strict clothes rationing and consequent ingenuity in making the best of a difficult situation, was not restricted to Britain.

Helmi Spitze

As the war progressed, shortages of almost everything became commonplace. I remember the white satin shoes I wore for my First Communion were made by the local shoemaker but what my grandmother paid him with was never told to me. My mother made my First Communion dress from parachute silk.

Rita Blackie

The shortages started to count after about late 1941. There was no renewal of clothes or shoes - we children had clogs as there were no more shoes to buy, nor warm slippers. Neither was there wool to knit a cardigan, or any new underwear. My mother would take one old garment and with it would mend another old thing.

Monette Meulet (Simone Brustet, b.1936. Verdun-sur-Garonne, Tarn-et-Garonne.)

In the summer of 1941, my mother was doing some crochet with cotton thread - she was making a shoe! It turned out to be summer sandals. The uppers were crocheted, normal child's sandal-shape, with a bar strap and one button to fasten. The soles were made of several layers of heavier fabric. These were very light and pleasant for me to wear. Later on, I saw my father fashioning shoe soles from old car tyres, more solid and hardwearing.

Louise Milbourn

As the war progressed, rationing was introduced first for petrol and sugar then later butter and other food items (in America). The only clothing to be rationed was shoes; this was not a problem, especially for me, as at every opportunity I would go barefoot.

Anna Piper.

We had very strict rationing for clothes but clothing coupons were also good for trading for food. Make-do-and-Mend was my mother's great strength. I had a beautiful blue cape which she made from fabric that had been either an adult coat, or a rug (throw). It also appeared as soft toys!

From around late 1941, shortages became evident. By this time, knicker elastic had become but a memory or else it was very very tired. Knickers were knitted from all sorts of unravelled, multi-coloured wool remnants (they were scratchy!) and in the absence of elastic, the waistbands were knitted in knit 1 purl 1 rib. This was not very effective at holding them up! On Sundays it was, and still is, in Germany, the custom to go for a Sunday afternoon walk. We did a communal walk, 4 mothers, 4 girls and 3 boys. The eldest was Peter, 8. He got really fed up with one or other of the girls having to stop every few yards to hitch her knickers up. He threatened not to accompany us any more!

One similar consequential event I have never forgotten. During a visit to my great aunt in Innsbruck we were walking down the main street when suddenly my knickers succumbed to gravity without warning. I panicked; I wanted to pick them up as I did not have many, but my aunt, whose clothes came from the great designer houses in Paris and Rome, held my hand very tightly and said with great calmness "A lady never stoops herself and in this instance you must just step out of them and pretend they are not yours". So I did.

Our clothes were made of remnants of worn sheets, curtains and cast-offs, colour and interest being added by bits from other outworn items. Buttons were often wooden, made by the local wood turner; and as many people kept rabbits for the pot, fur trimming was de rigueur. One year I got a rabbit muff for Christmas. Shoes were very precious. When you had sandals that started to cramp your toes, if you didn't have a smaller sibling to wear them, a razor blade cut out a hole for your big toe!

In Britain, too, the supply of elastic trickled virtually to a halt by 1941. In the television show "Dad's Army" the portrayal of Private Walker, the spiv, with his constant offer of knicker elastic amongst his dubious wares, is an accurate reflection of the situation as it was. The writer recalls watching the girls from a senior class at school doing PE in the playground and howling with laughter as one girl's knickers slowly descended to a dangerously low level before the teacher allowed her to stop and rush indoors hauling the garment up, in search of a safety pin. The boys found her flight a disappointment!

How did we manage? If the elastic was struggling to function, it would be pulled tighter and knotted to keep it at a functional tension, but eventually there were so many knots that it was impossible to pull the knickers up, the stretchless elastic now being too tight, so safety pins came into their own. As children's knickers were eventually outgrown and fit only to be used as floor cloths, the elastic, if reasonable, would be carefully removed and saved for re-use. Should you be in the market and one of the stallholders have elastic, then you bought some as you never knew when there would be any more. It was so valuable that it required clothing coupons, the number being dependent on width, from half to three coupons per yard. Reflecting now, the supply would have been prioritised for the Women's uniformed Services, it simply could not happen for Servicewomen to be subjected to the same underwear indignities as civilians…!

There were some Board of Trade Make-do-and-Mend leaflets addressing the problems of underwear. The most amazing ones were about "reinforcing" clothing and underwear. It was quite reasonable, at the time, to advocate reinforcing the seat of boys' trousers, but little girls' knickers? Diligent yet discreet enquiries have failed to find a single person whose knickers sported a large reinforcing patch across the seat, as recommended by Authority! A worse recommendation was for ladies' knickers - how to reinforce and simultaneously patch, theoretically making one serviceable pair from two pretty-well worn out ones. The illustrations are depressing, the methodology hilarious; again, enquiry fails to discover anyone carrying this out. Most people would simply have used both clapped-out pairs as floor cloths or similar! The *pièce de résistance*, though, has to be the recommendations for corsetry - ill-fitting corsets spoiled the look of outer garments, so it was essential to keep them trim and well-repaired. Apparently, a girdle that had become too big because the rubber had perished could be reshaped by making strong seams down the sides and the centre back, or at the damaged point. The new seams should be as flat as possible and covered with tape. The mind boggles! How was the owner expected to get into it after so reducing its girth, let alone its residual elasticity? To let out a similar garment the side seams should be unpicked and a strip of strong fabric inserted, neatening as necessary and also inserting a strip of fabric down the centre back seam if still needed. Surely simpler to have bought a larger size initially! The final admonition was that corsets should be mended directly when needed. A safety pin should never be used as it would pierce and break the rubber threads. A patch, if needed, should be taken from the good parts of a discarded girdle...the whole set of ideas raises a hilarious vision of battalions of British Battleaxes clad in their reinforced knickers and made-over corsetry barging onto the beaches to repel the invading hordes! Thank heaven it never came about - and who ever went to all that trouble? Certainly no-one among the writer's acquaintance!

Despite these strictures, most leaflets were useful, including frequently, basic tips on darning and patching. Most of us born in the 1930s can well remember the sheets turned sides to middle, or rough-hemmed "handkerchiefs" made from the most worn patches that were fit for nothing else. (New handkerchiefs cost precious clothing coupons to buy.)

Brand new clothes could come from unlikely sources. A report in the Ely Standard of 19 January 1940 tells that £10,000-worth of children's clothing, footwear and blankets was on its way to the country, the gift of the Imperial Order of the Daughters of the Empire, in Canada, some of which was allocated for needy evacuees in the Isle of Ely. The gifts were to go to necessitous children including Czechoslovak and Polish refugees. Many of the articles were hand made and of very high quality. They included brightly coloured jumpers (these would often be in three colours, frequently beige, white and brown, or any combination with two toning shades and white as a contrast. The front and front half of the sleeves would be knitted all in one piece, similarly the back, so they could be swiftly sewn up and formed a T-shape), snowshoes (not the tennis-racquet type article for negotiating massive snowfields, but lace-up ankle-height, fur-lined boots) and Canadian knickerbockers (trousers that came below the knee but were not "long"). The reporter opined that these items should go far towards brightening the countryside of Eastern England - but given that the intended recipients of much of this bounty had already been mercilessly teased by English schoolfellows over the unfamiliarity of their clothing there was a fair chance they would be subjected to more of it! Many of the gifts had the name and address of the donor pinned to them so that a letter of thanks could be sent by the recipient to "express their gratitude".

More conventionally, Jennifer Bedford recalls that her mother had billeted in the house an American officer and his wife, a childless couple. They gave Jennifer a little red and white striped dress, at the time her pride and joy!

In Ely and district, there were many Jewish mothers evacuated as well as the children from specific schools and these people had nowhere to go during the day. After a short time, the W.V.S set up "clubs" for them, places, often in church halls or sports pavilions, where they could go during the day with their small children and "socialise". A sewing machine was one day introduced and was a huge success. Many of these ladies had been employed in the garment trade in the East End of London and with access to a sewing machine, set about making clothes again. The Jewish refugee boys were well clad by these ladies, who also sewed for themselves and their landladies' families, re-using old garments and small pieces of new fabric when it could be obtained.

After less than a year, in February 1942, the Clothing Coupon allowance was reduced to 48 a year. These really would not have gone very far and it was after this that the Children's Clothes Exchanges set up and run by the W.V.S came into their own. Here, mothers could take outgrown but not outworn clothing and exchange it for things sized to suit their children, or neighbours would arrange exchanges among themselves. Thus cash and coupon expenditure was minimised and wear of garments maximised. Shoes were frequently included - no mother particularly wanted her child to wear second-hand shoes but often there would be no choice. There was never any guarantee that a shoe shop would have any specific size in stock, nor did the retailer know very often if any of that size were expected in the near future, so mothers tended to take what they could where they could!

Again, children accepted these restrictions as part of everyday life, but the women found the restrictions increasingly depressing. In June 1942, Austerity Regulations banned pockets and pleats on all new garments (for adults and children alike) and also banned long socks for men. By the end of the war grumbles over the restrictions on fashion and the lack of anything frivolous had reached the level of real dissatisfaction; the war had lasted long enough!

CHAPTER 7

OCCASIONS AND CELEBRATIONS

Wartime celebrations were muted when compared with the same events in peacetime - but celebrations there were. Think of all the weddings and the time and effort put in by relatives, friends and neighbours of the couple to make the occasion memorable, despite everything. Many children have memories of being taken to a wedding and having new clothes for the occasion - even if the newness was of the made-over variety - and of there being a party of some kind as part of the proceedings.

Parents made great efforts to keep Christmas as a very special occasion for children with presents, decorations and a celebratory meal that meant planning and scrimping on the rations for months to bring about. And birthdays were made as special as possible even if it was impossible to have a party. Sometimes, though, the items given as presents had started out as something very different from the toy they became, or had quite a history attached to them, having been treasured by an earlier generation of children before being passed on to their new owners.

Decorations for the home were essential, but normally unavailable in the shops - there were more important uses for paper! Instead, most families made paper chains. It was possible to buy packets of strips of coloured paper which had to be stuck together. Paste made from flour was the general choice as glue or gum was rarely obtainable. Lengths of gaudy chains in primary colours were quickly made and adorned many houses.

Peter Rex

At Christmas I would visit my grandparents. There was no electricity in the house, the lighting was by gas. The living room was festooned with paper chains, all radiating from the centre of the ceiling and all close together, anchored just above the gas mantle. There was also a Christmas tree, a real one (Lord knows where they got it, perhaps people grew them on the allotments!) with small candles on the branches. These were always lit. I frequently wonder now how we managed to avoid incineration. Oh, and they lived in the garden flat (semi-basement) of their house!

One year I received as a present, a model of a Spitfire on a stand. It was made from heavy silver-coloured metal, quite small, but with wingspan true to scale. Someone had given the model to my father and he gave it to me.

Gloria Morgan

One birthday my present was a rocking horse. He was a splendid beast whom I christened Bucky. My dad had spotted his body on a rubbish tip, minus one leg and his rockers. He was rescued, refurbished and repainted, with marbles for eyes, and a leatherette saddle. My mother paid a visit to the stables where Mabel (the milkman's horse and my favourite of all the delivery horses) lived and came back with enough horsehair to make Bucky a beautiful mane and tail. He was my pride and joy, a triumph of ingenuity and the art of Make-do-and-Mend at a time of rationing, shortages and austerity.

My parents, along with many others, scrimped and saved to keep us kids provided with all the things we would have had if there hadn't been a war on. My doll's house was built out of scrap wood in dad's workshop and so was my scooter. Mum made dolls with celluloid faces and cloth bodies, and made dolls' outfits to match those she made for me.

Joy King

I can remember going to Croydon every December to buy a doll for my Christmas present, so some toys were still available, but one year my mother was able to buy a GAS MASK for my new doll. It came complete with case. Even Barbie doesn't have one of those!! One of my favourite toys was a kaleidoscope which my father made from an old mirror and scraps of coloured glass and counters from tiddly winks.

Ruth Stobart

I cannot remember much about receiving presents. My uncle made a splendid fort for my brother, which we all had fun with. It was a fairy castle when cousin Dorothy and I had it to ourselves. I had a favourite doll who was washed so often that all her hair had come out. My mother and my aunt both had long hair and often sacrificed bits to make paint brushes. One night, as I slept, they decided to cut some of their hair and fasten it to the doll's head. This they did with no small amount of effort. When I saw it next morning I burst into tears, declaring I didn't want my dolly to have GREY hair! Ungrateful little brat that I was!

Ruth Hixson

One night, near either my birthday or Christmas, we took shelter in the cupboard under the stairs. The raid over, I found a blue furry bag thing which I gave to mum. The next time I saw it, it had been transformed into the head of a teddy bear which mum had been busy making from my baby pram rug. There was only enough of the fawn side to make body, legs and arms, so he had a blue head. I kept him for years, he was much loved. I had probably helped to make the stuffing - any odd scraps of fabric which had no other further useful life were frayed to make stuffing for soft toys and the task was often mine.

Val Lines

Christmas was the highlight of the year. I don't ever recall having a Christmas tree but Father Christmas did attend, usually leaving a stocking at the bottom of the bed. Although only half-full and containing items of little worth, the excitement knew no bounds. A painting book needing only water and a paintbrush - the results always as disappointing as the colours were confined to about four insipid hues that always ran into an unseemly mess; a pair of gloves knitted by an aunt with recycled pre-war wool; a slightly wrinkled apple that mother had stored in the old servants' quarters, and supreme joy - a book! A love that lasted into adult life. The delight of the day was to tuck oneself into an armchair complete with a tin containing very sticky and damp cough sweets that I received from grandmother (along with a Bible, she made every effort to guide me along the narrow path!) and, shutting out all noise until the King's speech, I read and chewed in paradise. I believe the cough sweets were pre-war and contained ingredients that would have long been removed from current medicaments! Christmas decorations were made by making paper chains from strips of coloured paper stuck together with flour paste. One year I decided to make some sherbet for my sister, combining flavoured sugar with Andrews Liver Salts; the effect was remarkable; my sister spent most of the day visiting the bathroom!

Jean Runciman

Christmas 1943 looked like being a disappointment. Everything was in short supply. Toys were a luxury and toyshops mostly closed down. My mother had absolutely nothing for Father Christmas to bring me. On Christmas Eve there was a knock at the door. The caller was a lady in Red Cross uniform, delivering toys to children affected by the war. She gave me a dressed baby doll - it was truly a miracle as it was just what I wanted. Of course it was second-hand but to me it was the most beautiful doll in the world!

M. S. (b.1937. Northumberland)

The only toys I remember getting were a rag doll made by a neighbour and a kaleidoscope made by an uncle with some bits of mirror joined together with sticky brown paper filled with coloured foil taken from sweet wrappers, cut up very small. I really loved looking at it and in time eventually bought one for my own children. At Easter, no chocolate eggs but a small wicker basket filled with handkerchiefs.

Virginia Watkinson

I recall a wonderful Christmas moment; coming into the big room decorated with a glittering tree - and the doll's pram my father had made for me, painted in green and red with a peg doll in it, probably made by my father too. Also a book called "Buttercup Fairy". This I treasure still as being one of the few presents my father gave me which I kept beyond childhood.

Monette Meulet

One winter evening, it was Christmas; there was nothing unusual around the house, but in the morning, on the table, there was a present for me! No special bright wrapping paper round it, no ribbons, but the marvellous present was there, my eyes must have been shining in wonderment. A small cardboard box on the table, and in it were a red crayon, a blue one, one green and finally a yellow one, and even better, with it, a four-page book with pictures to colour. A better present one could not have imagined...oh the memories...!

Anna Piper

My father, promoted to "Oberscheutze" (Senior Rifleman) on 1st June 1941, had been killed in a guerrilla ambush in the Ukraine on 4 August 1941, a few weeks before my 4th birthday. I was now a half orphan, as war orphans were known, which meant that ever afterwards, mother and I were invited to Christmas Celebrations with speeches, Christmas Carols and the presentation of a gift. (The gifts we were given at Christmas consisted usually of a wooden toy or, on one occasion, a red-painted footstool. These toys were made in sheltered workshops.) The choir consisted of the local groups of the Hitler Youth and the Bund Deutscher Maedchen. I would so much have loved to join this latter organisation but was not old enough. They looked so happy when they marched along the road in their smart uniforms, singing. We lived not far from their meeting place.

Christina Watt

Christmas 1944 I will never forget. At school we had been read stories of "Little Black Mambo" and I longed for a black doll. Goodness knows where my mother and aunt had bought them (the aunt and two cousins were living with us to escape the V–weapons) but we woke on Christmas morning to find all three girls had received a doll and mine was black! I promptly named her Little Black Mambo and would not be separated from her. After lunch I rigged up a skipping rope as a swing and gave Little Black Mambo a swing, then persuaded my cousin to do the same with her doll. I pushed the swing, then the doll fell off and shattered on the stone floor. Mary howled in anguish. Mother seized me and made me hand my beloved doll over to Mary then gave me a tremendous hiding. I would not cry which probably made it last longer. Afterwards I read my new books, any sniff or gulp I made eliciting the comment "Do that again, you Tina, and I'll give you something to sniff about!"

I never played with dolls again and took a long time to trust my mother fully once more.

Christmas and other celebratory meals perhaps called for the greatest reserves of ingenuity on the part of mothers. In cities there was no guarantee of what might be available as the meat centrepiece, anything from turkey to rabbit could be offered, whereas in the country it was more likely that poultry of some sort would be available, or maybe a piece of pork. The actual creature cooked could by itself produce trauma in the children, mainly as people were encouraged to keep poultry or rabbits to supplement the meat ration, and these creatures often were regarded as pets by small children!

The pudding was another headache as little dried fruit was around - in newspapers and magazines the adverts from official sources were frequently for "one fruit" pudding, the "one" almost inevitably prunes, but we loved them nevertheless! If there had been some dried fruit get through, it was rationed very strictly so each family had a share and of course, it was not washed and cleaned, unlike nowadays when you would simply not find the unwashed product in the supermarket. The women cleaned the sultanas themselves, washing them thoroughly. They could not be used wet, so were put to dry in front of the fire, near the range if there was one. Such largesse of fruit drying off was a real temptation to sweetness-starved wartime children, but in the writer's family it was prudent to ask if one might have one. The reply was generally yes, with the rider "but remember I've counted them, I'll know if you have more!" We doubted if mum really had counted the things, there seemed an awful lot of them, but it was never worth trying to sneak an extra currant - she might just have done, and then we would have been in trouble!

As for a Christmas cake - sometimes there was a 'real' one if it had been possible to save some fruit over the year; sometimes there was a sponge-cake substitute, with icing if there had been an allocation of icing sugar to the shops. Marzipan was simply a memory for most of us...

Brenda Booker

Christmas 1943 must have been harder than 1942, as '43 was the one when we ate our rabbit for Christmas dinner - and I had thought it was my pet!

Jean Runciman

By about 1943 the "spiv" had become part of the general scene. One hung about my school, exchanging day-old chicks for old clothes. Being crazy about animals I ran home and surreptitiously grabbed my mother's only remaining good cardigan, shouted to her that I was going out to play and returned home with four day-old chicks! Next morning three of them had died, so there were many tears from me (and bad temper from mum who had discovered the absence of said cardigan). All the other children's chicks had died too. But my survivor must have been tough because he grew into a magnificent white cockerel. We had nowhere to keep him so we gave him to our neighbours, who had hens. Later, I was absolutely shattered to learn that they had eaten "my" chicken for their Christmas dinner.

Margaret Mould

We used to go to dad's sister, her husband and dad's parents for the holidays. Auntie Nan worked for a company that had moved to a requisitioned house in Weybridge where the gardener provided her with superb veg. And she always managed to acquire a huge turkey and many of the trimmings. And there was a Christmas tree from the grounds so tall it touched the ceiling - with REAL candles!!

Marlene Newson

My father grew all his own veg. and even our back garden was dug up to grow potatoes. Christmas was always a wonderful time even though we had few toys, but our dinner was always a chicken, homemade Christmas pudding, mince pies and jam tarts, jelly and blancmange! Mum trimmed the front room on Christmas Eve and a fire was always lit in this room for the whole of Christmas.

Margaret Wood

On Christmas Day, which was in the middle of South Africa's summer, we had the traditional turkey and Christmas pudding even though the weather was extremely hot. But on Boxing Day we all went down to the sea with a large watermelon and a carving knife to carve it. Then we sat in the sea munching it to cool down.

Glenda Lindsay

We, parents, two children and 'the aunts' from the stationer's shop, who lived in the flat above it, all went to Christ Church on Christmas morning, then we went to "the shop" for lunch. Each family was allowed half a turkey so (the four aunts counted as a family for this purpose) the two families put their half-turkeys together. On this particular memorable occasion both families had received right sided halves. When my aunt carried it into the dining room on the serving dish it looked as though the turkey was running! We all fell about laughing!

Jeanne Taylor (b.1941. Filton, Bristol)

Trying to gather the ingredients for a Christmas cake was both a feat and a trial. My mother hoarded odd amounts of dried fruit for ages, but ground almonds for the marzipan were totally unavailable. One day, by great good fortune, a food parcel arrived from relatives in America and contained, miracle of miracles, ground almonds! Mother was absolutely delighted and managed to find enough icing sugar to finish the job. The cake was duly admired and eaten by friends and family. The following January we received a letter from these distant relatives in the States apologising for omitting the explanatory letter with Great Uncle Charles' ashes! No-one complained at the time that the old boy had made the "marzipan" a bit gritty!

Wendy Walton

The window of our walk-in pantry looked out over a neighbour's orchard in which a flock of geese roamed free. Several of them came to the window for my sister and I to feed them with scraps. Our favourite, George, grew fat.

At Christmas dinner we were preparing to eat when one or other of us asked mum what the meat was and she replied "Goose"! We had noticed the recent absence of geese in the orchard, thinking little of it, but we both burst into tears, sobbing our hearts out for George and his/her fellows. We ate little of the first course but for days after we unsuspectingly ate "mince".

Claire Hardisty (b.1937. Upper Norwood)

My father, with many of his friends, was a Conscientious Objector. Both my parents were members of the Peace Pledge Union and were actively 'political' in the pre-war years. On PPU advice, father worked on the land while awaiting his Tribunal hearing. We moved around a great deal as when some farmers discovered his C.O. status, he would be sacked. We were living mainly in Oxfordshire where there was widespread rural poverty. Children often didn't have food before school. A small boy was sick once and the teacher asked him what he had eaten; he replied "a slice of bread and margarine Miss".

Our turn for margarine came one December 25th, when, it being my father's only day off in that Quarter, he rode eight miles to see another farmer about a better job. He wrote an account of the War years and he described how "Joan (my mother) had eaten bread and margarine with the children for Christmas Dinner and there were no presents".

Gwen Pritchitt

Birthdays - I have such admiration for my mother, she was so cheerful and tried so hard to give us a happy time. She would hoard tins of peaches, jellies etc. to make lovely birthday teas for us. All the children in the street would come and we had to put a plank between chairs to provide enough seating. The best thing she did, though, was to save the stamps and paper from any parcels that dad sent us from Ceylon and wrap a present from him in it. She also kept the cards he drew for us of scenes there, later also of Burma, should they arrive too early; we were so pleased that daddy had got our cards and presents to us on the very day!

CHAPTER 8

FOOD – BUT HARDLY GLORIOUS!

Food was a constant preoccupation during the war. As small children, we were not directly aware of this, but we lived constantly with the exhortations of the Dig for Victory posters, with the knowledge that food should not be wasted and with (in the towns) the ever-present pig bins in almost every street for vegetable peelings and any food scraps to go to the nearest pig farm to help with the swill.

Kathy Jackson
In 1942 my daily job was to take the scraps to the "pig bin". I used to take a deep breath and hold it while I removed the lid, put in the scraps then replaced the lid!

Gloria Morgan
We didn't 'dig for victory'. My parents were no gardeners and we didn't have a compost heap or grow our own veg. We did, though, have a metal 'pig bin' in our street where we put our vegetable parings for regular collection and distribution to the ad hoc pig keepers of the area.

Even before the war, this country imported more than half the food needed to feed the population. On the outbreak of war, merchant shipping, which transported the foodstuffs, became a target of the U-boats, so the country had to maximise agricultural production, especially of the staples, wheat and potatoes, to save seamen's lives, shipping space and use of precious oil for other purposes. A 50% increase in crop-growing land was achieved on farms by ploughing pasture, draining marshy tracts and planting on hillsides. Inspectors from the various Ministries involved "encouraged" the farmers to increase their arable land as far as they were able, but the public were expected to "do their bit" as well.

The public responded by digging up flower beds, lawns and tennis courts (if they had them) for vegetable and fruit plots, and municipally-owned parks and sports facilities soon became allotments. Even the moat round the Tower of London was used for vegetables, while sheep grazed in Hyde Park! (Domestically, the soil covering Anderson shelters was almost always turned into a plot for cucumbers, strawberries, or anything edible which would grow there.) Anyone travelling by train saw the embankments near the station had been dug and were growing potatoes, beans, peas and other vegetables. The honesty of people in respect of these allotments was amazing - the big London parks and open spaces boasted innumerable plots, as did the other cities, yet there was little theft of produce. Those people who later shared some of the vegetables and fruit were very pleased with it. Shortly after the war started, about 1.5 million people had taken these allotments - and the land surrounding fire and police stations was enthusiastically dug up and cultivated by the station occupants. By 1943, more than a million tons of vegetables were being produced annually by these "domestic" growers, on its own no small contribution to the war effort.

Marlene Newson

I cannot remember going short of food even though we were rationed. My father grew all his own veg. and even our back garden was dug up to grow potatoes.

Jennifer Bedford

I don't recall food ever being short but no doubt this was partly because in addition to a garden, there was an allotment opposite the house on the land surrounding an electricity sub-station, and we always had chickens to provide eggs and meat. A certain amount of bartering went on to acquire the other things needed.

Jill Whalley

My mother, having been left on her own for the duration, managed to cope without inflicting any of the worry on us, she even managed to dig up some of the garden to grow our own vegetables.

Barbara Langridge

We had an allotment in the park opposite the house and apart from vegetables, grew flowers. In summer the flat was full of vases of flowers. I can remember helping my mother cut up home-grown runner beans then putting them between layers of salt in big china containers. They kept for ages.

M.S.

I spent most of the war with my grandparents in Northumberland. We were very lucky that we had a large garden and about 50 yards away an even larger allotment where my grandfather grew vegetables. One year, with a neighbour, he bought a piglet which they kept at the allotment and fattened up so we had quite a bit of meat when it was slaughtered.

Linda Zerk

The median strips in the roadways were dug up and things like potatoes grown; vegetables seemed to be grown on every spare patch of ground. The National Provincial Bank sports ground was ploughed and hay and crops grown. Us kids were encouraged to toss the hay around and jump in it, probably to get it dry enough to make into a haystack.

Christina Watt

We had not been long in the village when mum was able to rent a cottage where we spent the rest of the war. There was a large front garden, bisected by a central path. Mum dug up the lawns to grow potatoes one side and an assortment of vegetables on the other.

Ann Dix (b.1938. Ely)
During the war we stayed with my grandparents in Waterside. They had an allotment and as grandfather died during the early years of the war, my mother kept it going, along with all her other responsibilities. I was always given very tiny new potatoes, freshly dug. It was exciting going to the allotment as we played in the adjoining field making tunnels in the long grass!

In an age when refrigeration in the home was virtually unknown (and domestic freezers unheard of!) preserving the produce was a major concern. The season for any fruit or vegetable was quite limited so it was necessary to preserve today's glut for tomorrow's famine, which was done by "bottling", in "Kilner" jars for fruit, or salting of vegetables, (and preserving eggs in water glass,) quite apart from the making of jams, jellies and chutneys.

Maureen Jordan
We had two apple trees in the garden, one supplying eaters, the other cookers. My father had an allotment (as did most people, it was Government policy) and we were fairly well supplied with vegetables. The runner beans were finely sliced and packed with salt in tall jars and had to last all winter. We stored sacks of potatoes in our garden shed and one winter's day my mother pushed her hand in to get the potatoes for our main meal and screamed in agony. She had woken a hibernating hedgehog and the spikes were embedded in her hand. She was rushed to the hospital for immediate treatment.

Brenda Booker
Our back garden was dug up for vegetables. We had bottled tomatoes and fruit and salted runner beans from the produce, to help through the winter.

As the imports of foodstuffs had drastically reduced, it was necessary for all free foods to be utilised fully. In the autumn, rose hips were harvested to make rose hip syrup for children. The rose hips were purchased from the pickers at about 2 or 3 old pence per pound weight (1p or 1.5p in present-day terms) and many people were pleased to pick all day to earn the few extra shillings so raised! Similarly, crab apples were harvested to make crab apple jelly and the blackberries which abounded in autumn were picked. Around the country, jam factories paid for this and any other hedgerow fruit they could use for manufacture.

Ely Standard, 29th August 1941
A Board of Education memo to schools urges the need for making the best possible use of the autumn yield of fruit crops - blackberries, bilberries, crab apples, elderberries, rowan berries and sloes. Fruit collected by schools and not needed for immediate consumption could be sold to fruit preservation centres (jam factories!) or made into jam by the schools for their own consumption. Additional supplies of sugar for this purpose would be available from the local food office.

Jam-making in Ely (from the Evacuation Chronicle of the Central Foundation School)
J. Sparks & J.Good

On a September morning in the school holidays of 1942, three of us, with ladder and stepladder, went into the school garden to strip the two large mulberry trees of their ripe fruit, competing with the feasting song birds. Two of us picked, the third emptied the filled baskets into large fruit skeps which were eventually carried off by Miss Lenn and four other girls to the kitchen of Ely High School, where the jam would be made. There, the fruit was first "stalked" (the stalk cut off) then was washed and put into saucepans. Half our number in the kitchen then prepared and part-cooked apples while the other half measured out panfuls of sugar, after which the great pans of mulberries were tipped into the even larger pans of apples. Then we either stirred, taking turns, or scrubbed, cleaned or put the jars to warm. As we tipped the pans of sugar into the cooking fruit, the kitchen became very stuffy so we opened a window, but as the fresh air came in, so did the wasps. Thereafter we had little peace, every time a wasp approached the jam we all screamed, except Miss Lenn. One of our number declared war on the wasps, chasing them all off with a tea towel. When the jam was ready we allowed it to cool and ladled it into the jars, which were then labelled and topped. There were fifty six pounds of it! Miss Lenn gave us a lovely surprise for she presented each of us with a jar for the help we had given, but we all agreed the fun we had had was more than enough payment for our help.

Mushrooms, in season, were picked and used, and many more people discovered the use of tender nettle shoots for soup or of dandelion leaves in salad. In the countryside, sites of wild garlic were jealously guarded and the plant used.

It was not just vegetables and fruit, though, that the civilian population was urged to produce. It was acknowledged that meat would have to be strictly rationed and it was policy to encourage the raising of rabbits and poultry for the table by the population; it was also permissible for a small group of people to buy a piglet to raise between themselves as a future source of meat for their families but there were restrictions as to slaughter-weight.

If a family had a large number of hens they might be expected to hand over a certain number of eggs per week to the central authority but this could be quite difficult to police and enforce - people ate some of their chickens and it was not unknown for others of them just to go missing, an administrative nightmare to keep track of!

Pat Fulmer

After D-Day, mother and I returned to Catford, London, to live with my grandparents. Grandfather kept chickens but obviously didn't feed them properly because the eggs all had soft shells! We seemed to eat cabbage most days - my grandmother made me drink the hot cabbage water. I think that is why I've had such good health all my life!

Corinne Older

In a smallish garden we had chickens, ducks, a pig and for a very short time, a goat! This chased one of my friends home and dropped a load in the kitchen before we could drag it off. I think mother had a difficult time putting it right with my friend's mother!

Linda Zerk

We kept chickens. Some eggs had to be relinquished to the authorities, a constant source of frustration! At one time, we had no chickens but used to boil up food scraps and vegetable peelings with bran and pollard, then, when petrol was short, it was my job, with Lynne from next door, to deliver this to friends who had chickens. We had to tie the billycan of hot stinking slurry onto our bike handlebars. In return we received eggs which had to be brought home on the bike without breaking them! To foil the egg "police" we kept ducks for a while as duck eggs didn't have to be surrendered. Unfortunately, they never laid any!!

Strange things were done with eggs. We pickled them in some sort of slimy material in buckets and they were supposed to last for years.

Jean Runciman

At the beginning of 1941 mother decided we must get away from the Blitz for a while so we joined her sister and family who were in a small village on the Norfolk/Suffolk border. We stayed as paying guests with a Mr & Mrs Gould, an elderly couple. The Goulds kept rabbits and chickens in their back garden to help with the meat ration. I was overjoyed to find lovely rabbits in hutches. I helped to feed them and cuddled them. One was my favourite but one day I couldn't find him. At lunch, we were eating a very tasty casserole and I asked what the meat was. Mrs. Gould told me it was my beloved rabbit! I turned white, refused to eat my dinner and have never eaten rabbit since.

Pam Wellsted

If chicken was for dinner I had to go with my uncle to the coop at the bottom of the garden, watch him catch one, wring its neck, and then put it on the ground where it would run a few more steps before collapsing. If rabbit was on the menu I had to go with him, holding the sacking bag with the ferret in, which kept leaping up and down, really scaring me. He would put the ferret down one hole while I had to stand over another with a bag in which to catch the rabbit when it rushed out of the burrow. Terrifying for a young "townie".

Brenda Booker

We kept chickens and rabbits for eggs and meat. My dad could never kill them, so had to ask the man across the road, who was a real countryman.

It was not only in Britain that food was rationed: Germany already had quite strict rationing in force in 1937 when most of the contributors to this book were born; rationing was imposed on Holland when the Nazis over-ran the country and there was rationing in France after she fell in 1940. Reading the stories of those years, the escapes, the imprisonments, brings home the general shortages of food all over the combatant countries and the desperate measures that were sometimes resorted to, simply to stay alive another day.

Compared with most, we in this country did not fare too badly. What is a very salutary thing to do is to visit the Imperial War Museum and look at the exhibition The 1940s House, which has on a normal-size dinner plate a display of one adult's rations for a week of butter, margarine, sugar, lard, cheese, tea, meat, bacon and eggs. Most of us would have problems now stretching this beyond one day, yet our mothers fed us successfully on this for six years (more, in fact, as there was rationing, albeit of a gradually diminishing number of items, until mid-1954).

Ruth Stobart
Dried eggs! These made lovely scrambled eggs or omelettes. After the war, my brother wouldn't eat fresh eggs, he wanted proper ones! We had milk puddings made with baby milk; one I particularly liked was Creamola.

   Whale meat!! It looked like meat and tasted of fish. We ate it because it was available. My mother, aunt and grandmother must have been good cooks because I can't remember anything really horrible. My father, in the RAMC, swapped his cigarette allowance for sweet coupons then sent them to us, meaning we had additional sweets!

One outcome of the concern over food supplies was the implementation of school dinners and free milk for all schoolchildren. There was official disquiet over the evident malnutrition of numbers of schoolchildren whose parents had been victims of the Depression, concern over feeding of those whose mothers had chosen to do war work and general concern that with the cessation of imports of citrus fruit all the children could suffer vitamin deficiencies. The dinners were largely appreciated at least in part (some of the milk puddings were intensely disliked!), the third-of-a-pint of school milk probably less so. The cod liver oil was almost universally detested and the orange juice tolerated. (In later years this was found to go very well with gin!)

Valerie Bragg
At school in Stratton-in-the-Wold I spent a lot of time dodging classes. I would volunteer to feed the caged chickens at the back of the school. I was terrified of arithmetic and got out of it by taking the milk crates round to the three classrooms.

Marlene Newson
I vividly remember the free school milk which on frosty winter mornings was placed around the hearth of the open coal fire to be warmed up! And how I hated it!

Christina Watt
My main 'food' memory is the school milk. We had to drink it, cold with crystals of ice in it in winter, (unless the teacher had stood the crate near the fire in which case it was warm and smelled even worse), evil-smelling in summer as it seemed to have passed the point of "turning". I had it down to a fine art - I drank it, then I just had time to make it to the girls' loos before it all came back. Every day. The headmistress insisted all children must have milk, no reprieves. Mother told me to give mine to one of the Palfrey brothers (from a large, poor family) which I did. They thrived as they had lots of milk and quite a bit of extra food at dinner as well, they ate all the sago, tapioca and rice puddings and vegetables like swede or spinach, that the rest of us turned our noses up at. But to this day, I cannot tolerate milk!

Ruth Hixson

We had milk every morning. The teachers had to pour it into beakers, three to a pint. Some beakers had straight sides, some were curved. How it started I do not know, but the children who helped distribute the milk insisted that the boys have straight beakers, the girls, curved.

Wendy Walton

My over-riding recollection of school was the smell of the glue pot, inside the fireguard near the fire and the milk we were forced to drink at break time ... oh how I hated it, it made me feel sick and I tried my best to get someone else to drink it for me. The worst thing was when they put the stuff on the radiators to warm on a cold day. It's making me feel sick now, writing about it!

Ely Standard, 4th December 1942.

Milk supplies to schools in the Isle of Ely were described as extremely unsatisfactory by the County Inspector of Weights and Measures in a report to the Public Health and Housing Committee. In his opinion over half the milk supplied to schools was unsuitable for the children. Schools had priority of supply but no priority of quality and because the supply to schools was of necessity intermittent due to holidays and weekends, the suppliers had been providing "accommodation" milk which came from dairies outside the county, nominated by the Milk Marketing Board, over which the County authority had no control. The supplier preferred to keep his T.T. milk for private customers when he got an extra penny per pint. A price subsidy was agreed because of the potential threat to childrens' health.

Ely Standard, 11th December 1942.

In Ely, the Medical Officer of Health expressed the view that the recent outbreak of paratyphoid fever in the city had been due to contaminated milk. The Council was far too lenient in dealing with a few offending places where some of the cowsheds and cows were found to be in a filthy condition.

(These reports followed a lengthy correspondence over the previous weeks about unclean milk churns.)

There were some foods unrationed - offal and sausages at the butcher's, although only a small quantity of offal was ever in any one shop, and the percentage of meat in a wartime sausage was another of life's mysteries. But these items were prized to eke out the rations.

Peter Rex

One day towards the end of the war, I was on my way home when I passed two ladies talking about their day's shopping. They were closely watched by a little black and white dog sitting gazing with rapt attention at the package held by one of them. As I passed, the first unwrapped the package to show off its contents to her friend - a large slice of liver. As she did so, her hand wobbled, the liver slipped and fell straight down the little dog's throat!

1 Archer House, Ely; Wartime base of the C.F.S.

2 Bernice, Desmond & Melvyn Zerk, South Australia: a Special Occasion during the War.

3 Monette Meulet, standing on front bumper of car, 1942.

4 Linda Zerk (l) & elder sister Jennifer, siren-suited ready for a night in the shelter, ?1940/41.

Above left: 5 Joan Hardy on beach at Ramsgate ?1939.

Above right: 6 John Taylor (r) on beach at Bournemouth with Austrian Jewish refugee boy, September 1939.

Above left: 7 Four cousins in 1944:- l-r Bill, Mary, Wendy & Christina Watt.

Above right: 8 Dad (Capt. M.D.P.Watt), mother, Aunt May, Uncle Peter Watt, RN. 1944.

Above left: 9 Ruth Stobart, parents William & Sharly, brother John. Anderson shelter in background.

Above right: 10 A 500lb landmine caught in a tree next to Linda Zerk's house. Defused and landed.

11 Some of the Sunday Walk children. L – R
Anna Piper, Peter Friedrichsohn, Inge Kurrle, Suse
Friedrichsohn, c.1942.

12 German Informal Knitting Circle.

Below: 13 Anna Piper's Sunday walking group.
Anna held by her father (r), 1940.

Right: 14 Margaret Wood, aged 12,
broadcasting home from Cape Town, July 4th
1941.

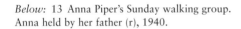

15 C.F.S. Production "Ward Scenes", Ely 1940. Muriel Gent, front row, second left.

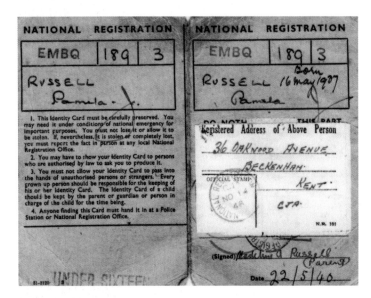

Left: 16 Inside View, Child's I.D. Card.

Below left: 17 Cover of Child's I.D. Card.

Below right: 18 Interior of Clothing Coupon Book.

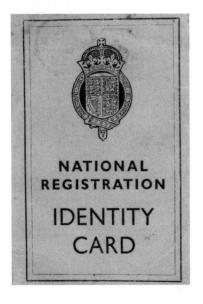

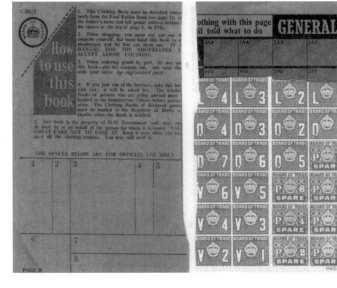

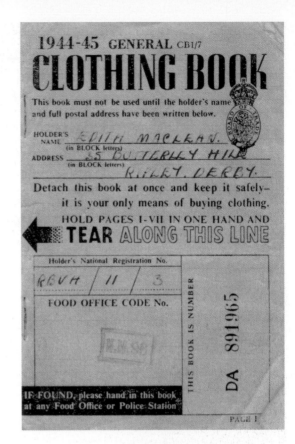

19 Clothing Coupon Book.

20 Hereward Hall, Ely; Wartime base of the J.F.S.

21 Margaret Mould, age 5, in her grandparents' garden, 1942.

Above left: 22 In Kilbirnie, Ayrshire, late 1940. Christina, Irene, Wendy Watt, Grandma Mary B. Watt at back.

Above right: 23 Ruth Stobart, parents & brother.

Left: 24 Helmi Spitze with her mother, 1940.

Below: 25 Inner pages, Joan Hardy's father's Pay Book.

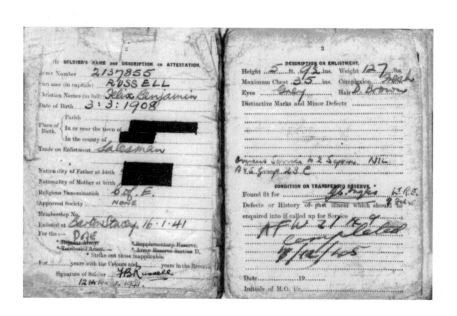

Above left: 26 Goldman sisters, evacuated to Ely, with the daughter of the host family, Renee Goldman, Maureen Goldman & Pamela Blakeman, Pearl Goldman.

Above middle: 27 Linda Zerk & Jennifer with their home help/nanny, just conscripted as a bus conductress.

Above right: 28 Joan Hardy with her father.

Below: 29 A picture of the red stool Christmas present to Anna Piper.

Right: 30 Jennifer Bedford's red striped dress; woollen bonnet & baby blanket made from "other fabrics".

Above left: 31 Glenda Lindsay & sister Valerie with Mother and family dog, c1942/43.

Above middle: 32 Mrs Ethel Smith, Gwen (now Pritchitt), Valerie.

Above right: 33 Gwen Pritchitt with doll "Daddy Soldier", elder sister Valerie, Oct.1943.

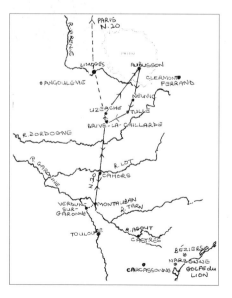

Above: 34 Monette Meulet's trek to Aubusson. Picture realised by Nancy Voak from a rough sketch by Monette Meulet.

Left: 35 Monette Meulet's round trip journey, Montauban - Aubusson - Montauban.

Above left: 36 Anna Piper, held by her father and wearing his formal Wehrmacht cap. 1940.

Above right: 37 Christina Watt, clutching her beloved Grumpy, November 1939.

Above left: 38 Salute for a dead comrade, Egypt 1944.

Above right: 39 Jean Runciman's father Charles V. Woodward, Royal Corps of Signals, near Cairo.

Above left: 40 Valerie Bragg with her parents. Her father committed suicide 4th September 1939.

Above right: 41 C.F.S. girls working in school garden in Ely. Marie Sternlight, Peggy Skepelhorn, Winnie Noble.

42 Prime Minister Churchill & Harold Macmillan in Beckenham c1943. Anne Gordon third little girl on right.

Above left: 43 Joy King's "Victory" Street Party, S.E. London, 1945.

Above right: 44 June Thomsitt with her parents, brother and younger sister, in Wales before 1945.

45 Ely Market Square: Club Hotel sign and entry lane, right. (Originally published 1906).

Right: 46 Jennifer Bedford, parents & brother, just before father's posting to the Med. for three and a half years, 1941–44.

Below left: 47 Gloria Morgan, aged 5, in bridesmaid's dress, 1942.

Below middle: 48 Ann Dix riding her pedal car, c1943.

Below right: 49 Glenda Lindsay, c1944.

OPEN-AIR THEATRE.   **JULY 24th, 1943.**

"THE TAMING OF THE SHREW"
By WILLIAM SHAKESPEARE
At Looe Rocks, Manor Way, Beckenham.
(By kind permission of Mr. and Mrs. Percy Jones.)

CHARACTERS IN THE INDUCTION:

CHRISTOPHER SLY, *a tinker*	ERNEST R. OSBORNE
HOSTESS	EDITH HOWE
A LORD	VERNON JONES
ATTENDANTS	KENNETH BRADFORD, SIDNEY COLLETT, G. J. GOODWIN E. J. DENT, A. THORN
PAGE	HENRY CLEERE

SCENE: Before an alehouse; and a bedchamber in the Lord's house.

CHARACTERS IN THE PLAY:

LUCENTIO, *son to Vincentio*	F. M. PERRY
TRANIO, *his servant*	R. G. C. BROWNING
BAPTISTA, *a rich gentleman of Padua*	HARRY THORN
KATHARINA, *the Shrew* } *his daughters*	EILEEN DAVIDSON
BIANCA	IDA POOL
HORTENSIO } *suitors to Bianca*	F. D. L. BURGE
GREMIO	JOHN FLYNN
BIONDELLO, *servant to Lucentio*	BENNET HATCH
PETRUCHIO, *a gentleman of Verona*	VICTOR THORNTON
GRUMIO, *his servant*	ELLIS GUBBINS
SERVANTS TO BAPTISTA	ANGELA THORN, CHRISTINE THORN
CURTIS	HENRY CLEERE
SERVING-MEN } *servants to Petruchio*	KENNETH BRADFORD, SIDNEY COLLETT, G. J. GOODWIN, E. J. DENT
A PEDANT	VALENTINE CARTER
A TAILOR	E. J. DENT
VINCENTIO, *an old gentleman of Pisa*	FRED J. CLYNE
WIDOW	EDITH HOWE

SCENE: Partly in Padua and partly at Petruchio's country seat.
The play will be presented in two parts.

The play produced by VICTOR THORNTON.
Orchestra directed by VIOLET ELWELL-SUTTON.
Stage properties and furniture by ERNEST POOL and E. J. DENT.
Wigs and costumes by B. J. SIMMONS AND CO., Covent Garden.

Producer's Note. — Shakespeare's share in the writing of "The Taming of the Shrew" is the subject of much debate. What is indisputable is the existence of another play, "The Taming of a Shrew," and the two have many interesting parallels. The character of Christopher Sly is, in the Shakespeare version of the story, completely forgotten after his one interjection at the end of Act I, scene i; whereas in the other play, his presence as spectator throughout the players' performance is preserved by some half-dozen snatches of dialogue sprinkled here and there. As an experiment, I have ventured to restore all but the last of these comments to Sly. In defence of this action—should anyone bother to challenge it—I see no greater heresy in tinkering by addition where there is some excuse, than by subtraction where there is none—the latter a common practice among presenters of Shakespeare who cut to suit their taste, convenience or the supposed susceptibilities of a twentieth century audience.—V.T.

PREVIOUS PRODUCTIONS AT LOOE ROCKS.
"Twelfth Night," August, 1941; "Much Ado About Nothing," June, 1942; "The Merchant of Venice," July, 1942; "The Rivals," June, 1943.

"The Taming of the Shrew" will be played in Kelsey Park next week from Wednesday to Saturday inclusive, at 7.30 p.m., with a special matinee for children only on Saturday at 2.45 p.m.; and on August Bank Holiday in the quadrangle of Bromley College at 2.45 and 7.0 p.m.

Above left: 50 Programme of *Taming of the Shrew*.

Top right: 51 "Taming of the Shrew" produced by Victor Thornton (father of Glenda Lindsay), centre stage arms outstretched.

Above right: 52 Jewish Refugee Boys in the Dining Room of their Ely hostel. Rev'd (Rabbi) Kon, Hostel Supervisor, seated.

Above left: 53 Teaching Staff of J.F.S., ?1939. Dr. Bernstein, front row, centre.

Above right: 54 J.F.S. (Ely-based) Pierrot Troupe, 1943. Mr Joseph, who wrote and produced the shows, seated centre.

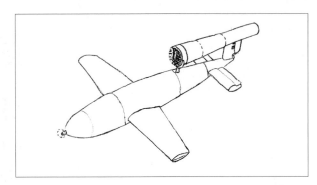

55 Sketch diagram of V1 weapon, Doodlebug.

Above left: 56 Kathy Jackson's cousin Jeanne's wedding, January 1943, to an American serviceman, Walter. Kathy in front of bridesmaid.

Above right: 57 Cover of C.F.S. Prize Day programme.

Above left: 58 Llanrug, north Wales, after village Sports Day, before 1945. June Thomsitt and her sister on left of second row.

Above right: 59 Christmas Card from Daddy, serving in the R.A.M.C.

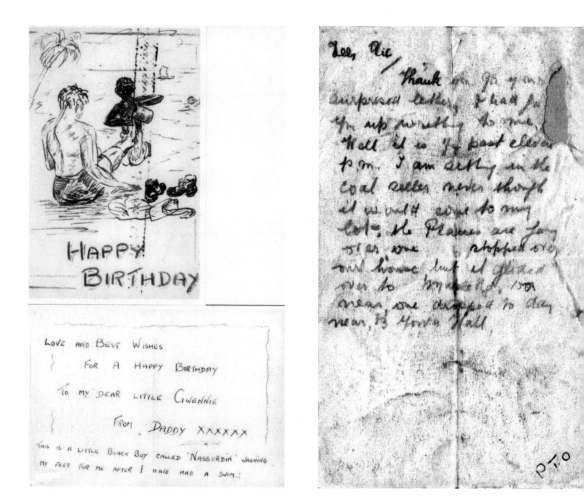

Above left: 60 Birthday card drawn by Gwen Pritchitt's father, stationed in Ceylon (Sri Lanka).

Above right: 61 Letter being written by Ann Gamêt's grandmother, sheltering under the stairs, when a doodlebug fell, destroying the side wall of the house.

Above left: 62 Pat Manning, mother & brother on beach at Margate, ?1939.

Above right: 63 Sunday School class in patriotic fancy dress.

64 Figurenlegenspiel - game played with by Ruth Hixson.

Above left: 65 Joan Hardy with Red sailboat.

Above right: 66 Jewish Refugee Boys in their hostel, Ely. ?1940.

Right: 67 Linda Zerk, sister & cousins, Great Barford, 1944.

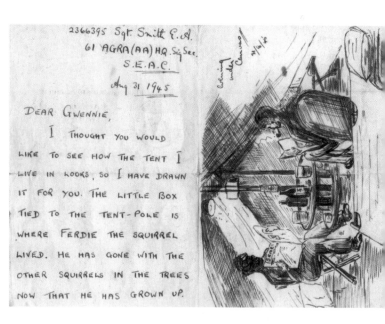

2366395 Sgt. Smith E.A.
61 AGRA (AA) HQ. Sig Sec.
S.E.A.C.

Aug 31 1945

DEAR GWENNIE,

I THOUGHT YOU WOULD LIKE TO SEE HOW THE TENT I LIVE IN LOOKS, SO I HAVE DRAWN IT FOR YOU. THE LITTLE BOX TIED TO THE TENT-POLE IS WHERE FERDIE THE SQUIRREL LIVED. HE HAS GONE WITH THE OTHER SQUIRRELS IN THE TREES NOW THAT HE HAS GROWN UP.

Above left: 68 John Taylor, summer 1939.

Above right: 69 Illustrated letter from Daddy, to Gwen Pritchitt.

70 Group of neighbours of Gwen Pritchitt and their children, Hayes (Kent), sometime during the Second World War.

Above left: 71 Margaret Mould aged 8, in the Brownies.

Above right: 72 Ann Dix on her tricycle, c1941/42.

Above left: 73 Jennifer Bedford & brother with "their" American serviceman's wife.

Above right: 74 Christina Watt in costume for Fancy Dress parade, 1945.

Above left: 75 Children's Victory fancy dress parade, W. Yorks., 1945.

Above right: 76 Wendy Watt, in costume for Fancy Dress parade, 1945.

Letf: 77 Composite picture of Ruth Stobart's family; made in Egypt.

78 Margaret Mould, 6th birthday party, July 1943.

Above left: 79 Three soldiers. Gwen Pritchitt's father, centre.

Above right: 80 Jennifer Bedford, American serviceman's wife and her friend, early 1944.

Right: 81 June Thomsitt (l), younger sister (r) and a friend, Wales, pre-1945.

82 Wendy Watt sitting on the front garden wall,
W.Yorks. c1943.

83 Margaret Mould on holiday at Bournemouth
1944. Note Coastal Defences!

There were other "perks" to living in the depths of the countryside.

June Thomsitt
Living in the country we ate well. We could buy eggs and my father had the shooting rights of a local estate as it had been taken over by nuns for a 'transplanted' school for the duration of the war. They would not kill any of the wildlife. Consequently rabbits and pigeons supplemented our meat ration.

Margaret Haynes
One day I went to the village shop with my mother and there was a large pink slab in the cabinet - SPAM! I can still smell the aroma when the door was opened for the lady to slice it.

Richard Ellison
I really enjoyed Spam - and the little Perch of which we could catch many at the edge of Lake Windermere - no longer there now!

It was axiomatic that no food could be wasted because there was only just enough of it. The writer remembers reading, many years ago, about a family during the war whose grandmother had made them some vanilla flavoured cakes for tea. Unfortunately she had confused the bottles of flavourings and put eucalyptus in the cake mix, but the cakes were still eaten, odd taste notwithstanding. Too many rations would have gone into them which could not be replaced.

However, some things really could not be used.

Janet Ellison
A food parcel arriving from Orkney (where my father had been stationed) caused much excitement until we opened it to find that it contained one extremely smelly duck! However, we appreciated the islanders' kindness.

Food parcels were sent to many families from relatives in the Commonwealth countries or America, and were a huge treat, containing as they did unheard-of luxuries like tinned peaches, tinned pineapple or pears, various tinned meats and sometimes dried fruit. All items were either unavailable or needed a number of points to buy at the grocer's. (Again to try to ensure fairer distribution, most tinned goods needed little coupons, known as points, to buy them. The grocer had to snip them from the pages of the ration books in exchange for tins of sardines or baked beans, let alone anything more exotic. The system of points applied to virtually every food item in the grocery, but not, during the war years, to bread or flour. These were briefly rationed in the period of hyper-austerity immediately after the war.) It was later in the war that food parcels started to arrive, possibly when the people in the donor nations had received direct evidence of the lack of such items in Britain and realised how much pleasure a parcel would give. After a short time, generous people in these countries would contribute money and a parcel would be sent which would go into a general distribution system, usually to households where there were children.

Mary Hardcastle (b.1937. West Wickham, Kent)

One memorable day we received a food parcel from Australia. These were delivered down our street by a slow-moving lorry crawling along the road where normally only the milkman's horse-drawn cart or the coalman's dray were seen. The back of the lorry was open and loaded with brown paper parcels. Mothers ran over, waving their children's ration books and begging for a parcel. My mother seized hold of my hand and dragged me over, calling "I've got a little girl. Can we have one too?" To our immense joy, a parcel was handed down.

We ran into the kitchen and placed the parcel on the table. No cutting of string or ripping of paper - these were prized themselves as commodities almost unobtainable in ordinary households. At last the contents! My mother was actually weeping with joy as we lifted out first a large tin of peaches, then one of pineapple chunks, a packet of icing sugar - my eyes were goggling! But mother was busy unwrapping hand-knitted white socks, new white handkerchiefs and other small luxury items which she squirreled away for future occasions. Soon we were reading the enclosed letter from our new Australian friend and started to compose our letter of thanks. The tinned fruit and the icing sugar were saved for my approaching birthday party. For the next six months tinned peaches and pineapple became the usual treat at parties. The kindness of the Australians lives on in my memory and the importance of such gifts organised by the Red Cross and similar caring organisations today will always gain my reciprocal support.

Ruth Hixson

At about the end of the war we received a food parcel from Australia. The only edible item that I remember was a large tin of mango jam (what was a mango?). There was a letter too, from a girl called Grace Frencham. We exchanged several letters. The main thing I remember of the correspondence is that she told me she had just knitted herself a dress. That must have made me feel inferior because I don't think I wrote any more. Blackboard rubbers, which is what I knitted then, didn't quite compare with a dress!

Peter Rex

In 1942 or '43 we received an overseas food parcel (quite rare as there wasn't much space in the convoys for non-essential supplies) which came from my Aunt Edith Pinkney in Canada. It contained some fairly unusual North American foodstuffs. I recall some quite repulsive powdered egg and, of all things, packets of 'Jell-O' which did not taste like British jelly! My aunt seems to have had a very odd idea of what rationing actually entailed, and of course, the food sent had to be concentrated so that it would not go off.

Margaret Mould

Pre-war work friends of dad, in the New York office, occasionally sent us food parcels. One contained a large, catering-size box of cloves. When I cleared mum's cupboards, in 1984, there were still quite a lot left in the box!

With the continued call-up of men to the Services, there was a shortage of agricultural workers. For the normal running and work around a farm, the Women's Land Army proved to be invaluable, despite farmers' initial extreme scepticism about female labour on farms. (Yet in virtually every other country in the world at that time, the women worked alongside the men in farming, and the Land Army had been invaluable in the First World War.) But some harvest times needed extra help. It was normal, in the areas where potatoes and root crops were grown, for schools to have a two-week break in the autumn term so that the senior pupils could help with the work; where the writer went to school in Yorkshire, this activity was known as 'potato picking'. Senior boys, and frequently younger ones in the higher classes of the junior school, were only too pleased to do this work and earn themselves some welcome pocket money.

It was fruit picking which could pose a problem, an activity which is labour-intensive. As many fruit harvests happen during the school summer holidays, it became customary to arrange Harvest Camps for young people, so they could do the picking.

Pam Daymond

After our return from the Exeter evacuation, we went to school Harvest Camp, August 1942 or '43, in Goudhurst, Kent. I was allocated to a fruit farm, picking plums and apples. We weren't allowed to pick cherries as the trees can be dangerous (with the branches so heavily laden) and special ladders have to be used. Even with them, it is possible for the branch to give way. On the first day we were told we could eat as many apples as we liked (!) and of course, the novelty soon wore off. When it came to weighing the fruit, we were heaving forty-pound boxes around! Some of the girls had been allocated to hop-picking and the rest of us didn't like the smell of the hops when they came back to the billet - it clung to them until they had washed and changed!

We were paid for this work, but I can't remember the rate. For taking our own blankets we were paid a shilling (5p) per week and the same for taking our bicycles. We had to pay for our keep out of our earnings, but we did not know what that sum actually was. We were told we would get our money back at school, but it was after Christmas when I received the grand sum of eight shillings (40p) for the four weeks!

To keep the country working while the men were fighting, women were either encouraged or conscripted into work. Married women with children under 14 were exempt, but many chose to work anyway, frequently from patriotism, wishing to do their bit' or from economic necessity. A soldier's pay was not very much and families had to be fed and clothed somehow! It was necessary to feed these people. In factories, there was usually a works canteen to provide a meal, but the British Restaurant was born in these times. These provided a meal of the meat-and-two-veg. style, with pudding and generally a cup of tea, at a very reasonable price, for the workers who could not get home for lunch. The menu would be fairly restricted but adequate. Many women exempt from other work would help in them as their war-work.

Jean Parrott

Once the raids abated we returned to Wickham and I eventually went to the County School at Beckenham on a scholarship. At the same time, mum started to 'do her bit' by working at the British Restaurant in Glebe Way, West Wickham. I remember her sitting taking the eyes out of potatoes that had been de-skinned by machine.

Linda Zerk

British Restaurants were set up in local halls to provide cheap meals for people working for the war effort, although anyone could eat there, for about 1s. 2d (one shilling and two old pence, about 6p today). I can remember having the odd meal there when Mother was working there. Good stodgy food dished out of enormous containers and I enjoyed it! Rather like school dinners. The restaurant seemed to be run by the WVS - ladies who wore green dresses and funny hats.

In the cities, restaurants still opened and nightclubs were still popular, as people needed and wanted meals out sometimes. As early as July 1940 it became illegal for protein to be served in more than one course in a restaurant. The prices that could be charged were governed by rationing, eventually being fixed at a maximum of 5/- (five shillings, or 25p in current terms) per meal. Sourcing the protein could be a problem and on some menus an unlikely beast started to appear - "roof rabbit", a euphemism for the domestic cat. (What is more odd is that there was the same phenomenon in Germany where the term Dachschwein (roof pig) was coined for the pet cat raised as food by people suffering severe meat shortages. Similarly, there was the term Quatschschwein, (balcony pig), a rabbit raised on a balcony or in a porch, for food.) And, of course, in Colditz Castle the French officers kept a cat to which they fed all manner of scraps until it grew into a magnificent creature, whereupon they killed and ate it! Food supplies at home were limited, certainly, but generally not to the extent that people had to eat the family cat!

John Taylor

As a child during the war food did not seem to be much of a problem. I'm sure we were helped by my father having two meals a day in the works canteen and I know mother sometimes went without to feed the children. She used to get lumps of unrationed fat from the butcher to make beef dripping and lard. We kept chickens and ducks in the back garden. Mother would make dried egg omelettes and sweets from dried milk. During the last part of the war my Uncle Jack was in charge of stores on a local army camp for a battalion of troops who had all gone to France on D-Day. He had a mountain of food with no-one to eat it so he brought us a whole range of goods from cake to blankets! Very little food was ever left over, but any that was, was fed to the ducks and chickens. One treat I do remember. A cousin was in the Royal Navy and on one leave he brought home a banana for each of the youngsters. It was the only one I had from 1939 to 1946!

Louise Milbourn

In America butter was one of the food items to be rationed along with sugar. I well remember the alternative to butter, called Oleo Margarine. It arrived as an unappetising lump of white fatty substance into which we had to mix the little packet of orange dye accompanying it to make it have a closer resemblance to the butter it was replacing though the taste was hardly in competition with butter.

Throughout the war, the one unrationed protein source was fish but the supply was limited. Trawlers could not put far out to sea as shipping lanes were mined, once out into open waters: indeed a proportion of the fishing fleet was taken over for mine detection and removal duties! Some supplies were available though, and the queue at the fishmonger's, on the days there were supplies, were extremely long. Fish and chip shops were supplied every so often - the shop in the writer's village, from memory, seemed to have fish on a Friday and possibly also Saturday, but certainly not every weekday. They quickly sold out, although there always seemed to be plenty of chips. Again, the greengrocer, who had a horse and cart (a lorry when he had petrol) for trading in those villages, had some fresh fish on Fridays but rarely otherwise. There is no recollection of freshwater fish...salmon came in tins and was a very rare treat!

For many, the dish known as "Woolton Pie" is likely to be the abiding memory of wartime food. Lord Woolton was Minister of Food from 1942/43 and this vegetable pie was named after him. It is made without meat but with a selection of nutritious and fibrous root vegetables instead. The crust could be a standard pastry or of potato. Made well, it is a good dish though badly made it is probably awful!

The Ministry of Food published adverts throughout the war for vegetable dishes, urging people to make the most of potatoes or carrots. The consumption of the latter was greatly increased when word got around that pilots ate them to improve their night vision, so all the pilot-hopefuls among the young boys followed suit.

Many of the manufacturers also published economical recipes in their advertising campaigns, which made nutritious dishes with or without the product (Bovril, Oxo, Marmite) so there were always ideas to try, and the women's magazines co-operated in these campaigns in their cookery pages. Oatmeal became a staple "filler" in many dishes.

We were fed but after six years the lack of variety was starting to tell. The experiments with whalemeat were an unmitigated disaster and did not last long, the public, despite wishing for more protein, would not have that at any price! The fish snoek was similarly rejected. It was pretty repulsive and not in the least like cod! Many mothers refused these two, knowing full well their children would not look at them. The protein they represented might have done us good, though.

Joan Hardy
I shall never forget the taste - or the toughness - of whale meat!

FRANCE, HOLLAND & GERMANY

Concerns about the supply of food were not confined solely to Britain. After the Blitzkrieg of May 1940, the food politics of Occupied Europe changed almost immediately. Much of the produce and harvest was taken either to feed the occupying forces or to feed the

German people; that nation's food imports had been reduced to around 25% of the total consumed before the outbreak of war, but now the Occupied Territories were making up the shortfall, without payment. Their own people therefore suffered real hardship, in Holland to the point of starvation. The large cities suffered the most because of the difficulties of distribution and the claims of the Occupying Force on all foodstuffs. Country dwellers were, on the whole, far more fortunate, having gardens where they grew vegetables and kept chickens, and knowing what hedgerow fruits to gather for food.

France had been divided into two zones, the North being "Occupied", the South, "free", at least for a short time. After 1942 the Occupation of the remainder of the country took place.

Monetter Meulet

There was an outbreak of severe chilblains in winter, attributed to the lack of butter in the diet!

Children were entitled to chocolate with their ration cards, chocolate later kept in a tin. We would be given a "bar" with bread at 5.00 o'clock. When we broke the "bar" the chocolate was just a white sugary cream with the chocolate simply painted on the outside.

I remember in the warm days of summer, there were plums on the trees and my grandmother made jam from them with grape juice (not yet fermented). The jam was black, with a taste both sweet and sour – it was good!

My great-grandmother lived about two kilometres from our village. Every afternoon my mother would go to visit her grandmother, "Manti", to take her the day's necessities, returning with milk and eggs.

During all this time hunting was forbidden – no one was allowed to have a gun (they were all buried in the gardens), but there were rabbits ... my father was a friend of one of the gendarmes. This one sent the two other gendarmes to patrol to the east of the village and then he, my father and another friend would patrol to the west. The friend kept ferrets and in the evening there would be dead rabbits in our houses! There was a warren nearby – they put the ferret down the rabbit-hole and covered the exit with a bag. Soon there was a rabbit in it, which they killed.

But of course, the "boches" knew nothing of this!

In Germany, food shortages grew, and householders took similar measures to those in this country, but there was no official campaign to bring this home to people as there was here. Again, the countryside fared better than the cities, country dwellers being more aware of the abundance of free food to be found in nature than town dwellers.

Helmi Spitze

As the war progressed, shortages of almost everything became commonplace. My sister and I were fortunate because our grandmother had a vegetable garden and fruit trees on her property. We shared those items with people who did not have gardens. For meat we stood in line with our ration cards. We received dairy products from farmers who traded for household items that we had and they wanted.

After the war the Americans occupied Moosburg. Every Saturday there was "Open Haus" at the American House for the children. I would go there and be given a peanut butter sandwich and other treats. However, several of my friends were not allowed by their parents to attend those gatherings.

Geseke Clark

[Food recollections come from the immediate post-war period]

There were severe food shortages. My father, being a lawyer, did not believe in black market buying though my mother often did get a loaf of bread that way. We gathered nettles for vegetables, the nutty fruits of beech trees, mushrooms etc. At a funfair, a woman wanted my lovely blue bicycle for her daughter, so it was exchanged for a sack of flour.

There was once source of help which stood out – the warm school meals provided by the British Red Cross. Every day we were given a thick nourishing soup in our little pots with handles, and before any holidays we received an exciting parcel with dry food, for example a tin of chicken soup with rice, a bar of chocolate, a tin of sardines and other goodies. It was a great help. Sometimes we were allowed to take seconds home. In the cold winter 1946/47 I often had a full pot of soup, which was awkward when I wanted to slide my way home from school!

Anna Piper

Early on, probably in 1941, food shortages became apparent. We were lucky, as some friends were farmers and our grandparents had extensive orchards and a vineyard outside the town. The orchards made good vegetable gardens as well. Everyone with a little space kept chickens. As my mother was working, I was entrusted with the food shopping whenever possible. I was then probably five years old. (We went to school at 6, not 5). So my reading was not very good. That necessitated my memorizing the shopping list. Very often there would be large queues, so I turned out to be the secret weapon, as I recited the list aloud in order not to forget and was therefore quickly moved up to the front.

Our mothers made syrup of pears and sugar beet for sweetening and as a topping for bread. Pancakes were made with beer instead of milk. All the surplus fruit and vegetables were either bottled or dried and eggs and cabbage put in stone jars for the winter in waterglass and salt respectively, covered with wooden boards. These were stored in the cellars.

Vegetables and fruit suitable for drying were sliced and strung up and hung in the loft to dry, they made wonderful compotes and stews in the winter. At Christmas time we made gnome-style decorations from prunes, dried apple rings, pear slices, wire and nuts! My cousins and I hated to be sent for supplies; to put one's hand into the waterglass that was all slippery and cold was horrible.

My maternal grandmother lived in Bavaria, not far from the Czechoslovakian border. I was taken there for visits whenever possible. Grandmother possessed a very voluminous loden cloak. She would don this and a rucksack and take me to catch the local train out to our weekend cottage in the countryside. Once there, we walked miles through the woods, visiting farms and exchanging what we had brought against bread, usually baked in a wood oven, freshly churned butter, eggs, smoked pork, even potatoes and vegetables. We also collected mushrooms and berries on our journeys. My grandmother just tucked me under her cloak when it rained and I looked through the arm slit.

One farm was about twelve km. away. The grandmother there always gave me a cup of buttermilk and a big hunk of bread with butter that you could see your teeth in when biting into it. Butter was still churned by hand and sometimes I was allowed to help and would be rewarded with some small food item.

The cottage was on a farm above a trout stream, called the Lauterach. On the opposite side was a pub whose owner had seven children. The youngest son was my age and he taught me to tickle fro brown trout, another welcome addition to the table. It was a great treat at the weekends when the family joined us to eat at the pub as we could get fish, meat, eggs, and home made cakes. Sometimes the owner would give us food to take back.

Probably February/March 1945, the Front moved nearer to us and our school, a few hundred metres from where we lived, was closed and became a first-aid post. The doctors and ambulance personnel came to us in their breaks to listen to the news on the radio. They brought items of food, coffee and best of all, ration chocolate. This came sealed in round tins with circular markings and sectioned like a round cake ready for cutting.

After the end of the war, the school re-opened. An American person came to the school and we were weighed and measured to work out if we were undernourished. Those in this category got supplementary foods. I loved the dried milk; it was delicious in powdered form.

The situation in Holland was vastly different from that in rural Germany, especially the major cities of Amsterdam and Rotterdam, where the people lived with near-starvation for years. There, domestic pets became food, and even rats were eaten.

Rita Blackie

During the first winter of the war, shortages started to take hold in Holland. Clothes, fabrics, wool, leather shoes, were increasingly unobtainable, along with the absence of gas for cooking and electricity for lighting. Food was short – we were hungry all the time and it became worse every day. There was simply not enough, my mother walked through the streets seeking out food, and wood to burn for warmth. The trees disappeared. The refuse was not collected but was dumped in a central Rose Garden which backed onto where we lived. At first, rats swarmed over the dump but they were caught, killed and eaten. People died from cold and starvation. Our dad would go on hunger tours into the countryside, where he exchanged everything of value for food, some grain perhaps, or really anything edible. My mum lost all her jewellery, and my father, his violin and all his beautiful books. We lost the blankets from our bed – all for food. I cannot even touch upon the horror, the hunger, the cold and the absolute fear of those five years. , My elder sister and I were taken to father's relatives in the country to give our mother two extra ration cards for our baby sister, but that was no help because there was nothing available.

In the last year at nursery school the children got so-called meals supplied by the Nazi government. My sister had to take a bowl and spoon to school and she and the other little ones got soup. The potato peelings were cooked and the liquid was hot. The spoon scraped the sand at the bottom of the bowl because that was what they were given to eat.

When the allies invaded on 6th June 1944 we all though it would be over soon but the allies stopped in Belgium and Holland and had another year to go! That soon became the worst year of all, when we really started to scavenge for anything to eat. When the farmers reaped their harvest, we went over the fields to pick up any ears of corn left behind. We would pick up anything left – frozen potatoes, sugar beet, tulip bulbs. They said the bulbs were like onions! It was sheer misery and many people died. When the Germans at last capitulated we had the Swedish Red Cross and American Military rations handed out and that was heaven. But many people were sick and even died because of too much too soon after having nothing. The appalling misery did come to an end once the Americans started to bring food relief, and we were finally liberated by Canadian troops.

Over the Dutch 'Hongerwinter' (hunger winter) of 1944–45, 22,000 people died of starvation while tens of thousands more survived by eating tulip bulbs. Western Holland was the last part of the country to be liberated and those people had lived there. The Dutch Government in Exile had ordered a national strike that winter so the Germans retaliated by forbidding food to be taken to the towns. More than 90% of Dutch agricultural produce was taken by the Germans for their own use so there was little of anything left for the Dutch to use themselves. From the winter of 1944 no fuel of any kind was delivered to major cities. It was 'normal' for people to eat nothing at all for several consecutive days. Domestic cats disappeared. In Rotterdam people also ate rats, as in Amsterdam near Rita's home, and the bartering of remaining clothing and possessions for scraps of food was an everyday occurrence. It was not until early May 1945, when the war was all but over, that some of these towns were finally liberated and people were again able to eat.

CHAPTER 9

EDUCATION

Through the early stages of the war - the evacuation, 'the phoney war', the Battle of Britain and the Blitz - the priority for the authorities was that children's education should continue as normal, or as close to normal as could be managed. To evacuate schools en bloc was administratively excellent, allowing the authorities to know where the youngsters and teachers actually were, whilst simultaneously avoiding too great a degree of trauma for the children involved as they arrived in their new surroundings in a pre-existing, socially cohesive unit. It also meant that the pupils continued with teachers and teaching methods that were familiar to them, a factor which could be vitally important in maintaining morale.

However, the needs of the armed forces and the industry supporting them meant that as the war progressed, more and more teachers, especially men, were called up. Those evacuees who had returned to the towns against official advice were receiving no education at all, so some teachers eventually had to be brought back to supervise classes for them. But through all this, the children did receive their schooling even during raids and chronic shortages of materials, in village halls and W.I. huts or in shared premises, and passed their examinations regardless.

In the Ely area, the Jews Free School sorted itself out remarkably quickly. The girls were mainly in Littleport and Ely, the boys' Central School was at Soham and Isleham and the refugee boys were in Ely, at the hostel in St. Mary's Street. Both senior and junior boys were in Ely, where seniors attended Needhams School, at least initially. Apart from the refugee boys, for whom classes were held at the hostel, the Jewish pupils in the area either enrolled directly in local schools, if sufficient places existed, or else shared premises with the local school; one school attending in the morning, the other in the afternoon. An appropriate hall or room would be taken over for lessons or activities on the same alternating basis. Dr. Bernstein, the head of JFS in Ely, preferred the shared premises scheme as it allowed the same system of teaching to continue for his pupils.

The Central Foundation School also shared premises, with the Ely High School for Girls. There were additional premises in the town taken over for them as their base, a large house, Archer House, and the Club Room, (behind the Club Hotel) both on the Market Square.

Muriel Gent

School was my whole life. I started in the preparatory department at five, and after the VIth form I stayed on as Miss Menzies' secretary. In Ely we were split up into "families" under a teacher. This was our main social life and we were often invited to their homes for tea and games. I went back to school to Archer House in the evening, to do homework or practise on the piano. Our foster-father had a piano but sadly it was a new one from Liberty's in London, his favourite supplier, and although I had been learning since I was five, and my sister was just starting, we were not allowed to use it. This upset my mother, herself a wonderful pianist.

We always wore uniform in school; originally it came from Bourne and Hollingsworth, but I've no idea where we got it in Ely.

At the beginning of the war, in those parts of suburban London not subject to evacuation, school conditions were a bit chaotic.

Diana Scott

When we got back to Beckenham in October 1939, after staying longer in Hove through fear of Beckenham being bombed, we found all the schools were closed and we had classes in houses. I and about seven other children from Balgowan School, met in a local house where we sat round the table and were taught by our teacher for two mornings a week. The rest of the class was divided into similar groups and the teacher went on her rounds, so each group got about 1 day's tuition a week. After a few months, this scheme was abandoned and we went back to our primary schools.

Evacuation to the country brought different methods and standards for many London-area children.

Valerie Bragg

We went to Cirencester with our school and teachers. It was a church school of sixty pupils. In Gloucestershire we attended a church school in Stratton-in-the-Wold. The vicar came every morning to say prayers. My excuse for poor handwriting is that we learnt to write with relief pens. With the poor education I received, I ended up with my local authority's library service as a general assistant.

Sylvia Bunce

I was evacuated to Naseby in Leicestershire, with my gran and cousin Val, who was in the year above me at school. We went to a little country school there, where we were considerably advanced in comparison with the local children and we ended up helping the teacher with the other pupils.

Jill Moxon

My family eventually rented a small cottage in Dolton, north Devon, near the village school, where my father was to teach. Local children and London children were crammed into small classrooms and I was in the Village Hall being taught by a Guinea Girl. (She was 18 years old and unable to take up her college place, so therefore taught as an unqualified teacher for pay of a guinea a week. [A guinea was one pound and one shilling or £1.05 in present coinage.])

June Thomsitt

My education started in the village school in Llanrug. For our first year we were not given paper to write on but something that was very plentiful in that part of the world - slate - thin sheets of it in a wooden frame. We used a special slate pencil the marks of which could be easily erased. I once drew what I thought was a pretty, repetitive pattern and was sternly told by the teacher that the figure four did not have a closed top but an open one! I had not realised that I had been drawing fours!

I must have had a very good start because after returning to London at the age of ten and spending one year at Stewart Fleming Junior School, Beckenham, I passed the scholarship to Beckenham County Grammar School.

Brenda Booker

At Farncombe I went to a small country school. On the first day we were all given a 'tidy box' containing chalks, counting frame, slate and duster, etc. I spent a lot of time making 'bobbles' from wool wound around milk bottle tops, or doing French knitting.

Claire Hardisty

We lived mostly in Oxfordshire, where there was a large contingent of Conscientious Objectors around Buscot Park. While we lived at Fernham it became time for me to start school. A friend of my father's offered to pay my fees so that I did not have to go to the village school, but there was an insuperable problem; the drive to the school, as we had no car.

So I began my schooling at Little Coxwell Village School and was bored. I didn't fit in because I could already read and count and write numbers to one hundred and the others could not. I attended two more schools after this. My mother had suffered a difficult pregnancy and taking the elder children to school became too difficult so we attempted the long walk alone. But the village children terrorised us because we were different - we had a snake thrown at us once. Father moved to another job and my mother taught us with the help of PNEU. From that, mother was recruited as a teacher at a Quaker school in Hertfordshire and I became a boarder there. The school was run on progressive lines. If I felt like playing all day long, I did. If I wanted to read a book in the library, I could. We studied history - I loved it, music - marvellous, carpentry - I did fretwork for one whole week and made a crew of wooden elephants. I did all this and more and was blissfully happy. I managed to avoid English Grammar entirely - it still shows to this day; and only attended the arithmetic classes if I felt like it - which also still shows!

When the war ended my father returned to work in the City but mother stayed on at the school for another year. When we returned home and were sent to a normal primary school, we were like little fishes out of water. It was too late for me to acquire much "normal" education; I was lost in a fog where grammar and arithmetic were concerned. Of course I failed the 11+ and although I was fortunate in passing at 13 thus arriving at Beckenham County Grammar School for Girls, I never really caught up. And as a result of these experiences, I always felt like an outsider.

Joan Hardy

I attended at least two schools in Cornwall whilst evacuated privately there, one in Gorran Haven and Mt. Charles Junior Girls School in St. Austell, and then one small private one when I was in Bromley. Yes, my education was interrupted but I don't recall it being a problem.

Christina Watt

I started at the village school in Yorkshire when I was four. I loved every minute of it apart from the milk. Our teacher had masses of reading cards for us - all home-made, and as I had been able to read from the age of 3 I raced through them all at breakneck speed and was allowed to read real books! We had "band". The teacher played the piano and the class had an assortment of percussion instruments to play; we learnt to follow a (somewhat primitive) score and the value of the differing notes, also how to keep time and rhythm going. This was a favourite lesson that only happened once a week. Schubert's Marche Militaire is still a favourite!

The only way to get to school was to walk. It was almost a mile from our house so I had school dinners, it would not have been possible to go home at lunch time.

Getting to school was far less of a problem then. On the whole, you walked or possibly cycled or were carried on a child seat on a bicycle. Generally, car transport was not used. Most people did not have a car then, and even if they did, the petrol allowance was so small that there were far more important things to do with it than take the children to school!

Ann Dix

As my father was called up, my mother had to keep the newsagents' business going, learning to drive the van which was used for the newspapers. I was sent to a private nursery school for mornings only at the age of three and a half. My mother used the van to take me and two friends to school. Every time we saw a policeman - which was often - we were told to lie down flat, as petrol was rationed and the van was only allowed to be used for business purposes. We thought this was great fun, not realising the seriousness of the situation.

Corinne Older

I was five but I walked to school, a mile away, on my own, home for lunch and back again, then mother met me at 3.30pm - I was more frightened of a dog than I was of the war!

Gloria Morgan

School days began for me in September 1942. Every day I walked down Anerley Hill from where we lived, almost at the top, to the school behind the Town Hall, about three-quarters of a mile. It is a steep hill and coming home at lunchtime and after school, I would ride up on the number 654 trolley bus.

Classes there were crowded. In my class there were 51 pupils and folding desks were squeezed in at the front and in the aisles between the two-seater bench-type desks with lift-up lids and inkwells. I always hoped to be picked as ink monitor. I wasn't ever picked for any class responsibility - passed over for cleaning the board, distributing milk and handing out pencils!

Those of us who started school in the early years of the war accepted whatever conditions we found ourselves in as being the norm - this was school and obviously, this was how it was. Older children must have found it difficult, though, to adapt their continuing education to the variety of surroundings and differing syllabi they encountered, and to the very trying conditions under which they might have had to take public examinations.

Diana Scott

In 1943 I passed the scholarship and moved to the Beckenham County School for Girls. At the end of my first year the flying bombs started. These went on continually day and night, but school was still open and I remember on one day when I got there, we were directed to sit in the shelters as they were reinforced and we were given work there. There were senior girls taking their school certificates under exam conditions at one end of the shelters with notices up insisting on silence - not very easy when there were constant sounds of flying bombs cutting out and dropping!

Pam Daymond

The eighteen girls from Beckenham were integrated into Bishop Blackall School for Girls. With girls from Dartford County School and some evacuated privately, there were sufficient numbers of the 12 - 13 age group to make a separate class. Girls from other age groups were incorporated into existing classes. A difficulty was that in some subjects, Bishop Blackall was ahead and in others behind the standard attained in Beckenham. Then we ourselves encountered a similar position when we returned to Beckenham. We wore our own school uniform at Bishop Blackall; our parents would have sent any necessary replacements.

Miss Rabson, from Beckenham County, was in charge of the group. We met with her every day to tell her of any worries and to discuss things generally. She also occasionally organised outings for us on Saturday mornings.

Pam Wellsted

The time came when I had to take the scholarship exam. In those days, different counties and authorities set their own syllabus, which meant that the learning pattern varied from one area to another. Consequently I couldn't take the Devon exam but had to go to the headmaster's house on the Saturday to sit the London exam. I sat at one end of a long dining table while he sat at the other end. The whole room was filled with black ebony furniture which I found very intimidating. However, I managed to pass and subsequently transferred to Tavistock Grammar School where I was happy, although they had covered things which I hadn't and vice versa. After I returned home from Devon, I attended Beckenham County School.

Jean Parrott

Once the raids of the blitz abated we returned to Wickham from Colyton and I went back to Chase College. I passed the scholarship exam for Beckenham County School and started there in 1943. The following summer the doodlebugs and rockets began, so we evacuated once more, to my mother's cousin near Stoke-on-Trent. I went to Golden Hill Primary School, where my "aunt" taught. I was thought very snooty because I had already started at a senior school; it was soon the summer holidays and I was sent to a tutor for a while to catch up. Arrangements had just been made for me to go to the Grammar School at Newcastle-under-Lyme when it was deemed safe to return home for what proved to be the last time and I returned to the County School. One effect was that after the flying bombs, girls returned to school only gradually and with a smaller number we were divided into two instead of three sets for subjects such as maths. This resulted in my being put in the 'a' stream with the advice that if I worked hard I might be able to stay there. I shall always be grateful that I was able to take advantage of that chance.

The boys from the cities had parallel experiences with evacuation of schools but sometimes with a less satisfactory outcome than reported by the girls. At that time, perhaps it was not always considered at all important to provide for them the same degree of pastoral care as was provided for the girls.

John Taylor

Somehow in 1941, amidst the Coventry blitz, I managed to pass the scholarship and went to Bablake School. It was evacuated as soon as I joined it. On 20 September 1941 I joined a column of boys at Coventry station with my suitcase and gas mask. We were taken to Lincoln where we met our host families in a church hall. The headmaster and his deputy stood on the stage and lectured us. They were frightening to a small boy who had never seen anyone in an academic gown before. The head was a man I came to fear, for whom I lost all respect and came to recognise as a bully. He lacked compassion - that was left to the secretary, Miss Twigg, loved and respected by all of us.

August 1943 saw us return home for good and I returned to two brothers, one I hardly knew as he had been born the August before I went to Lincoln. During those two years away I had been dropped into an entirely different type of schooling with no-one to advise or help me. I'd learnt to cope with the new concept of homework, then not done in junior schools. When I returned, I continued to scratch out the homework at playtime or during other lessons. All I wanted was to leave school as quickly as possible and this I did on my sixteenth birthday - probably the greatest mistake I've made in my life - but not the only one!

Peter Rex's experiences, although not of evacuation, are disturbingly representative of many boys' wartime education.

Peter Rex

In Spring 1941 I took the local 'scholarship' examination (forerunner of the 11+). Although I did not pass, I went to St. Brendan's College anyway, as a fee-paying pupil. The system there was one of strict corporal punishment administered by the Irish (indubitably) Christian (open to question) Brothers (anything but!) who ran the place. Lay staff were not permitted to use physical punishment. The slightest offence, from being late for morning assembly or talking in class to handing in inadequate homework or failing a rote learning assignment, meant up to six strokes on the hand from what we called 'the Whack', the Tawse of Ireland and Scotland; a leather strap about fifteen inches long and an inch or so wide. It was the luck of the draw or the intent of the user whether it hit your palm, your fingers or even caught your wrist. And it hurt!

The result was that I spent the rest of the war more worried about an encounter with the headmaster, Brother Gibbons (known as Vinegar Joe), Brother 'Bomber' Harris or, for me, the lethal Brother Little (physics and Latin and for two years my form master; no nickname, only fear) than about anything Hitler could do to me. If you were a rugby star, that was fine, you could do no wrong and life was comparatively easy, but with my damaged hearing (partly as a result of a rugby scrum) and a consequent medical ruling not to play contact sports, I was not a rugby star! I was never flavour of the month - and legitimately avoided games during the winter and spring terms. I spent that time in the public libraries of Bristol reading widely and avidly, which has stood me in good stead since. Of course, there were never any staffing problems at St. Brendan's - all teachers were from the Irish Republic, and neutrals!

The Central Foundation School took to its wider new sports facilities with pleasure. In Ely the school had the use of the Open Air Swimming Pool during the summer and every form swam twice weekly. According to B. Phillips, Games Captain 1942–44, the standard of swimming rose steadily with the improved facilities and in 1941–42 many girls were successful in the Royal Life Saving Society examinations. It was also possible, in Ely, for the whole school to tackle tennis seriously; they played during normal school games lessons but also from 6.00 - 9.00pm they had the use of the courts. At the end of the summer term, matches were played against the High School, the Girls' Training Corps and the CFS staff.

In the first two weeks of the evacuation, CFS had their first ever lessons on hockey from Miss Noake, P.E. teacher, despite not possessing one hockey stick between them! The necessary equipment was soon forthcoming and hockey lessons took place at Paradise Recreation ground, on the former football club pitch. Before long, matches against Ely High School and the G.T.C. were taking place. All continued splendidly until the time when the military occupied Paradise and games tended to be interrupted by a soldier determined to mow the grass then and there, hockey players notwithstanding.

There were other nightmares to Paradise!

E. Lamb; CFS School Chronicle, April 1944

In future years many of us will recall the numerous happier and lighter moments of our Ely sojourn, one in particular typical of the sleepy little market town.

Most of the school was assembled to watch the First XI play a match against Ely High School, at the Paradise Field. All was going well until the pattering of many feet was heard from the far side of the fence, mingled with bleats. Then a woolly head thrust through a hole in the fence, closely followed by an equally woolly body. Sheep upon sheep squeezed through and began wandering across the pitch. Soon, the whole flock was waiting to follow to graze this new pasture. We were galvanised into action. Brandishing hockey sticks and various other implements we raced over the field, trying to drive the intruders back, but only increasing their panic; some galloped, terrified, in all directions, while others gathered in the centre of the field, bleating hideously. Miss Roberts, in a valiant effort to check the onslaught, stood up against the offending break in the fence, when, above the confusion, the herdsman, not wishing his flock to be split up, shouted in an unmistakably "fen" voice "Git away frem that there 'ole" - a remark which initially scandalised us but afterwards added to the hilarity of the moment. Finally, the leader of the flock was persuaded to return to the road, the others followed and they were driven away. Play resumed but the dignity of the occasion was lost and the chief topic of conversation was the uninvited visitors and the grins of the girls at the cry of "Git away frem that there 'ole"!

E. Windsor, CFS Chronicle, April 1944
A typical day in the life of an evacuated schoolgirl.

I usually left for school with little time to spare; I scarcely had time to hang my coat in the cloakroom and reach the VIth Form Room before the gong sounded. Prayers came immediately after roll-call, in Archer House for Jewish girls and in the Club Room for the Christian girls. We prefects lined the route from the Club Room (large meeting room above The Club pub on the Market Place) to Archer House while the exchange took place. My position was at the foot of the Club Room stairs and I had to combine the duties of prefect and "chicken-shooer" since the hens were apparently more anxious to go into Prayers than the girls were. The last teachers would come hurrying across the yard followed by the inevitable procession of chickens and Prayers would begin. After Prayers, the exchange between Club Room and Archer House took place again, the gong sounded and the ordinary work of the day began. After school I would perhaps go to the Choral Class (in the Club Room), home to tea, change, then back to Archer House for a meeting of the Dramatic Reading Circle. After an hour, home again (via the school garden to give encouragement to the gardeners,) to tell my small foster-brother a bedtime story, and then I would spend the rest of the evening doing homework, getting inspiration from the view when I was in difficulties with Latin grammar or history dates. Then supper, mending and letter-writing kept me occupied till bedtime.

The JFS School and refugee boys' hostel were becoming accepted in the town, too. Wild rumours as to what went on at the hostel had circulated rapidly after a large oven of a type never before seen had been delivered to the hostel, soon dispelled after the Dean of Ely, Dr. L.E. Blackburne, had made an unannounced visit one evening with the school headmaster, Dr. Bernstein, to see Rabbi Kon, who ran the hostel, and the boys. The Dean urged that the installation of the pottery kiln (what the oven actually was) should proceed as quickly as possible, then he used his influence to calm all weird speculation by encouraging councillors, clergy and other people of influence to visit the hostel to see for themselves. It was a normal hostel with the occupants pursuing normal activities in a pleasant and home-like atmosphere. They did visit, they reported and the rumours and gossip soon subsided.

On the 28th of June 1940 a display of gymnastics was staged in the large garden at the hostel, after which the audience heard Dr. Bernstein praise the progress the boys were making both in their physical education and their schoolwork, for which they were displaying remarkable aptitude.

During 1939 and 1940, most of the equipment from the school's London premises in Bell Lane was moved to Ely. The premises were severely damaged on February 1941, which Dr. Bernstein, in Spitalfields at the time, took very badly. The school had been his life. Back in Ely, he passed the news to staff and pupils, but remained obviously very upset. The Dean offered the use of Hereward Hall, part of The King's School, to Dr. Bernstein, allowing him to bring into Ely many of the children from the outlying villages. The transfer, from the start of the academic year 1941-42, was a success. Girls and boys were taught in separate classes, as in London, and there were separate dining rooms in Hereward Hall. The *Ely Standard* reported the moved premises, pointing out that many courses on offer, such as metalwork, were unusual in the Fens, and technical drawing for those who wanted to enter engineering employment. The pottery room, the paper said, had its own kiln. The school was as self-supporting as it could be, cultivating part of the garden at the Hostel so that there were chickens and eggs; they kept bees and had their own allotments apart from the garden. But Dr. Bernstein's health still did not recover and in August 1942 he retired, after 40 years' service at the school, 9 of them as Head of the Primary division, to be replaced by Miss Samuels, the first female head of the primary school.

In March 1941, the Ely Standard had sponsored an Essay Competition in connection with War Weapons Week. The results are interesting:

Class A, under 11s	1st prize, Celia Nyman, Jews Free School.
Class B, 11 - 14	Highly Commended, Israel Gelkoff, pupil of JFS Central School.
Class C, 14 - 16	3rd prize, Nathan Leff, pupil of JFS Central School.
	(Highly Commended, Betty Barst, pupil of CFS, Ely.)

Academically, JFS in Ely and District was certainly maintaining standards, but numbers were falling. As pupils in the Senior and Central Schools reached school leaving age, they returned to London to find employment and it was not possible to replace them. Many parents were no longer willing to send their children into the country. Staff of eligible age were conscripted into the military so there were teacher shortages as well. The Woodwork master of the boys Central School, which shared premises at Isleham with the village school, found himself teaching his subject to pupils of both establishments, his opposite number having been conscripted. There were other effects - the Headmaster of Needham's School in Ely (the boys' senior school which JFS boys attended) considered that the brighter evacuee boys had spurred his pupils on to higher attainments than usual!

In Amsterdam there were problems with teachers for the schools, especially senior schools, but for more sinister reasons than conscription.

Rita Blackie

My elder sister was eleven when the war started and turned sixteen when it was all over. She and all the students in her year were awarded their final qualifications without exams because the school was halved of teachers. All the Jewish ones were deported and it was impossible to replace them.

There were also problems in Germany. To escape the increasing bombardments of Hamburg, Geseke Clark and her sisters were several times evacuated from the city to the East of Germany.

Geseke Clark

Our mother's help, Klara (16), my younger sister and I got on a lorry and were taken to the nearest railway station which was functioning. After many delays we got onto a train full of soldiers. One of them gave us a few sweets. After two days and nights and half a dozen changes we arrived in Dorow. The family von der Linde had welcomed the three of us again and also more children from Berlin. A private teacher, Frau Smuda, was engaged and she taught the five of us well. She was a good organiser, but strict, with a terrible system of red, green and black points for each day according to how each of us had behaved. She was a firm believer in the Nazi regime and I heard later it was very difficult for the host family. If they said anything against Hitler in front of her they would have risked being reported to the authorities by her.

Anna Piper

I started school in the autumn of 1943. You learned to say "Heil Hitler" to everybody in uniform, or authority. You were asked what you did at home, always special attention being paid to whether the family listened to the radio or had lots of visitors. Sadly, some children's answers were acted upon and parents were subject to surveillance and interrogation. This made everybody very careful as to what they did or said, or how they acted, at all times. Some of the older children, who had joined the youth organisations, became very keen to tell on their parents who might have been listening to English language broadcasts, and occasionally one heard of people being questioned or ending up in a concentration camp.

As the war front got nearer to us, our school was closed to become a first aid post, but by the late spring of 1945 it re-opened and we returned to school. On our first day back, a friend came to collect me, he was a little older. We were skipping along near one of the houses occupied by troops, when an officer came out of the door. We smartly saluted (Heil-Hitler) and smiled as we had been taught - this was not appreciated. This officer was one who spoke German, he told us never to do this again, then took us by the hand and marched us the last hundred yards to school, took us to our classroom and instructed the teacher to make sure that this never happened again.

Other people had differing reactions to the war. So much depended on circumstance.

(Heath) Robin Hazelton

I started school at Kerrywood in Westmoreland Road in 1943 and used to get there on an open-topped bus, the 138. Our French teacher was, I now realise, a Jewish refugee and she used to go into complete panic whenever the sirens sounded; we had no understanding of the horrors she had been through before escaping to England.

Peggy Davies (b.1937. Cheshire)

We had been staying in London, leaving the comparative safety of our Cheshire home. On our return we found that Sale (where we lived) had been hit that very weekend. The next week, several children were missing from school; we developed a very fatalistic view to life.

CHAPTER 10

TOYS AND ENTERTAINMENT

At the outbreak of war, the government declared that this was no time for frivolity so radio became a dull medium of informative and instructional talks, all to do with the various precautions to be taken in every imaginable situation of conflict. As the theatres had also closed, the population rapidly became fed up with this deprivation of anything to lighten the load; fortunately the government listened and saw the error of its ways. Radio returned, but not television. Again, at the outbreak of war, Britain's television service was far in advance of the rest of Europe - here, there were 20,000 sets in private houses in 1939 but transmission stopped immediately the day war was declared not to return until some years after the end of hostilities. By January 1940 there was the BBC Forces Programme, which broadcast dance music and comedy for the troops and the Home Service, which broadcast a range of programmes for the Home Front, like Music While You Work, Workers' Playtime and (not in the modern understanding of the term) the superbly named Let Us Be Gay - all of them morale raisers as well as being intended to maintain a high rate of productivity in the factories, where the wireless (as the radio was known) tended to be on, loud, all day. There were evening programmes such as Henry Hall's Guest Night, and radio plays were enormously popular as were concerts of light music. We children were as avid in our listening as the adults. The evening comedy shows were especially popular, Tommy Handley's ITMA being a great favourite with most people. It had a kind of manic quickfire surrealism, although "peopled" by characters particularly relevant to war, such as Colonel Chinstrap or "Fumf", which put aside for half an hour the tensions most people felt.

In London, the treasures of the National Gallery had been removed to safety far from the risk of aerial bombardment, leaving a large empty building. The pianist (Dame) Myra Hess, on tour in the U.S., returned and began the organisation of the National Gallery lunchtime concerts there. Nearly 2000 were held, every weekday, over the 6 years of the war, for anyone who found themselves near Trafalgar Square. Admission was one shilling. It was not permissible to eat sandwiches (or anything else) during the performance, but sandwiches were available before and after the event. The entertainer Joyce Grenfell was one of those who attended whenever she possibly could and was a frequent maker of sandwiches there. All the finest musicians in London appeared, generally without fee but sometimes a small one was offered and accepted. These concerts were for thousands of people remove the highlight of their wartime experience, the calm and peace of the music a temporary setting aside of the worries of the time.

The cinema was, after the radio, the second great source of entertainment, the kindly light amid the encircling gloom! Throughout the war, 25 million tickets to the cinema were sold every week. The newsreels were popular and if the audience was young enough, could elicit cheers for Allies' exploits and hearty boos whenever Axis forces made an appearance.

Dances and dance music cheered the population. A dance was an immediate response as a fund-raiser for all the special "weeks" such as Savings, or Spitfire, of which there were many during the war. And there was a dance almost every week wherever there was a village hall or suitable venue to hold one, often the social highlight of the week, a popular rendezvous; whether the music was live or from a gramophone made little difference.

There was a real hunger for social life and entertainment, be it dance, beetle drive, whist drive, or local concert. The day to day conditions of life were hard and anything that provided relaxation was very welcome. But one does wonder about one item: during the bombing of Plymouth, some people sheltering in the communal shelters were treated to the unusual spectacle of their M.P., Nancy Astor, (62), turning cartwheels in the shelter as a means of entertaining them!

This apart, much of the live entertainment on offer consisted of "home grown" events of all kinds, from the concert in the local hall to the domestic show prepared by children.

Muriel Gent

There was lots of music of all kinds, especially the wireless, then always, Saturday cinema at the Rex, in Ely. Going to the pictures was very important and my diaries are full of the films we saw. My first experience of seeing nursing mothers (from the new Maternity Home) was feeding-time whilst watching Errol Flynn in "Sea Hawk"! Then there was dancing in the Corn Exchange to the music of "Tangerine", with my friends Winnie, Marie and Peggy, with whom I also worked in the school garden. There was always something going on at Chapel and I entered Scripture exams with them, and we won the Shield. There were numerous Fêtes and the travelling fair in Market Square, riding on "Jollity Farm" - and of course, trying to do homework in Archer House with all the fun of the fair going on outside! Our foster-parents also took us on visits to their friends - an old lady in Broad Street gave us lavish teas; on one visit she had trays of hundreds of golden baby chicks on the settee in the living room. We were fascinated.

Glenda Lindsay

One Christmas, after lunch and opening the presents, Valerie and I decided to present a Nativity play in the Drawing Room with Auntie Doffie playing the piano. We wore angel wings made by my father. Auntie Connie sat with her large bosom heaving as she tried to suppress her laughter; Auntie Gertie smoked furiously, rubbing the fallen ash into the carpet; Auntie Edie sat smiling benignly and I can't remember what my parents were doing. I was cross that Auntie Connie was laughing and started to cry, so Valerie hid under the piano! The Nativity didn't get very far! Every year, after a similar afternoon interlude, it would be tea-time - potted meat sandwiches, celery, and then the *pièce de résistance* - the Christmas cake made by Auntie Gertie, always sunken in the middle and covered in VERY rough icing. After this we played games - consequences, charades etc, until it was time to go home and to bed.

Diana Scott

We had a lot of fun in the war. Holidays had to be taken at home and in all local parks, entertainment was provided during the school holidays. Concert parties, circuses, fairs etc. were organised for all ages. We had a lot of home entertainment - people were very hospitable despite rationing and we had sing-songs etc. My friend and I were very patriotic and raised money for the Red Cross by holding a garden fête in my garden where we raised the princely sum of over £6. We attended many musicals which were put on at the Davis Theatre in Croydon. They revived all the old ones - Rose Marie, The Desert Song and many others. I can well remember seeing Bitter Sweet which was very good but sadly the hero was elderly with a humped back - all the young and handsome heroes were at war!

Glenda Lindsay

My father was always a keen performer, both in theatrical productions and in musical presentations, and was aware of the hunger for live entertainment during the war. He produced and took part in Shakespeare plays for outdoor performance in the natural amphitheatre of a neighbour's garden, and was also a member of a small musical company which presented concerts around the area.

Maureen Jordan

Theatre outings were rare but I was taken to pantomimes every Christmas/New Year and I remember Arthur Askey having a 'jokey' conversation over the garden wall during one of these shows in Croydon. The grown-ups probably laughed more than the children.

Val Lines

I remember going on a train journey with my elder sister, who was about 12 at the time. She was as addicted to books as I was so she didn't notice that I had left the carriage and wandered up the corridor. When she found me I was entertaining a carriage full of GIs by singing, complete with all the actions, a rendition of "You are my sunshine". Her wrath soon disappeared when I was laden with chocolate and chewing gum - the Americans were always very generous to children!

Molly Oakley

Our entertainment was simple - playing cards, board games and listening to the wireless, this is what family life was all about.

Jean Parrott

I joined the Brownies in Colyton and once had to recite "Christopher Robin is Saying his Prayers" at the last minute because another Brownie was ill. Why me?

Margaret Mould

I joined the Brownies as soon as I was old enough - I loved it and remember my first 'stage appearance' was as Streptococci. We had a raid during the performance and I had a black hood over my head - that would have frightened off the Germans on its own! I must have been a real pain, with an acting 'bug' - at Christmas, Auntie Nan and I would make up a play to entertain the family; every year Uncle Bill was cast as the 'Smelly Pig' because he'd snore in the armchair after Christmas dinner!

Valerie Bragg

Pat and I were in a play called "The Wishing Well". I was the wicked gypsy and Pat, the farmer's daughter. (I went on to do amateur acting for many years, also verse-speaking competitions.)

John Taylor

In Lincoln, Thursday afternoons were free of lessons. If we were not in detention, we would go to the cinema but the only two films I recall are Mrs. Miniver and Moon over Miami! Back home in Coventry, I enjoyed going to the theatre and the pictures. Seats cost about ninepence (approx. 3p). Popular music formed a staple diet in our house, bands like Geraldo, Billy Cotton, or Henry Hall along with Sandy Macperson at the theatre organ. And there was comedy from the likes of Arthur Askey, Richard Murdoch, Cyril Fletcher, Norman Evans and Tommy Handley, to keep up morale and spirits. All this from the wireless!

Jean Runciman

My parents had always been very keen on music. Mother played the piano, father the violin. I was used to hearing music and wanted to learn to play the piano. Accordingly, mother found a delightful elderly piano teacher, Mr. Bates (irreverently referred to by me as 'Old Beethoven'). He would travel to our house on an old bicycle and became a great friend but I had no musical talent, lacking the self-discipline of frequent practice. Later in the war, to avoid the terror weapons, we went to St Anne's-on-Sea, near Blackpool, staying at the house of Mrs Gerrard and her 15-year old daughter Margaret, who was anxious to go on the stage. She would dress up in all kinds of improvised costumes and make-up (then in very short supply) and sang and danced. We had to be the audience and clap heartily. Margaret kindly tried to teach me ballet dancing - a rather hopeless task!

We had no difficulty finding entertainment - reading was a great standby, with one fiction and one non-fiction book a week from Beckenham Public Library, and the news bulletins on the wireless, very heavily edited and emphasizing Hitler's setbacks. There were two cinemas in Beckenham, the Odeon at Elmers End (near our house) and the Regal, about twenty minutes' walk away. The programme changed weekly and there was a main film, a "B" film, a cartoon and a (very patriotic) newsreel - if you had really enjoyed it you could sit through the whole lot again without paying as the programme ran continuously! We went to the cinema most weeks. We also had regular sessions of cards and board games with neighbours and their children; we collected everything imaginable like stamps and shrapnel, we "dressed up", we went to Sunday School and, when my mother managed to get hold of a couple of antiquated bicycles we managed to travel around the district a great deal.

M.S.

Just before the end of the war I went to the cinema with my parents and while watching the news my mother suddenly called out "There's your Uncle George!" The scene was of soldiers crossing the Rhine as they were on their way to Berlin. When my uncle was demobbed we found it had indeed been him.

Certainly the cinema was a great favourite for entertainment, but perusal of six years of advertising for the three cinemas in Ely does lead to the conclusion that we sat through a great deal of unmitigated cinematographic tripe - the saving grace being that it was escapist unmitigated tripe and we relished every cheesy minute of it!

Not all entertainment was the wireless or the pictures, though. We also had many healthy outdoor pursuits!

Les Oakey

Queen Adelaide was the scene of great excitement in March 1944 as the Oxford and Cambridge Boat Race was rowed on the straight stretch of water between Ely and Littleport. The usual Thames venue was considered too dangerous owing to the flying bomb menace. A vast crowd of people gathered to watch. Much amusement was felt when one of the local special constables went to apprehend some lads who had strayed from the roped off area and were larking about, as lads are wont to do. (I was one of them.) The bank was slippery with mud and the unfortunate constable slid gently down it into the river, to the cheers of the assembled crowds. He was soon hauled out and sent off to dry, leaving the grinning youths still in their place of advantage. (He was my boss at the brewery where, after leaving school at 14, I was working.) Incidentally, Oxford won!

John Taylor

Around Lincoln there was also a network of canals with barges carrying munitions etc. Carbide lamps were quite common here. We used to drop a piece of carbide into a pop bottle containing a small amount of water, screw in the stopper and drop it into the canal. The bottles exploded like depth charges - highly dangerous but great fun!

Ann Dix

I remember the unofficial Boat Race in 1944 which took place locally. My Aunt took me to watch it and I remember the crowds of people and the boats.

June Thomsitt

At weekends, usually on Sundays while my mother wrestled with the range to cook our Sunday dinner, my father would take us on long walks. As the mountains stretched up behind our house this was one of our favourites. However, we had to be sure that the Commandos were not up there training. The training was serious and live ammunition was used. My brother and myself were always instructed to watch the traffic in the early mornings and ensure that the army lorries of Commandos had not passed by on their way to train. One particular day we missed them and off we went for our walk. We were lucky. A few bullets whistling over our heads soon had us on our stomachs and crawling for safety accompanied by father's best and ripest language.

Our entertainment in the evening was provided by the wireless which was powered by batteries that consisted of charged acid held in large glass containers about the size of a present-day juice box. These had to be recharged periodically. To do this, we had to take the accumulators, as they were called, into Caernafon, our nearest town. The journey was by bus and we were constantly reminded to take great care as any spillage of acid would be extremely dangerous.

Wendy Walton
We walked to church at Campsall, the next village, a long way to walk when you are only 4 or 5. One day I was told not to look in the field. I couldn't have looked anyway as the hedge was much taller than me, but there were Prisoners of War working there. Quite what would have happened to me if I had seen them was never explained - but as I didn't see them, all was well.

Ruth Hixson
There were some Italian P.o.Ws in a camp somewhere nearby. I would see them, as I walked past, in a group with a soldier guarding them. They were a work party. Mum said I shouldn't look at them - why, I don't know!

Anna Piper
One very happy memory of the Sunday walks tradition, was the occasional trip, for all of us, on Peter's grandfather's truck, for a picnic. Our home town was surrounded by extensive woodlands. Peter's grandfather had a wonderful hut which in the past had been used as a hunting base. In the clearing near the hut we played war games, climbed trees and were just allowed to run wild and get dirty.

In Ely, the JFS, having settled down, began to establish itself in the town. In London, the school was renowned for its entertainments - musical productions, choral groups - indeed the well-known wartime entertainer, Issy Bonn, was a former pupil of the school - and having had to move out of the capital for safety reasons, there seemed to be no reason why the tradition should not be continued. A Pierrot troupe was a fixture, started and continued by a staff member, Mr. Joseph (specialism, P.E.) and the troupe continued in Ely. Their first show in the town was at Christmas 1939, in Trinity Hall. There were sketches which contained references to well known Ely personalities in the non-stop show of songs, dances, sketches, one-liners, performed by about a dozen boys under Mr. Joseph's direction. He wrote all the original material used. All the work of rehearsal was done in the evenings. The audience for this first show was mainly the foster-parents along with members of the school. The Eleans present greatly appreciated the "thank you" to them that the show represented.

Along similar lines, the Central Foundation School put on a dramatic production, Our School in Days Gone By, in the school room of the Countess of Huntingdon Chapel. The play told the story of the school's 200 year history, firstly to pupils of the Ely High School for Girls, then for foster parents, and finally two public performances which raised £15 for the Red Cross.

Dramatic performances were a constant happening during the CFS stay in Ely, being acted at the Grange Maternity Hospital, among other venues, for foster-parents, families and friends, for fellow-evacuees from London, and at school parties. From newspaper reports, all appear to have been well received and were certainly well attended.

JFS tradition continued with productions of Gilbert and Sullivan by the younger children, more specifically, The Pirates of Penzance which was performed in April 1940, when the producer had to take over the role of Frederic as the young boy playing the part had his voice break just before the performance, then another production of it received four performances in December 1943, with a different cast. (The producer of the G & S, Mr. Cousin, also became a leading light of the musical scene in Ely, founding a group of singers who gave concerts in aid of various war charities and being concerned with the schools' music festival in the Cathedral.) The girls of the JFS were also involved in musical productions; in their stay in Ely they performed three 'fairy operettas', The Magic Key in January 1942, The Quest of Imelda in February 1943 and The Enchanted Glen in June 1944. These were all presented to the foster-parents and friends, along with some public performances, and raised funds for war charities, the last-named raising more than £50 for the British Prisoners of Wars' Relatives Association.

Some of the 'public' entertainment given by the JFS was inadvertent! There is a report in the Ely Standard, 17 March 1944 of a "happy, unexpected and unrehearsed incident". A party of American soldiers and one American nursing sister were returning to the station from a day's sightseeing in Ely on the afternoon of Thursday 9 March, when, as they passed Hereward Hall, they heard the sound of children singing. They entered the building and asked to be allowed to listen to the youngsters because it reminded them of home. Miss Samuel, Head of JFS, invited them in and arranged an impromptu concert which lasted an hour. Then she served refreshments. The leader of the party thanked her and the children for giving them a most happy and unexpected hour's entertainment. They asked to be allowed to return in the near future with a larger party and pledged that they would not go back to the United States until all was well again in Europe and the children had returned to their homes.

The Schools Music Festival took place in late March 1944. All the schools in Ely took part - the Cathedral Choir School, Kings School, Ely High School, Ely Senior Boys (Needhams), Ely Senior Girls, Ely Junior Boys, Ely Junior Girls and the Jews Free School, a massed choir of more than 1100 voices. It was unique because all of the schools in the city were participating. The County Music Director reported that he was very pleased with the concert and thought everyone had done extremely well. In December that same year there was a follow up to it, a Children's Music Recital in the Cathedral, which consisted mainly of listening to good music with an explanation beforehand, then the singing of carols conducted by Dr. Conway, Cathedral organist, in which all the schools again took part.

There was other entertainment provided by the young people by themselves for themselves. On 20 June 1941 there was a debate in the Ely Porta, in which three schools, Kings, Ely High School and the Central Foundation School took part. They decided that Town Life was better than Country Life.

But by far the most important entertainment for young children during the war was toys, and there were few toys about. The country's factories were working flat out on the production of military equipment, there was little or no industrial capacity for manufacturing toys. Some was spared approaching Christmas, as some toys did appear in the shops, but the supply nowhere approached fulfilling demand. So what toys the children had were jealously guarded and looked after. The Dolls' Hospital establishments flourished, toyshops where the proprietor did a flourishing trade in repairing dolls whose limbs had become detached or were hanging out of their sockets (this largely due to failed elastic and elastic was in very short supply!) while any boy fortunate enough to have a train set was usually not permitted to play with it unless there was an adult around to make sure it was not misused!

Many of the collective childhood pastimes were seasonal. In the writer's Yorkshire village, marbles, whip-and-top and hoops were associated with spring and in summer were put away until the next year. Other pursuits, requiring a ball, were subject to improvisation - the older boys would use an inflated pig bladder as a football and were not put off by the irregularity of bounce and flight that was often encountered. The girls were most unlikely to allow the boys to kick their precious (if balding) tennis balls around, these being reserved for games of twosy or threesy (playing with two or three balls at the same time, games of throwing and catching them as they bounced off the wall, and having all sorts of agile variations on how they were thrown or caught). Skipping was also seasonal; a piece of old clothes line made an excellent skipping rope, a longer piece, a rope for large numbers of girls to play counting-in-and-out-of-the-rope games. Given the precarious nature of the rope once it had collapsed to being used as a toy, this type of skipping rope tended not to be hoarded from one year to the next, but to be used for whatever other purpose it was deemed suitable, reliance being placed on someone else's family washing line giving out in time for the next season! If the boys were able to acquire a small ball, then games of cricket were played in the road, the only place where vegetables were not growing and traffic being no more than half-a-dozen vehicles daily, four of those generally being horse-drawn so there was no danger to life or limb.

Marbles, though, were cherished possessions and you hung on to them for dear life, generally refusing to take part in the marbles contests that took place on the way home from school, along the gutter, and where somehow, the older boys always managed to "win" the best ones from the younger children. Most of us found the rules incomprehensible!

Pat Fulmer
Toys were virtually unobtainable during the war. I was lucky to have a beautiful scooter, which my grandfather made for me. Most of the time I played with my small collection of coloured marbles all of which were given names - my heroine was called Carol. By the time I was six I was reading well and spent a lot of time with my nose in books. My grandmother used to make dolls' house furniture from matchboxes - I still have one of her armchairs in my Victorian dolls' house, which I inherited soon after the war.

Ann Gamêt
Mum was a needlewoman, making all our clothes and I remember having a rope of empty cotton reels to play with. Also she made me little miniature sandbags. There was a spinning top that gave the 'All Clear' sound as it whistled round. Uncle once spun the top outside the kitchen window, whereupon Grandma dived under the table! She was very angry when she found out!

Val Lines

There were many playground games; hopscotch was a surefire winner and the way to get your stone to land in the right square was to scramble over a bombed site and retrieve a piece of broken hearth tile - it slid beautifully! We were also good at improvisation - old paint cans with long string handles made stilts, and wooden cotton reels made perfect tanks when attached to a small piece of candle and an elastic band (but getting hold of the elastic band could be difficult.) The boys still played 'flicking' cigarette cards, which were still plentiful even though no longer produced. And there were many skipping songs for the girls, not all of them polite to Mr. Hitler!

Helmi Spitze

Toys were dolls made by my grandmother. We read a lot, took part in sports like gymnastics and ice skating, and walked a great deal.

Jill Thomas

Toys were difficult to obtain during the war, but my mother managed to buy me a second-hand baby doll from a friend. She was so pretty and my mother knitted her a set of clothes from left over scraps of wool. I loved that doll so much.

Margaret Wood

At home in Kenilworth, Cape Town, we played French cricket on the vast lawn and hopping games like hopscotch. We had our own stamp collections and cigarette cards so there was a lot of swapping between us. I belonged to the Girl Guides and went camping at least once a year. I also stayed on a grape farm for two holidays. That was great fun eating grapes straight off the vine, then playing tennis before 7.00am, before the sun became too hot.

Anna Piper

By 1944 the day and night bombing raids had become very frequent. After the first raids on Stuttgart, Manfred arrived. His parents were friends of the family and lived in the centre of Stuttgart. Manfred was our evacuee and he occupied my room while I moved into my mother's bedroom. All my possessions stayed with Manfred who defended "his" domain fiercely. He was not settled, he thought of all sorts of things to cause mischief. I had a beloved doll, the size of a small baby, made from a kind of *papier mâché*. One day, as Manfred still slept, I crept into the room to collect my doll from the toy cupboard. Oh - what a horrid smell! Our guest had prised off the sole of one of the doll's feet and filled her with excreta! Needless to say Manfred and I never became friends and lost sight of each other after his departure!

Merrill Drzymala (b.1937. Bromley)

Many gifts came from Canada. At our primary school in Shortlands, the children were given toys donated from Canada, possibly through the Imperial Order of the Daughters of the Empire. Mine was a jointed doll which was made by the ABC Toy Company in Toronto (now unfortunately defunct) which was my one and only doll. I treasured it close to my heart, so much so that I brought it to Canada when I emigrated and kept it for my own daughter.

Joan Hardy

While at Gorran Haven my memories are mainly happy ones, for example the day my precious red-sailed toy yacht was carried out to sea, only to be returned the next day by a kindly local fisherman to its distraught owner! I have photos of myself with easel and chalk, a dolls pram and doll, so there were some toys. I got a Brer Rabbit book and some pastel-coloured wooden letters (some of the alphabet missing) at a school jumble sale in St. Austell. My cousins and I tried to build a clubhouse by glueing together planks of old wood found on the cliffs in Gorran Haven!

A cousin in the forces came home with a model RAF plane which ran along a string dropping "bombs" on the "enemy" below...

Maureen Jordan

I used to play with the other children in our street; there were 'alleyways' at the back of our gardens which were ideal for secret games. I always enjoyed make-believe and acting and I apparently (according to his mother) scared the pants off a little boy who lived opposite, in my portrayal of Sweeney Todd, the demon barber!

Expensive toys were not usually received. I remember always looking forward to receiving the 'Annuals' and puzzle books as well as books on original party games. The Pooh books by AA Milne, Beatrix Potter's works, Enid Blyton...these were the usual Christmas presents.

Christina Watt

We did 'craftwork' at school and one day I decided to make a toy boat, which most of the boys were making (knitting, the alternative, did not appeal to me very much at that age!). This involved much crouching near the evil-smelling glue pot, awaiting one's turn to daub the stuff on the various pieces of wood. We none of us heard the bell at the end of the lesson. Miss Carroll was in a bad mood that day. As I continued to stick my boat together she kicked my backside to make me hurry from the glue pot. (The same happened to the boys lingering there.) After school, clutching the sticky boat, I told my mother. She, aghast, checked my statement twice, then took my hand and marched back into school, to Miss Carroll's classroom. She confronted her with my statement, to have it firmly denied. Mother looked at me. "Let's find out the truth" she said, then "What happened, Tina?" she asked. Both women were strong and terrifying if you even thought of telling a fib. I looked at the teacher. "You kicked me, Miss Carroll", I said. She blushed and started to bluster. Mother was dangerously quiet - "Don't you ever let me hear of anything like this again" she almost hissed at the head of the Infants school. When we got home, she put the rather horrid boat which was sticking to my glove, on the fire. Its fate seemed appropriate, somehow.

Wendy Walton

We played outside a great deal; we were in the country and there were farms and lots of birds to see and flowers, we could give our mum a bunch of very wilted wild flowers from our meanderings. It was lovely and I never once felt deprived. Cards featured in games at home and we loved playing at Post Offices using the fire guard as the grille and stamping bits of paper. We were happy and for me the war was a long way off. We didn't have any bombs and I don't recall any planes though there must have been some.

The nation's children really did entertain themselves throughout the war, despite the lack of manufactured toys. Imagination was stimulated and ingenuity called for in the making of their own toys and radio and the cinema played a huge role for children and adults alike. Children were fortunate in that they could run free in the countryside and the towns without fear of molestation, older children could cycle all day in safety. Many of them feel they had far more freedom of action, in a war, than their grandchildren have in peacetime.

CHAPTER 11

HEALTH AND MEDICAL CARE

The National Health Service did not exist at the time of World War Two. Medical care was provided by doctors, but every visit to the surgery, or home visit by the doctor, had to be paid for, also any medicine or treatment provided, so a person was usually quite ill before ever a doctor was consulted. Instead, for the normal run of coughs and colds, and childhood illnesses, home remedies were relied upon, or remedies were bought over the counter at the pharmacy after having sought the recommendation of the pharmacist. There were also many bottles of commercial brews available, such as Liqufruta, Gee's Linctus, or Dr. J. Collis Browne's Chlorodyne, with all of which many of us became unhappily familiar as cure-alls for our coughs and sneezes! If you fell over and grazed your knees, then you washed the grit off (or your mother did) and possibly put some Vaseline on, or an Elastoplast. An improvised bandage was highly prized, even if it did sometimes consist of a quickly converted handkerchief! These measures seemed to do the trick without involving any health professionals.

Also, only two vaccinations against illnesses were then available, for smallpox and diphtheria, and under the various Child Welfare programmes, most of us received these two in early childhood. The programmes were initiated in the 1930s and do seem to have had the effect of drastically cutting the incidence of these dreadful diseases, a factor that can only have helped when the effects of saturation bombing and mass-destruction of housing became a reality, when disease would have spread rapidly among the ruin and rubble. As for the other childhood illnesses, children were expected to catch them and acquire immunity that way. If a child in the area went down with mumps, measles, German measles or chicken pox, then 'parties' were likely to be held so that the rest of the children in the age group could catch it and get that one over and done with.

Schoolchildren's health was checked by the School Medical Service, but as the demand for military personnel increased so the number of doctors was reduced through many of them having to go to the Forces. Schoolchildren seemed to be under the care of increasingly elderly practitioners coaxed from retirement by the exigencies of the national emergency, but they carried out their tasks to the best of their ability and we do not appear to have suffered. The same might not necessarily be true of the school dental service!

The other fixation of our childhood was nits - headlice - for which our hair was regularly checked. These wretched little beasts seemed to flourish during the war, perhaps all the dust and general upheaval helped them, and a secondary war was raging in homes up and down the country as mothers and foster-mothers battled to eliminate this affront to their cleanliness and hygiene!

Brenda Booker

I had measles which led on to whooping cough and then pneumonia with a long stay in an isolation hospital without visitors. At home, chesty coughs were treated with a hot poultice (frequently kaolin) spread on flannel and pressed on the chest.

Maureen Jordan

Rickets was fairly common and a major health target was to prevent it. Children were given cod liver oil, orange juice and sessions under ultraviolet radiation. I can still smell the rubber goggles we wore.

TB was rife among larger, lower income families in overcrowded accommodation, as was Bovine TB, which was caught through contaminated milk. I remember being taken to a clinic in Bromley for a patch test which in my case was negative, but there were a number of people there with typical swellings on the neck, indicating Bovine TB.

The school nurse was an institution in our wartime childhood. She checked for nits in one's hair but she also took regular measurements of height, weight and the length of feet. If one had feet above a certain length at a given age, then parents were handed vouchers to be spent against new footwear. My feet appeared to feature regularly in this category, so new Start-Rite or Clark's shoes were always being bought for me.

Joyce Kitching

My sister got scarlet fever during the war but wasn't taken into isolation. (Amazingly, I didn't get it.) Just as the war was starting, she was in isolation as a diphtheria carrier, although she didn't actually have the disease. Swabs had been taken at school, unbeknown to our parents, and she had to go away for six or seven weeks with absolutely no parental visiting.

Val Lines

There are fleeting memories of school friends sporting wonderful purple patches where a strong solution of gentian violet had been applied to battle the common skin problem of impetigo. Unfortunately, they were treated almost as lepers by some of the youngsters.

Joan Hardy

I was quarantined with scarlet fever while I was in St. Austell. I also had my tonsils and adenoids removed at a cottage hospital somewhere there. I distinctly remember lying on the operating table, the gauze mask being put over my nose and mouth and the anaesthetic (ether? chloroform?) being sprinkled directly onto it.

Corinne Older

If we were ill and had a temperature the doctor came. We always had to stay in bed until the temperature had been down for 24 hours, then stay in the house for a couple of days or so, then back to normal. We were, on the whole, healthy children!! However, my sister became very ill and nearly died. We had a very good doctor - I think he must have been invalided out of the services - and he managed to get some M.M.B tablets for her - the first antibiotics - we were so lucky; she recovered.

John Taylor

I recall having flu at some stage and being prescribed sulphonamide tablets, which made me feel terrible.

June Thomsitt

Probably the most serious illness we had in the family was when my youngest sister contracted scarlet fever. Today it is considered fairly trivial but then, pre-antibiotics, it was regarded with great apprehension and usually meant the patient being nursed in a hospital isolation unit. Because we lived in a rather isolated house on the edge of the village the doctor agreed that Jean could remain at home but stay isolated from the rest of the family, to be barrier nursed by my mother. It is to mother's great credit that Jean made a complete recovery and the rest of the family remained healthy. However, there was one casualty and it is probably the reason that I remember the episode. I had always been a great reader and owned many lovely books, presents at Christmas and birthdays. As Jean began to feel better I suggested she might like to read some of my books, which were taken in to her. On her recovery the doctor insisted that anything in the sick room that could not be sterilised must be burnt. That meant all my beautiful books!

Some of our number had the fortune - or bad luck (!) - to encounter some very strange remedies for commonplace conditions when they were living in the depths of the countryside, made more hazardous for these displaced city dwellers by the inescapable presence of livestock.

Jean Runciman

At the height of the Blitz mother decided she must get away for a while so decided to join her sister and family in the East Anglian village of Hopton, staying with an elderly couple, Mr and Mrs Gould. I did not have to go to school, being only four, but my nine-year old cousin did.

She promptly caught all the childhood illnesses which she passed on to me. Medical treatments in 1940/41 were very limited; few effective drugs were available and no antibiotics to the general public. I caught measles and whooping cough at the same time and was very ill. There was no doctor in our tiny village and I was not well enough to be taken further afield, so my mother, who had little knowledge of nursing, had to do the best she could. I eventually improved but the terrible cough would not go away. One of the local women, who had a reputation for knowledge of folk medicine, assured my mother that the only thing that would cure the whooping-cough was to place the patient among a flock of sheep. The smell from their wool was supposed to work wonders! Accordingly, I was wrapped up in a blanket and taken in a pushchair to a local farm which boasted a field of magnificent sheep. Mum left me in the middle of them and retired to observe the miracle cure. Being only four and still very weak and poorly, I was petrified and cried loudly. Eventually I was taken out (still coughing!) and we started to take a "short cut" home through another field. A single large "cow" was in this field and seemed to take an unhealthy interest in the unusual phenomenon of a London mother and daughter alone on a strange farm. Whether it was due to the fact that my mother was wearing a smart red felt hat shaped like a halo I cannot say, but the cow, now clearly a bull, became angry and started to charge. Luckily we were very near a gate and escaped without injury. My whooping-cough was not cured and poor old Mr Gould (who was 84) caught it and nearly died.

Mother decided to go back to London and face the Luftwaffe!

Mostly, though, illnesses and remedies were more conventional.

Geseke Clark

I had been evacuated to East Pomerania. One of the happiest days there was in October 1942 when I received a card saying that my youngest sister had been born. At home for the Christmas holidays we had a lovely christening. During these holidays I developed whooping cough and so did the baby. It was difficult during air-raids to get to the shelter without waking the baby in the pram. We feared that if she had started coughing we would not have been allowed inside! On one of those walks to the shelter my mother, finding herself alone with me, told me the facts of life. She thought it pretty urgent to do so as the farm children in Pomerania were much more knowledgeable in such matters and had tried to tell me in rather an unpleasant way.

Because of my whooping cough my stay in Hamburg was extended… how I enjoyed those precious weeks with my mother and baby sister. I remember roller skating all morning and then sleeping after lunch in my mother's bed, near an open window. I cannot remember what medicine I had for whooping cough - perhaps a soothing cough linctus, nothing more.

Helmi Spitze

We were fortunate to have good health. There was a town doctor, too old to go to war, who was a family friend and who made house calls should we have been ill, but we did not need to call him.

Rita Blackie

Our G.P. was a Dr. Cohen. One day he was gone, and replaced with a German doctor.

In Ely the school medical services were overstretched.

CFS Gazette, April 1944. B. Phillips

When we were first evacuated there were no means of supervising the health of the school. The Ely Clinic was understaffed and inadequate to deal with minor ailments, teeth and eyes. When girls were ill they used to go either alone or with foster-parents, or with Miss Alexander, to the surgeries of the four Ely doctors. There were, however, many difficulties and after some weeks Dr. Maurice Smith got in touch with the other doctors and offered to hold a Clinic twice weekly for CFS girls. Miss Alexander helped with the organisation and secretarial work. Records were kept; girls were free to come of their own accord. Severe cases were sent to Addenbrooke's Hospital.

Later, Dr. Maurice Smith became School Medical Officer, which meant that weekly medical inspections for part of each term were arranged and each girl again had a regular medical inspection. During 1941 eyes were tested, on the recommendation of Dr. Maurice Smith, at Ely Clinic and teeth were inspected and treated at regular intervals by Mr. Wolfenden.

Muriel Gent

We had Dr. Maurice Smith as School Medical Officer during our evacuation to Ely. There were regular health checks. We hated having to strip to the waist in front of him and our gym mistress, Miss Alexander! I cannot remember missing any schooling (on health grounds) but Phyllis, my sister, caught everything that was going and had to stay in the Isolation Hospital (old workhouse) in St John's Road. Our room, books, toys and clothes had to be fumigated.

School Medical Services were not the only health provision overstretched in Ely. The evacuation from London had brought into the area a large number of young women with small children. A considerable number of these young women were pregnant. The local maternity services simply could not cope, so a building, The Grange, on Nutholt Lane, was taken over and converted into a maternity home. (The girls of the C.F.S. gave several of their dramatic presentations at The Grange, to fellow London evacuees.)

The evacuation of the Jews Free School brought in its wake young Jewish mums from the East End, among them Ruchla, nee Sawicka, who had been born in Warsaw, where she married in 1935. Shortly after, she and her husband came to London, to the East End Jewish community. Two years later, their first son was born. In the summer of 1939 she thought of visiting her parents in Warsaw but they dissuaded her. So Ruchla joined the evacuation. On 25 October 1939 she gave birth to her second son in the newly established maternity home for evacuees, the first child to be born there. It was reported in the Ely Standard. The Bishop of Ely went to bless the baby and attended his brit (circumcision). The baby was named Norman Eli, in thankfulness to Ely for its hospitality at the family's time of need. The Jewish Chronicle was told of the birth and reported it as the birth of the first Jewish child in Ely for more than 650 years.

The maternity home flourished but then was taken over, decades after the war, and much extended as the Offices of the East Cambridgeshire District Council!

There were occasionally problems arising that needed the intervention of the hospital to put them right, generally some accident to a limb requiring either stitches or plaster-of-paris, or, the scourge of children then, removal of tonsils and adenoids.

Ruth Stobart

My brother, cousin and myself used to play on the top of the air-raid shelter which was covered with the earth from its excavation. One day we were planting seeds when a bit of an argument broke out, followed by a bit of pushing and shoving and I slipped and cut my leg quite badly on the corrugated iron. I had to be pushed to the hospital (fortunately not too far away) in my brother's pushchair. I was "put to sleep" and had seven stitches in a cut that was a good six inches long. I still have an impressive scar.

Anne Gordon (b.1937. Beckenham)

The only thing I had to access the health services for was to go into hospital to have my tonsils out. There must have been restrictions on changing bed linen because I had to keep the same blood-stained pillow case for several days, which shocked me, even as a child.

Christina Watt

My constant chesty, bronchitic coughs (legacy of measles and bronchitis aged four months) drove my mother mad and eventually she prevailed upon the doctor to send me to a specialist at Doncaster Infirmary. He recommended the removal of tonsils and adenoids, but then, as now, there was a long waiting list - nearly two years. Mother was determined that the procedure be done as soon as possible so I was booked into a private Nursing Home in Doncaster for surgery just two weeks later. I still have nightmares of the anaesthetic - no pre-med., just lifted onto the operating table, a rubber mask over my face. As the anaesthetic dripped onto it and the roaring in my ears got louder and louder, I was held down by two people to keep me still, I struggled so much. Then I came round, sore and very bloody with my nose packed with gauze. I kept bringing up quantities of blood and they kept changing the sodden gauze dressings. This continued for four days to mother's alarm but she was allowed to take me home on the fifth as by then the bleeding had stopped. I hadn't eaten much while there as I didn't want anything, it hurt my throat, but I did have jelly and a memorable ice-cream. After the nine mile taxi journey home mother let me rest on a reclining chair and prepared something to tempt my appetite. "How about some nice bread and warm milk" she asked. I hated milk, which well she knew, but she was totally convinced of its curative powers when warmed and poured over small cubes of bread with sugar. I did not share this conviction and asked if I might have some soup. No luck. The bowl of bread and milk was placed in front of me, on a tray. Being hungry, I shudderingly got it down. Mother removed the tray to the scullery. There was a croaked yell "I'm going to be s ....." and I was, bread, milk and stale blood, everywhere. When she'd cleaned up, mother made me a cup of warm Bovril, which I remember as delicious.

Neither of her daughters was ever offered bread and milk again!

Some conditions that befell us, while not needing hospital treatment, were nevertheless very unpleasant and a source of discomfort until cleared.

Jennifer Bedford

In 1944 we went to Devon because, mother said, she was weary of coping on her own. Travelling by train was an adventure, and staying at grandfather's pub was very different. I do remember a large kitchen there, and being bathed in front of a fire in some kind of foul-smelling disinfected water as we had caught scabies, presumably on the train journey to Devon. We also had to take some strange little silvery pills which I think were to combat some other little parasites we caught, much to my mother's disgust. At that time, any little cut was treated with iodine, which stung and turned bright yellow on the skin.

Ruth Hixson

During and after an air-raid all sorts of people would be mixed together in shelters, refuges, first aid stations and hospitals, leaving them open to who knows what bugs and germs. There was an occasion when my whole family had to go to the local clinic. Apparently one of us had either been in contact with someone who had scabies or else showed symptoms of it. We all had to take a special bath and were then painted with a pink lotion. My mother, I remember, was very ashamed, she forbade me from telling anyone at school what had happened. This thing called scabies was something that only 'dirty' people would have. Today I guess the most likely reason for the outbreak was that my father, in the course of his ARP duties, had been in contact with someone with the condition and caught it himself.

Despite Jean Runciman's bizarre experience with the sheep, traditional remedies were taken seriously, provided they were actual remedies and could be seen to have some effect.

Anna Piper

Herbal Teas and Tinctures were always the first line of approach if anybody in the family had a medical problem. Herbs were grown in the gardens and found in the wild, there was never a shortage. Alcohol was also no problem; quite a few of the local farmers had their own stills and fruit and grain could easily be turned into alcohol. It was necessary to label these bottles well, as the spirit was absolutely clear and was usually stored in any kind of bottle available. Both of my grandmothers, my aunts and our adult friends were expert at making these tinctures, infusions, ointments and poultices. When you had a tummy problem you got a bitter tincture, the upside of this being that it was dropped onto a real rarity, a sugar cube, of which my grandmother had a stock for such occasions.

I had pneumonia at an early age. My nursery school was only a few hundred yards from home with only a minor road to cross; I was four and was allowed to make my own way there. School finished at noon. In the opposite direction to home, through a delightful midden, was the cattle market, held weekly. I loved animals so decided to go alone. The pigs with litters were my favourites. They were brought to market in great square woven baskets, very generously sized and straw-lined. On that day, I must have been really tired. German children were used to a nap after nursery school, so I climbed into a basket without the farmer noticing or the sow objecting, and went to sleep. I was found when the market packed up and was returned to my, by then frantic, mother. The minute the door closed behind my deliverer, Mutti took a huge wooden spoon, meant for stirring the copper on washday and proceeded to belabour my backside. The spoon broke in half. I was put to bed sobbing. When I awoke (I now know) some days later, I learned that I had contracted pneumonia and that things had been touch and go.

I vaguely remember Mutti, grandmother and other family members sitting by my bed day and night. But being ill was great. You got an egg yolk stirred with sugar and a little red wine fed to you with a teaspoon. Best of all on this occasion, being centre-stage, I told everybody that Mutti's beating had caused the pneumonia. (I can only surmise that Mutti's reaction had been due to her having just lost her husband.)

Some medical experiences probably could only befall the children involved during wartime. There might be a less harrowing version occur in peacetime, but there would certainly also be a far greater degree of support for them than was available during those years of havoc.

Janet Ellison

One incident I remember was the time my mother had a miscarriage. I can remember her trying to hang curtains, perched up a ladder; she wasn't feeling very cheery. The memory continues a bit later on; it was dark and mummy was lying in two easy chairs that we used to push together at times of illness so that the patient was not up a flight of stairs. I sat beside her, holding her hand, not old enough to realise what was happening. Eventually she gave me a large bundle of newspaper to take upstairs and leave in the toilet. I felt very frightened going up the dark stairs, my mummy, the centre of my world, was in trouble and there was no-one to turn to for help. The bundle unravelled and contained what looked like a huge lump of liver. I can remember thinking, is that really a baby? I ran next door as that house had a telephone, but there was no reply. The rest is rather a blur, but I know that it was the following morning before the doctor arrived. I think I spent the night lying on the floor.

Brian Hardisty (b.1935 S. London)

I caught scarlet fever in 1944 at the age of 9 and was taken to an isolation hospital. Once I had recovered, my mother came to collect me and on the way home, upstairs on a bus, told me that while I had been away for two weeks our house had been hit by a flying bomb. My brother and sister had been inside with her, sheltering under the stairs, when this happened. My sister, who was 6, still vividly recalls the violent sensation of everything whooshing outwards from the house and the flying dust. Our father, who was too old to be called up, was out in the street on duty as an Air-raid Warden. He was badly injured and died shortly afterwards.

Our house was uninhabitable and had to be knocked down and all our possessions were gone. I never saw my father, my home or my things ever again, yet I still have vivid recall of the family home and the disposition of furniture, books and music. It was very traumatic. I remember mother sitting in the top of the bus telling me my father was dead and crying. I found the crying embarrassing and didn't take in the news about father. I was taken to an aunt's house where I stayed until the formalities were concluded and my physical recovery complete, then we moved in with my grandparents.

The School Medical Services did their best to fulfil their duties to care for the health of all schoolchildren, no matter what the circumstances nor how low the level of personnel might be. To many of us, the least successful of these undertakings had to be the School Dental Service. From a twenty first century standpoint, the very idea of taking dental services into schools seems close to barbaric. In the cities, it tended to be only the initial inspection which took place on school premises, but out in the sticks it was a very different situation!

Jean Runciman

The only downside to school, as far as I was concerned, was the dreaded annual dental inspection. The school dentist was an elderly man, all younger dentists having been assigned to the forces. He was appallingly overworked, being responsible for all the schools in the area, and his equipment was somewhat rudimentary and archaic. We had to line up at school for inspection and, if any cavities were noticed (practically always!) one's mother would receive the terrible appointment card for a filling or (worst of all) an extraction. The clinic was situated behind the Town Hall, and the miserable patients and their mothers sat in a row of chairs, moving up as each patient was seen, until the words "next, please" pronounced one's doom. The chairside assistant was a large, gloomy lady, much feared. She was very good at holding the patient down while the dentist drilled and probed. There were no such refinements as local anaesthetics, and the pain from the old-fashioned drill was excruciating. Even worse was an extraction under gas (no breakfast allowed!). The gas/air machine belonged in a museum and the frightful rubber mask clamped over the whole face gave us the sensation of being suffocated. The war seemed quite innocuous by comparison.

Christina Watt

The West Riding County Council did its best to look after our welfare; the nurse visited regularly, there was a doctor who put in an appearance or two, but our little village was out in the wild so the visitation from the school dentist (I recall only one in my almost six years there) was an occasion to remember if not to cherish! I don't think we had any warning of his impending arrival, we were just taken out, a class at a time, and lined up outside a door - it was not a classroom, at this stage I can only imagine it was the headmaster's office. One by one we were called inside to encounter an antiquated dental chair whose leatherette was shedding stuffing everywhere, and which creaked when you sat in it. Next to it was an elementary spittoon; there was no running water to it (there was no supply in the room) but there was a tin mug of water to rinse your mouth. The nurse was a vision in her brown warehouse coat - she was a rather large lady and the coat seemed designed for a stick insect so she had a strained, cylindrical appearance. The dentist was a little old man (or so I recall) with a bit of a stoop. He probed and peered at my teeth. One was hanging by a thread, ready to come out at any time. He took something and tweaked it out, dropping it in something for disposal. I gurgled indignantly - how would the tooth fairy give me my threepenny bit without the tooth? - but he barked at me to be quiet and keep still, then to spit! I spat obediently and rinsed my mouth. There wasn't much blood! "Out" he said, so I went. The odd thing is I can see him vividly still, clad in his blue-and-white striped apron! (Could it truly have been that?)

Mother was quite accepting of the removal of the tooth but unhappy at the cavalier treatment of the children so that was the only time I went to a school dentist. She let it be known that henceforth our dental treatment would be with a practice in Doncaster. Funnily enough, the tooth fairy managed the threepenny piece, regardless!

The other scourge of being a child in wartime and suffering the ministrations of the School Medical Service was the visitation, on a regular basis, of the School Nurse. This worthy lady was charged with several tasks, like keeping statistics of our growth, height, weight and foot length, but most of all, checking us out for the dreaded nits - headlice. The presence of these was generally seen by mothers as something shameful, to be hushed up, a sign of something being amiss with standards of cleanliness and hygiene, but the children were lined up, class by class, and the hair thoroughly inspected. Any unfortunate child found to be infested was taken to one side and either given a bottle of the special product to treat the hair, or told to be sure to hand a letter to its mother, so we all knew who had nits! The letter was presumably notification of infestation with instructions as to what to do next. The writer seems to recollect that those with nits were excluded from class until the condition had been remedied.

Muriel Gent
"Nitty Norah" had always visited the school at the start of every term in London and this continued during our evacuation to Ely.

Wendy Walton
My sister and I were forbidden to play with the evacuees!! Poor things, possibly because mother and our aunt thought they would be the cause of the dreaded nits. The nit nurse was a feature of school life - we all dreaded her visits because, whether you had them or not, your hair had to be done with the nit comb. Oh dear, my hair was very thick and naturally curly and was worn in long ringlets...IT HURT...!

Anne Gordon
My father served in Italy. His civilian profession was a Book Illustrator. He wrote home "at doorways you get scenes of family affection worthy of Raphael, but they turn out to be looking for nits".

Margaret Haynes
For a short time we had an evacuee family living in part of the house. They came from Paddington but they only stayed a few months then went back to London. My mother always said they found it too quiet in the country! We had paraffin on our hair because they had lice - I can remember my mother being very cross about that.

June Thomsitt
Nits were common in the village and my mother was determined that her children would not have them. Every week our hair would be washed with a special brown soap - Derbac soap - and then our hair would be combed with a very fine metal comb, each pass through the hair being examined for eggs or live nits. I am sure this is why my hair has always been so fine and difficult to manage! BUT we never suffered from nits.

Brenda Booker
We had nits! Our hair was washed over a bowl in the garden and then rinsed in vinegar.

Val Lines
Nits! Well, I have to confess to having an inspirational mother as nits became a huge competition at our house. It entailed catching as many of the beasties as possible during daily sessions with the special comb. Head down, comb at the ready and the race was on! I cannot remember what the reward was, but I do know we had the cleanest heads in no time. Wasn't Derbac soap used for this?

Rita Blackie
During the last six months of the war my elder sister and I were sent into the country, to family of my father's. That is where I became infested with headlice. My mother had kept us clear of headlice in Amsterdam until those last six months. Not nice.

Infestation was a major public health problem which seems to have been exacerbated in September 1939 with the evacuation of the children. There seems to have been a great deal of cross-infestation as a result of this massive movement of people.

In Ely, the foster parents soon noticed that many of the children they were caring for had nits and sometimes scabies as well, but being sensible, level-headed people did not panic but simply set about dealing with the problem. They had realised that for many of these evacuee children from the East End a bath was something they had never experienced and the first thing they did for their little guests was to run them one, so disclosing the problems. The teachers who had travelled with the children were as horrified as the foster-parents and co-operated in the efforts to get rid of these infestations.

Scabies meant being stood in the bath and being scrubbed from head to toe, and then the body from the neck down was painted with a special lotion. Head lice were dealt with by washing with paraffin mixed with sassafras oil. The adults took all these events calmly and did not complain to the authorities, although the child victims were taunted mercilessly in the playground! A teacher at the JFS treated the situation by writing a poem designed to counter any tension, depicting the hunt for nits as "doing their bit", the work of a heroine dealing with the nits!

There is much reference to "isolation" in any discussion of illness in the 1930s. There were few drugs available to combat serious illness, so to remove the patient from the home to a hospital where it was possible to be nursed without infecting the rest of the family was seen as the only solution. There was little consideration then of the trauma inflicted on the child from having no contact with parents or siblings for several weeks. There were many Isolation Hospitals throughout the country to cope with this need. The major purpose, though, was to shield the community from the very serious illnesses that were still encountered. The Ely Standard of 1 March 1940 reports that there were six cases of diphtheria in Ely Isolation Hospital, five from Haddenham and one from Stretham (both satellite villages in the Ely Rural District). A four-year old Haddenham boy had died from the illness. In this instance, the Isolation Hospital (allied with the vaccination programme) kept at bay the possibility of a major outbreak.

CHAPTER 12

A HEDGEHOG CALLED DOODLEBUG AND OTHER SNIPPETS OF DAILY LIFE IN WARTIME

For almost six years of our childhood we were surrounded by the physical evidence of warfare, be it military personnel parading, the warden insisting we "Put out that light!" or the Luftwaffe raining high explosive down on us in our air-raid shelters - much of the landscape we lived in reflecting the results of this last-named hazard - but we carried on with our everyday life regardless. Most of what we did we would have done anyway, but the fact of wartime put a different slant on things, making something of the unique from the commonplace, or the riotously comic from the normally mundane. There were also experiences encountered which would probably never have happened but for the fact of the war, journeys to unlikely places, family weddings to bridegrooms who would never have been met under other circumstances, and for many city children, the staggering encounters with primitive rural sanitation. These events do not fit into any category yet are important to the story of wartime childhood to illustrate how the ready absorption and acceptance of the ethos of war imbued everyday occurrences. Other snippets are simply made more hair-raising by the fact that they happened during a war, their inherent danger being highlighted by the already dangerous climate in which they occurred.

Ann Gamêt
The garden of the house we rented near Leeds had a huge barn filled with hay for the cows. A local boy and I found an old cigarette lighter and went into this barn to start a little bonfire. We struggled with the lighter but just couldn't get a spark from it, thank God!

However, most of the people appearing in this section were not incipient arsonists, simply those who were in a particular place at a particular time and observed.

Joan Hardy
When we lived in a flat over a shop in Clock House Parade, I remember sitting on the stairs, watching a grown up party down below. They were obviously having a great time, presumably living for the day. With a little too much to drink, they were playing a combination of spin the bottle and strip poker. I never did get to see the end of it!

Pam Daymond

At the Harvest Camp a group of us were taught how to chlorinate water. As the war was at a low point and the enemy only just across the Channel, it was felt that there was a possibility that in the near future the mains water supply could be dangerously and purposely contaminated. There was a well at a nearby laundry and this would have been used in an emergency. Thankfully we did not have to make use of any of this knowledge.

During the London Blitz, a bomb fell in the main road near my home and all the services were severed. My grandparents had not turned off their gas at the mains that night and on turning the gas taps on, got jets of water from the rings and were without gas for three weeks. Fortunately my parents had turned the gas off at the meter, but we were without gas for five days - "great fun" cooking on the open fire in the range in the dining room! I cannot remember how long we were without water, but we used the water in the storage tank in the loft, only not drawing it through the tap, to obviate an air lock. Fresh water was distributed by the authorities in a tanker, on one occasion at midnight, so many people appeared in their night clothes!

Jill Jones (b.1941. Beckenham)

I had a visiting hedgehog which I called Doodlebug. My mum would sit me on the back step to listen out for doodlebugs and, as I had no idea what they were, the little chap got his name when he came wandering up the garden!

A source of great concern to many people, including children, was the plight or fate of animals during the war. At the outbreak, the owners despairing of being able to look after the animals properly, many thousands of dogs and cats were put down. (The writer's family had a little white Westie; one day I returned from a morning visit to play with a friend to be told the dog had run away. This now seems unlikely; given the peripatetic nature of father's employment at the time, going to take over at a moment's notice wherever a pharmacy manager had been conscripted, it seems more probable that the dog was either re-homed or put down. It would have been difficult for my pregnant mother to cope with all the removals, her morning sickness and the dog getting upset as well. He was a rather nervy little thing. But I missed him horribly.)

Jean Runciman

I must mention the tragic plight of animals during the war. It was hard enough to feed one's children without having to find food for pets. Many dogs and cats were abandoned (when families left for the country) or they fled in terror from bombed buildings. The RSPCA and other charities did a wonderful job, but the scale of the problem was too much for them. One such sad case was a border collie cross, which had been wandering the Elmers End area for many weeks, becoming thinner and more frightened as time went by. The police wanted to shoot her on sight, the fate of most lost animals. My mother used to put out scraps of food for her. One day, I was in bed with chicken-pox and the poor exhausted dog managed to get into our house and came upstairs to lie quietly under my bed. When my mother realised what had happened she was appalled as the dog might have been vicious. The dog was in such a pathetic state and so grateful for shelter - and certainly not vicious - that poor mother could not bear to give her up to be shot. We called her Peggy and, after a struggle with the police, who thought we were mad and made mum sign a document accepting responsibility for the "dangerous" dog, she became ours. A month later she gave birth to nine puppies in our kitchen. Of course, finding homes for them was hopeless and the saddest day of the war was the day I came home from school to learn that five of them had been drowned by a neighbour. The other four found homes for a little while, but when they grew into lovely, healthy dogs, the new owners could not feed them and they were all put to sleep. But Peggy remained a much-loved companion for the remainder of the war.

Jill Thomas
We had a small black cat given to us and it had one kitten one day, in the garden shed. My brother and I loved this cat and kitten so when my mother needed to get away again we begged her to take the animals with us. Of course this was not possible but she did manage to find a new home for them. We were heartbroken to leave them behind.

June Thomsitt
As I grew older I was given the job of going to the local farm to buy eggs and milk. This was how I learned to run fast. Geese or turkeys always guarded the gate. They would advance on me with necks and wings outstretched, hissing or gobbling, threatening to peck my legs!

Gloria Morgan
We had space to keep half-a-dozen hens which were pretty good layers. I hated the smell of the mash we fed them. We regularly went to Brixton market and bought a few day old chicks to rear to supplement the meat ration. When they were ready for the pot it broke my heart as I had made pets of them.

Milk, bread and coal were delivered to the door. Because of petrol shortages, delivery rounds were all horse drawn. I loved all the horses and particularly Mabel, who pulled the milk cart.

In the depths of rural England, sanitation was often extremely primitive, frequently being either a privy or an earth closet. To city children accustomed to indoor flushing lavatories, these were horrifying. They meant wandering down the garden path in the dark if anyone needed to use the loo at night (the use of a torch to light the way was not allowed under blackout regulations) - or else there was a chamber pot in the bedroom, which would have to be emptied in the morning.

Ruth Hixson
My middle sister was evacuated to Yorkshire. We were able to travel and mother took me with her to visit Billie, a very long train journey away. The house was in the country, one of about a dozen, half on either side of an unmade-up pathway in which there was a block of privies which were shared by all the houses. I'd never experienced anything so horrid. An outside flush toilet was one thing, but this! It was awful if it was raining, worse if it was dark and you had to take a torch (blackout notwithstanding!). I hated the creepy crawlies and the pong! I don't know how my sister coped with it, but to my memory she seemed quite content.

June Thomsitt

The cottage we rented had an earth closet at the end of the garden. One incident I remember threatened to strain my parents' excellent relationship. With all the stress, my mother lost a considerable amount of weight. Even her fingers thinned, to such an extent that her wedding ring became very loose. On one memorable day for us all, during a visit to the toilet the ring fell off into it! Unfortunately, she did not notice immediately and other family members made visits. When the discovery was made, mother was distraught. To her, the loss of her wedding ring was a very bad omen for the marriage. An extensive search ensued until eventually there was only one place left. Yes, that's it! My father promised that the next time he visited Caernarfon a new ring would be bought. Mother would have none of it, only her original one would do. After some considerable time and discussion father, displaying the extent of his love for my mother, went out and heroically retrieved the ring! After considerable scrubbing and sterilising, the size of the ring was reduced by winding thread around one part of it - there was definitely not going to be a repeat of that episode!

Jill Thomas

The first of our unofficial "evacuations" was to Acton in Suffolk where I was horrified to discover the toilet was a hut down the bottom of a long dark garden. I was terrified of going there and would only go with my mother firmly holding my hand.

On a later occasion, my aunt and uncle were on a farm in Soham, Cambridgeshire. At this farm, the toilet was again down the garden but this time it was a double seated one, so two of you could use it at once! I soon got used to it and in the end thought nothing at all to sharing the toilet with my aunt or mother.

Jean Runciman

The only snag with the cottage where we stayed in East Anglia to get away from the Blitz for a while was that it had no inside sanitation. The loo was in an extremely malodorous hut at the end of the garden. I was very upset about this and promptly refused to go in there. Fortunately, a very pretty bed of sweet-smelling violets was situated outside the hut and my mother managed to persuade me to pick a bunch of violets each time I needed the loo, so that I could inhale their perfume instead.

As the war proceeded and started to turn the way of the Allies, prisoners of war began to arrive in this country in large numbers. There had been prisoners from the time the shooting war really started and German planes were being downed, although not in vast numbers, but once we had broken out of Tobruk and later, the Italians capitulated, then large numbers of soldier prisoners were brought here. The Italians were amiable prisoners and seemed to make the most of their surroundings, happily working in the fields or wherever else they were taken.

Marlene Newson

My friend Ann (Dix, nee Burrows) lived opposite to me; there were workshops and stores in her big yard, something to do with the brewery. I remember two Italian prisoners of war working there and they made small rings for Ann and me with our initials on. We really treasured these and thought they were silver, but were probably made from polished aluminium. I kept mine for years, but as with so many things it got lost in the course of time. I remember the big P.o.W. camp in Cambridge Road (where the golf course now is) and seeing men in their rust-coloured clothes with large yellow squares (or maybe circles) on them.

Ann Dix

Ely had some Italian prisoners of war housed at the Barracks, now the Ely Golf Course. My friend Marlene and I were each given a ring made by them, with our initials on. I cannot remember the name of the Italian but he was very kind and friendly. I lost the ring when we moved back to our own house and very much regret that. My initials A.R.B. were intertwined and I see it clearly, even now.

June Thomsitt

For a while Italian prisoners of war worked on the farm where we got milk and eggs. My father thought they considered themselves lucky to be in Britain. They seemed very fond of us children, especially my little sister. I never felt threatened by them. In fact I was far more terrified of the occasional nun that I encountered.

Wendy Walton

It must have been towards the end of the war, for I was at school, (which I started aged 4). On the way home on a sunny summer day, we had stopped at the house of our friends - their mother and ours were also good friends. Barbara and I were outside, my sister and Neville (Barbara's big brother) indoors with our mothers. A lorry pulled up with lots of soldiers in the back. Barbara told me they were German prisoners of war who had been working in the fields. We were not supposed to look at, let alone talk to, prisoners, but we had an idea which we put into practice. As gales of laughter rose from the lorry, mothers, sister and brother rushed out to see what was happening and there we were, feet planted well apart, ankles gripped, and, heads upside down, we glared balefully from near ground level at the poor young men and pulled faces at them. We were taken unceremoniously indoors and told off!

When the U.S.A. entered the war, hundreds of thousands of their servicemen were stationed in the United Kingdom, many of them in the East of the country, from where they flew bombing missions. They also made themselves at home in the towns and villages, entering enthusiastically into whatever social life was on offer - so often, the pub and warm, weak beer, or the local dance. These young men really were exotic beings to most who encountered them, as back then, no "ordinary" person had a hope of travel to America, and it was almost a mythical country known only through the cinema yet suddenly here were Americans living in our village or town. They were very hospitable and generous, giving parties for children on the base or providing amazing refreshments at the dances they gave - food which to their guests, accustomed to wartime rations, was simply out of this world. They were popular young men, the local girls were in great demand and many romances flourished...

Kathy Jackson

My eldest cousin was courted by an American soldier while she was living with my maternal grandparents in Huntingdonshire. Mum and I went down there to stay for a while. Walter used to bring American sweets, candy and chewing gum. I believe he also brought nylons for the older members of the family. My cousin Elizabeth and I used to barter with the sweets and were allowed even to join in the boys' games in exchange for some chewing gum! Walter made Jeanne his G.I. bride in January 1943. She was one of the lucky ones who had a long and happy marriage, in Ephrath.

Muriel Gent

We had spent some of our holidays whilst in Ely with an aunt who had a pub right in the centre of what is now Stansted Airport - the airfield built by the U.S.A.A.F. This was filled with Americans every night. The piano was taken into the garden and we danced on the lawn. When I was old enough, we were collected in a truck and taken to the airfield to dance. The bands were top-class.

While in Ely I did some "war work" for my foster-mother. I ironed handkerchiefs in Nash's laundry for an hour every week night. I also walked the dog before I went to school. This was entered on a chart, along with a record of my mopping and dusting our room! Cowslips are a memory of Ely. I used to pick these, pack them in a box, take it to Ely station, give it to the guard and he would hand it to my mother who would be waiting at Liverpool Street station. Those were the days!

Journeys by road were made difficult by the severe restrictions on the supply and use of petrol, which was rationed almost entirely to essential users; so many vehicles were off the road for the duration. But there were some ways round the problem if you knew about the technology involved. In France, the use of charcoal to power vehicles was well established in the 1940s.

David Elcome

I remember a car up our road which was powered by coal gas stored in a large bag roped to its roof!

John Taylor

I travelled about by cycle or on foot. There was little traffic on the roads and what there was, was very slow. Steam lorries rarely travelled above 20mph. In winter I enjoyed riding behind them in their warm exhaust. Horse drawn carts delivered bread and milk. Towards the end of the war buses began to increase in number, many of them powered by gasbags which were towed behind the bus. The gas was coal gas from the local works.

Monette Meulet

France was divided into two zones, the north being the Occupied Zone. We lived in the South. Grandfather was born in the Creuse, near Aubusson (Occupied Zone) where his parental home and farm were. Because of this, he had permission from the German authorities to go there for a month's stay every year. Late July, 1942, grandfather and all the family left for the Creuse.

He had to think of everything - he needed a car which could tow a trailer containing a month's provisions. It was a Peugeot, with a "Western" model trailer - two rubber-tyred wheels and covered in tentcloth, like a covered wagon.

At the back of this trailer were a barrel of wine, sacks of potatoes, crates of fresh vegetables, sacks of flour and grain and large flasks of water. In the centre, wire mesh cages of chickens and ducks, behind a small pile of wood, suitcases and the two dogs.

Seven of us were in the car. Behind it was a bin, containing wood, bolted to the back. This wood (or charcoal) powered the car, not petrol and it worked well. Only on the steepest hills had everyone to get out and walk, except for two people, the driver and his helper, whose role was to sit on the mudguard with one finger permanently on a button which he pressed every three seconds to clear the charcoal debris from the engine and save it from cutting out.

From Montauban, where we started, it was 290 kilometres to "Mas de Saint Sylvain" and the journey would take two days. The first was best as we used the main Paris - Toulouse highway, N20, properly maintained and well-used. At Uzerche we turned off to stay overnight in the hotel there, the next day continuing driving towards the Massif Central. There wasn't one straight stretch of road - I was ill, I don't know about the others.

That August was glorious. There were white cows which gave creamy milk and we had butter! Hens and young chickens wandered between the hooves of the cattle. One day, an accident - a cow plonked her hoof onto a chicken's foot - calamity - it was broken. I hospitalised the chicken in the house. He had wooden splints (I had no plaster), lots of rest and a great deal of attention, surviving this excessive care to become a real friend, acknowledged by the dogs.

The day of departure came, but as the trailer was now considerably lighter without wine, potatoes, grain, vegetables and poultry, it was decided the journey would be completed in one day. Leaving very early, we were in a small village called Neuvic by early afternoon. In the centre of the village square was a fountain. It was very hot - grandfather had decided on a stop to freshen up. The village, succumbing to the heat, appeared deserted. We got out, tired, suffocating with the heat and happy at the prospect of splashing some water on our faces. We all had the same idea, but I hadn't forgotten my animals. Someone opened the trailer door, the two dogs jumped out, ecstatic at their freedom. They leapt madly to my shoulders, followed by the chicken with a flap of his wings. I cradled him in my arms. The dogs chased around me and I watched, fascinated by their games. My long black plaits twirled around, my heavily tanned skin gleamed. It was then that a small group of children appeared from the far side of the square, which we had thought deserted; the biggest boy shouted "A circus! It's a circus!" I don't know what grandfather said to him but we left very quickly after having a drink of water.

Walking, in the country, was the normal means of transport; buses were not all that frequent and often did not go to the point you were aiming at, so you went on foot!

Christina Watt
Every Sunday we walked to church - about three miles away in the next village! My sister was generally in the pram, this being a long walk for a three year old. We did not go if it was raining hard or there was snow.

My recollection is that we sang the National Anthem every Sunday, immediately after the sermon. On this particular sunny, early autumn day we had sung it as usual, after a sermon about harvest time. We were walking home, sunk in thought. Suddenly I asked "Mummy, why does the king want all those plums?" Mother stopped dead in her tracks. "Plums?" she asked, "what plums are you talking about, Tina?" "Oh mummy, you know what plums. All those we sing about in the song; 'Send him victorias'" When mother finally managed to stop laughing she explained to me that this was a very old way of saying 'let him win'. All the three miles home I grumbled on about stupid ways of saying things with mother giving the occasional giggle. Kids said the darndest things even in wartime!

Glenda Lindsay
Mother collected scarce coal, and wood from the garden, in the pram and wheeled it down the High Street to the "shop" for the Aunts. If she saw a queue outside a shop she always joined it because there was sure to be something worth having in the end!

In April 2007, travelling back from Cambridge by bus, the writer was talking to another local passenger. She said how at the start of the war her family were living in Durham. Aged 8, she was sent to boarding school in North Wales. When she started there, she was escorted on the journey, but after that she travelled alone. The journey meant changing train twice, at York and at Manchester. She was never accosted by anyone and always felt absolutely safe even though the trains were packed and the stations swarming with troops of all nationalities. It would not be possible to allow a small child to do that today.

Barbara Langridge
My father was in hospital in 1944. To make things easier for my mother to visit the hospital at the other side of London, I was sent back to the Wirral to stay with an aunt. I was put on the train at Euston, the guard was informed I was on my own, I had a packet of sandwiches and at seven years old I managed this six hour journey on a steam train! Perfectly safely!!

In London, throughout the war, the trams kept running. They were very noisy as they rattled along their tracks. Travelling inside them, it was quite difficult to hear a conversation under normal circumstances; in wartime conditions this became worse. On some routes, it was possible for the siren to be drowned out.

John Buckingham
One day I was going for a haircut, travelling to the barber's by tram. It was a very noisy journey that day and the siren must have sounded, but we on the tram did not hear it, the tram just trundled along. Somewhere near the barber's a bomb had exploded. I arrived there to find him

sweeping up all the glass from his windows, which was all over the floor. He looked at me and said "Sorry, I won't be cutting any hair for a while, I've got to clear this up".

(The authorities were very quick to do emergency repairs, boarding up and emergency glass.)

A cinema near us had an advertising banner across the front - *Gone With the Wind*. The cinema was bombed - all that was left of it was the banner, streaming across the front. Everything indeed was gone with the wind!

In Ely the mundane daily life of farms and the countryside became a source of wonder for the girls of the evacuated Central Foundation School.

R. Kerstein. CFS Chronicle, April 1944

When I arrived in Ely I was billeted on a farm. At first the country noises disturbed me but then I got used to the strange sounds and I began to realise the advantages of living there. The fresh, rich and creamy milk was delicious, but I put on pounds at an alarming rate. The thin tasteless milk of London dairies seemed like water in comparison with this.

The huge orchard knew me as a constant visitor; in London I never had the experience of going to a plum tree and having all the fruit I wanted. The one drawback was that to reach the orchard I had to pass through two chicken runs, and initially the hundreds of chickens scared me. I had never seen such a horde of hens in London, but I soon overcame my fear.

Winter approached on the farm. I do not think I shall ever forget that cold, bleak winter, with the snow in the fields that looked like an enormous carpet of down spread for miles over the countryside. But the spring made up for everything. The pink and white orchard was an indescribable picture, reminding me of tiny babies surrounded with white sheets and pink blankets. As they matured they discarded their baby garments and began to wear their green dresses.

The harvest will soon come and mark the end of my year as a farmer's girl, but I shall always be proud to argue, when I return to London, that a farm life is the healthiest life anyone can lead.

B. Greenberg. CFS Chronicle, April 1944

As I climbed down from the big car bringing me to my new home, I was not really conscious of the fact that I was beginning a new life, yet such was the case.

I went blackberry-ing with my foster-sister then made jam from the fruit. The autumn trees were lovely with their golden-brown leaves which gradually floated down to make a crackly path for passing pedestrians. The winter turned out to be far more exciting than expected, with some falls of snow which settled, then after a time constant frost made skating possible. I went home to London for a holiday, leaving Ely with bare trees and damp streets. On my return a very different sight met my eyes as the trees were once more covered with leaves and some were beginning to blossom. As spring has drifted into summer and Matriculation has passed, I am noticing that grass is green and also that the sky is very beautiful in Ely. The sunsets are particularly lovely and any troubles seem to melt away as that vivid ball vanishes over the horizon.

In this way a year has passed. There have been times of acute homesickness, not due to any fault in my new home, only to my love of my old home. In fact it scarcely seems six months since I entered the gates of a strange house to begin a new life.

The boy refugees of the Orthodox hostel in Ely were also starting a new life.

Herman Kon (b.1927. Stettin, now called Szechin)
JFS alumni magazine, September 2006

I was born in Stettin, then in Germany, in 1927. We had kept our Polish citizenship to visit our family annually. My father (Rabbi Kon) had no illusions as to the nature of the Nazi regime in Germany and had been trying to get us exit papers since 1937. Just before *Kristallnacht*, all Jews living in Germany who were Polish citizens, were expelled to Poland. We were fortunate, as my father had been trying to get us out for some time, to get papers to come to England in 1939.

I was sent into JFS for the last few weeks of the summer term and found myself evacuated with the school to Ely where I was placed in the hostel for Orthodox boys. I was the youngest of the family and my parents were determined to be near me, so eventually they got the job of running the hostel. I was already of secondary school age so was sent to Soham Grammar School, in the next village, where I was the first refugee they had seen, indeed the first Jew they had seen! I didn't speak a word of English but came to an arrangement with Mr. Johnson, the Deputy Head. He taught me English and I taught him German. I quickly learned English and rose to become House Captain and Captain of Sport. The difference between England and Germany could not have been starker. Mr. Johnson could not have been more kind. He had two very frum (strict, Orthodox) boys living with him and he kept separate cutlery and crockery so they could keep kashrut (so everything was strictly according to kosher dietary rules). Later, he attended their weddings in Stamford Hill.

Mr. Cousins ran the school for JFS boys (seniors). I remember little except that the poor man was once chased round the hostel by an angry mother shaking her umbrella at him.

There was little to do in those days for leisure - no television, and blackouts were something of a limit. Considering that many of the boys were already orphans and the rest had no idea what had happened to their families, the atmosphere in the hostel was remarkably calm. Indeed, in their own way, they were happy days.

Family life continued in its normal way, despite everything.

Gwen Pritchitt

Dad's youngest brother was in the Merchant Navy, having lied about his age to get in. We were staying with grandma (his mother) when he came home on leave. He brought all sorts of exotic presents, a fancy stool and tiny inlaid table (which I still have) and a pineapple. He called to my mum saying "Catch, Ethel - a shrunken head for you" and tossed her a coconut complete with 'hair'. She screamed and dropped it - and did not appreciate the joke!

His sister was a WAAF, based on the South Coast and she brought home a succession of boyfriends. One, 'Mac', from America taught me to jitterbug and fed me chocolate and gum. Another friend played the 'squeeze box' and we had some good parties.

CHAPTER 13

FEAR & LOSS

Fear was not a great part of our psychological make-up, as young children during the war. We were on the whole accepting of the explosions, we scavenged for shrapnel and played happily in bomb-damaged buildings, all of which were pursuits fraught with danger we now recognise, but were simply part and parcel of everything put there for our amusement, as far as we were concerned. On occasion, fear would overtake us, as when we realised someone had been killed, for example, or friends had been bombed out of their house, but this fear did not stay with us as a permanent feature throughout those years. And we were far too young to transfer fear into the future; our parents could worry about what might happen should the Germans invade, if the bombs did score a direct hit on the house, or if a husband were killed in action overseas, and that fear could be and frequently was so transferred, but on the whole they kept such concerns from us. That did not stop us from picking up on the fear occasionally but it did not normally overwhelm us even when the V2 weapons came along towards the end of the war. There were things that happened to us that in the telling become terrifying, but at the time, again, were taken as part and parcel of everyday life despite the note of terror in the adult voices that shouted warnings to us. And some of the fears of the time manifested themselves later in childhood, when to go down to a dark cellar, in peacetime, became a venturing into the realms of monsters which, some of the older children had assured us at the time, lived at the back of air-raid shelters!

Sometimes the fears of their parents were obvious to the other children, when the fear was for a child who was in danger and could not be traced for a long time.

Corinne Older
I can remember the day my mother sent my brother to shop in Sainsbury's and the shop was bombed. I remember her anguish when he didn't return until hours later, then came in with the shopping and was all excited by watching the fire and the fire engines. My poor mother was nearly passing out with the delight of having him back.

Jill Thomas

I remember being in Beckenham and I was holding my mother's hand as she was speaking to a neighbour in the street. I must have picked up the anxiety in her voice as I clearly remember her saying "What shall we do when the Germans come?" This must have been at the fall of Dunkirk and I can remember being worried, although not really understanding the significance of it, as my mother was obviously so worried. I also remember waiting at the front gate with my mother, because she had heard that the school my brother went to, had been hit by a bomb. But as we waited my brother came round the corner of the road on his bicycle and my mother's relief was palpable. I can feel it now. The bomb had dropped next to the school but no pupils had been killed or injured, they had all been in the shelters.

When the Nazis moved into the previously Unoccupied Zone of France, in late 1942, the people of that region experienced the full rigours of having German security measures put into being among them. Not just the military in their midst, but the full attention of the Gestapo was turned upon them and there was a justifiable element of fear in their daily life.

Monette Meulet

My great-grandmother's house was a large square building with a central hallway and rooms leading off it on either side. On entering through the front door, the kitchen was on the left hand side then the large dining room, furnished with a wood-burning stove and a large table. Beyond that room were two bedrooms. On special occasions Great-Grandma would have all her family at the house, ten people in total. There would always be one of these gatherings when we slaughtered a pig, cured hams and made sausages - a lengthy task but eased with many helpers. On one of these occasions I was woken at 4.00 in the morning by a shaft of light - I slept in a room opening off the dining room. By the dining room light I saw everyone gathered there, in their night wear; they were all talking animatedly and I saw a bottle of alcohol on the table. Everyone held a glass of it.

I learned later on that somewhere in the hamlet a resistance member was thought to be hidden. The Gestapo considered he might be in our house, or in a loft, a stable or a barn around the farm, so, at 1.00 in the morning they arrived, compelled my grandfather to get up and made him take them to every nook and cranny of the place - all with a machine-gun in his back! Had the man been hidden here? No-one knew, that was the point of the exercise.

They found no-one, so eventually went away around 4.00. Everyone else was in dire need of a good stiff drink at 4.00 in the morning! The Gestapo had been there, poking around...!

Perhaps, back in England, it was shock rather than fear that played a part in children's lives. The warning siren before an air-raid was extremely loud and very unpleasant to the ears.

Gloria Morgan

When an air-raid was imminent a siren was sounded to warn people to run to shelter. The piercing wail of the siren is one of the most potent memories I have of the war. If I hear it now, in a film or in a wartime re-enactment, it still upsets me. After the raid, an 'All Clear' was sounded and life returned to normal.

Val Lines

It was always a shock when the siren suddenly started and I remember on one occasion standing in the playground sucking a blue button that had just become detached from my cardigan. I was talking to young Freddie who was proudly wearing a pair of Wellingtons. The sudden noise from the siren made me swallow the button and poor Freddie fill his boots, with much wailing and distress. Milk of Magnesia was duly administered to me on my return home. I don't recall what happened to Freddie!

It is not just in films that aeroplanes fly low, firing bullets at people who happen to be there. In the most terror-inspiring manner, many children and young people were the targets of returning enemy planes, flying low and strafing civilians.

Gwen Pritchitt

It was not just the raids of the night-time we had to worry about. One day we were out for a walk round the suburban roads, my mother pushing a neighbour's baby in a low pram. A plane flew low overhead firing randomly and my mother pushed me to the ground and laid over the baby until the plane had passed.

Janet Ellison

Once, I was running out of school, aged 5, and a teacher screamed at us to lie down. I clearly remember the fear and urgency in her voice. I lay down in a puddle and tried to wriggle to one side and again the teacher shouted at us not to move. There was a low drone as a German plane flew low over our primary school. Then great relief and we were allowed to get up. German fliers had apparently been strafing small towns and any pedestrians who were in the way. It was rumoured that we were an invasion point and this made the adults jumpy but they were good at keeping calm for our sakes. We were living in Worthing at the time.

Joan Hardy

I remember an instance when I was living on the top floor in Clock House Parade when a plane flew so low overhead that we could see the German markings. Later we heard that it had fired on the school playground in Catford, killing many of the pupils.

The incident referred to by Joan was one of the worst involving bombed schools during the war. By 1943, there were what the papers called "scalded cat raids", which took place during the daytime, where small groups of up to six German aircraft flew in very low to avoid the Thames defences, bombed and strafed to produce maximum damage in and around London then got out again "like scalded cats". (The other name for the raids was "tip and run", after the children's cricket-type game where, if the batsman tipped the ball, he had to run; the bomber struck then ran!) Most of the aircraft involved were Focke-Wulff 190 fighter-bombers or Messerschmitt 110s, speedy with the ability to fly in low under the radar cover, so avoiding detection or alerting British planes with the possibility of the siren then sounding to warn of danger. The first of these raids took place on 17 January 1943. Then, on Wednesday 20 January 1943, at lunchtime, a Focke-Wulff 190 on such a raid, dropped its 500 kg (1,100 lb) bomb on Sandhurst Road School, Catford, London SE6. As it had come in low enough for its markings to be read, there was no siren, although some teachers, seeing the plane circling, began to lead the children down into the shelters. Being lunchtime, there were 150 children in the dining room. The bomb passed through the wall of the three-storey school into the dining room where it exploded. The building collapsed on top of these children, burying them under rubble. There were many casualties, with thirty-eight children and six teachers being killed, and another forty children badly injured. (Other reports give the number of children killed as forty.) The older children, aged around 14, did marvellous work to help, taking home younger pupils, strapping up wounds and even helping in the rescue work. War brought a strong sense of maturity and responsibility to older children.

The sense of anguish and fury at this outrage was so strong that around ten thousand people were there for the burial service on 27 January.

Why deliberately bomb a school? The pilot had flown in low enough for the markings on his plane to be easily seen and he was observed circling above the building, so it is reasonable to assume he had to have seen some of the children in the playground or just outside the school perimeter, on their way home for lunch. It would have been difficult to mistake the school for a factory, being in a residential area and of an architectural style typical of school buildings all over the country, not just London. The inescapable conclusion has to be that the pilot's target was deliberately chosen either by himself or by the Luftwaffe high command. As the small town of Oradour-sur-Glane, France, showed a little later, the truly fanatical Nazis had no compunction in killing children if it suited their purpose.

Diana Scott

In the summer of 1941 I returned to Beckenham from Gerrard's Cross as there were few bombs, although I do remember one incident in early 1943; we were playing in a field at school when a German aircraft came over low and we ran as fast as we could to the shelters while he machine gunned. No-one was hit, fortunately, but he continued on and bombed a school in Catford where there were many fatalities.

Joy King

Back in Penge after my evacuation to Worcester, I returned to school. One lunch time we were let out of school just as the air-raid warning sounded. My friend and I continued to wander home when we were suddenly aware of an aeroplane above us, very low - we could see the pilot - and it was firing. On some instinct (probably fear) we ran into the grounds of the church we were passing and lay low on the ground near the building until the plane eventually went away. Quite scary for two 7 year olds, but we still went back to school after lunch.

Linda Zerk

I think of this still as The High Street Incident. Early on in the war, I was in Beckenham High Street with my sister who is three years older than me. A low-flying German plane at about the height of the parish church steeple zoomed up the High Street firing its machine guns. Jennifer pushed me against a shop wall and protected me with her body.

Molly Oakley

Most of my memories are quite vague but I do remember my sister and I returning from school running along the road with a German plane machine-gunning the centre of the road and we dodged in and out of shop doorways. I really don't think we realised the danger we were in until my mother came running to meet us, in an apron with a turban round her head - it must have been Monday and wash day!

These incidents of strafing, as opposed to scalded cat raids, were not confined to London. John Taylor's recollections of being shot at while delivering papers along the Holyhead Road in Coventry have already appeared and he is not the only Coventrian to have suffered this.

Virginia Watkinson

I don't remember being machine-gunned into the gutter but apparently my mother and I were, while my mother's closest friend, Cissie, screamed from her doorway.

Similar things happened in Bristol and in Stuttgart!

Peter Rex

My father served as an Air-raid Warden and had several fairly hair-raising adventures. One day, during daylight hours, a German bomber came in low over Clifton and as it passed over Park Place the tail gunner opened up with his machine gun and shot up the area. My father had taken shelter in the doorway of our house in Bruton Place and narrowly escaped injury when bullets struck the front of the house, leaving scars in the brickwork which were still there the last time I visited in the 1970s.

Anna Piper

By 1944 the day and night bombing raids became very frequent. The local train on which my grandmother travelled was attacked in a day raid by US low-flying aircraft which shot up the train. My grandmother died on the railway embankment of an upper thigh injury, bleeding to death. Her terrier was used as target practice as he escaped through the carriage window, according to eye-witnesses. There was considerable loss of life on that occasion.

Loss of a parent or close relative as a result of conflict was not something we all had to cope with, but when it happened the shock to others around was considerable. The writer remembers the day on which her class teacher was called from the classroom by another member of staff, possibly the headmaster, with a third person taking over the lesson. A little while later, one of her two sons, who was in our class, was also taken out, along with the other son, from a class junior to us. They were not seen for a few days, although the pupils in the senior classes told us that the teacher's husband had been killed in the fighting and this news had had to be given to her by the head. They had heard her sobs and were upset by them, which quickly spread to the other pupils; this was something way outside our experience which we did not know how to handle. When she and the boys came back, we said nothing as we had no idea what to say, that sense of helplessness and unknowing haunting us for months with nothing in the way of guidance as to how to deal with it. Those of us with fathers in the forces were brought face to face with the possibility of daddy being killed, but that, at least, we were able to shrug off with the insouciance of childhood! But the memories of such incidents are long-lived.

Brenda Booker

We lost family friends in the London blitz. My uncle was taken Prisoner of War and lost his life on the infamous Burma Railway.

Joyce Kitching

Just before the war, uncle Frank (mum's youngest brother) joined the Royal Artillery and went off to the Far East where the Chinese and Japanese were in conflict. My sister remembers sitting on a back step and him telling her he would bring her a doll when he came home. He never returned as his regiment was involved in the defence of Hong Kong in 1941 and he was taken prisoner by the Japanese. He was killed when the boat he was on - with other P.o.Ws being transferred to Japan - was torpedoed by an American submarine (the Japanese had contravened the Geneva Convention by not marking the boat as a Prisoner ship). My abiding memory of him is that he was a very handsome man - an Errol Flynn look-alike.

Gwen Pritchitt

There were always lots of visitors to our house, 'aunties' who were the wives of dad's army colleagues and another who was the fiancée of my dad's younger brother. She was with us when the news came through that he had been killed in a training flight over Nottinghamshire - the anguished sobs will stay with me forever.

In Australia, the loss of life on their own shores was more than was permitted to be known at the time. Australia was a major target of the Japanese.

Melvyn Zerk

Later in the war, when the Americans came in after Pearl Harbour, there was a narrow bitumen road built from Alice Springs to Darwin so that troops could be transported by train to Alice and from there to Darwin by road. Darwin received quite a battering from Japanese aircraft and the loss of life was considerably greater than was admitted to at the time. We were told that only nine people had been killed, and were relieved. It was around twenty years later we learned the actual total was well over 300 lives lost. It must have put the wind up people there, though, as parents dug shelters for the children at the local schools and some really panicky ones dug their own shelters at home, too. Wyndham, a port in West Australia, was also attacked. Caucasian and Asian women and children were evacuated south and Aboriginal women and children were evacuated to Balaklava, South Australia, where they were billeted at the racecourse. According to Barney, who married cousin Lucy, it was not a happy time for them. Barney's mother was one of the evacuees.

On the East coast, three Japanese mini-subs. were launched from a larger submarine which was off the coast. They came into Sydney Harbour and two got caught in the net which was strung across from shore to shore. I'm not sure whether they perished there or whether they were able to get back to the mother sub. The third one managed to get through and torpedoed a small ship. It was thought they were aiming for a USA vessel which was in the harbour, and got the wrong one. This was regarded as a minor event. The people were told that all the Japanese had been caught or drowned, (which wasn't absolutely true,) so there wasn't too much panic about this close encounter. That small ship was sunk and there were some lives lost. No-one was sure whether the sub. involved got away until 2006 when the wreck of a small sub. was found by divers outside Sydney Heads. It was proclaimed to be a war grave so off-limits to divers and Japan was invited to take charge of it.

The child's traditional fear of the dark, however, had conditions in which it could thrive during the war.

Pat Fulmer

After the D-Day landings my mother and I returned to Catford, London, to live with my grandparents until our house was rebuilt - it had been bombed in the Blitz. My grandparents' Victorian house had no electricity at that time. Mother and I shared a bedroom - and bed - at the top of the house, two flights up. My mother and grandparents were all hard of hearing and always had the radio on at full volume in the evenings. When the siren for the next area sounded I could always hear it and would scream for mum to come and get me. Without a light I was too scared to creep downstairs in the blackout. Eventually our local siren would start up and mum would race upstairs, wrap me in a blanket and hustle me down and out through the garden to the Anderson shelter, where we huddled until the 'All Clear'. I remember having nightmares about Germans and for decades afterwards the sound of planes at night always frightened me.

It was fear of loss in another sense entirely that is the basis of this vivid memory.

Jeanne Taylor

We lived in Filton, Bristol, on the perimeter of the Bristol Aircraft Corporation where my father worked. His was a reserved occupation so he never went to war, but the war did come to us. The aircraft factory was a magnet for bombs and on Easter Sunday in 1943 (I think) there was an enormous raid over Bristol which destroyed most of the centre of the city. It must have been night time for I remember the cold mouldy dampness of the Anderson shelter in the garden and as the curtain was pulled back from the doorway I vividly recall the patterns of the searchlights in the sky. In the middle of the raid, with bombs crashing down, my mother suddenly remembered that she had left the precious Easter Eggs in the house and in her fear that they might be lost, she made my father run up through the garden to rescue my brother's egg.

In country areas in East Anglia, which became almost one vast armoured camp of airfields and military bases, one might expect to have found a great deal of fear among the children, but no, they became accepting of the situation and adapted to the new circumstances of their lives.

Marie Jordan

Even when we had an aerodrome right on the edge of the village we didn't get worried over much with air-raids. The German raiders did drop anti-personnel bombs called butterfly bombs on the airfield. They looked like an old tin can but if disturbed had a lethal detonator that could maim if touched. We had to learn about the different types of bombs so that if we came across any we could give a good report as to what and where they were. Also we learned the different types of aircraft, both ours and foreign.

Living on the edge of an aerodrome we could hear the bombers revving their engines getting ready to take-off on a bombing mission, usually early evening. The aircraft were Stirlings and Lancasters, big four-engined planes, so they made quite a racket when about to take-off. In summer we would rush up to the front bedroom window to see them taxi along the runway ready to take off. (I was talking with a friend, in adult life, who flew bombing raids from RAF Mepal, as the aerodrome was called and he said the RAF personnel that were off duty used to wave the crews off, then further along, the crews would see the villagers waving to them and so right along they knew they were being thought about.)

One evening when they were preparing to take off there was an air-raid warning and of course they tried to get all the aircraft into the air when one of them crashed into the pair of houses that was close to the runway. All the crew were killed plus a WAAF as she tried to help the crew get out. There were also two civilian firemen killed because they went into one of the houses thinking two female teachers were trapped inside. They had gone out to visit friends without telling their landlord where they were going so the two brave men died.

When the plane crashed into the two council houses all the families were evacuated from their homes, some in their night clothes. They all ran to the bottom of the road and sheltered in the ditch alongside Sutton House Park. The explosion caused the plate glass windows of Greene King's shop to shatter with a loud noise. As this was where we lived, it was a bit frightening. That evening my mum had allowed me to go to bed with Dinkie curlers in my hair. When I awoke I thought there was a thunderstorm so I started to snatch the curlers from my hair, thinking I might be struck by lightning if I didn't.

It was possible for the young people to be the cause of fear in their elders and betters, even unintentionally.

Leslie Oakey

During 1942, two Ely lads appeared in court and a cautionary tale unfolded before the stunned bench.

The lads found their way into the large military camp at West Fen Road, then occupied by a sizeable contingent of the British Army. Evading the sentries, they made their way to the armoury which they found unguarded. Then finding the door unlocked they helped themselves to revolvers, anti tank missiles and ammunition.

After that, they made their way to West Fen, where they proceeded to blaze away at anything that happened to be passing, including some land workers on their way home. Alerting the local constabulary, the workers crept back under cover of a hedge to await developments. Retribution in the shape of PC Vail soon overtook the lads, but not before they had taken a shot or two at him. Greatly daring, he disarmed them and marched them off to the local lock up.

At the subsequent court hearing the officer in charge of the camp astounded the magistrates when he stated that he did not know anything was missing until the police informed him! The lads were duly punished and later were called to the forces where they put their firearms skills to better use!

CHAPTER 14

D-DAY, DOODLEBUGS AND THE DEMI-DIASPORA

This chapter has to start in mid-1943 when the tide of war turned decisively in favour of the Allies. On 10 July, they landed in Sicily and on 7 September, the Italian military surrendered. The war in Italy continued, though, as the Germans held out, but it was a very lengthy war of attrition fought bitterly along the whole of the country. The campaign was complicated by a kind of simultaneous internecine warfare going on between the remaining Fascisti and the Partisans (usually communist) for control of the country post war. Both of these factions would assist either Germans or Allies as and when it suited their purpose to do so. This bitter campaign continued virtually up until the end of the war in 1945. Many of us whose fathers served in that theatre have realised since that the intensity and loss of life sustained there bore an uncanny resemblance to parts of World War I, and that our dads were fortunate to come through it, but we were unaware of this at the time.

However, this change in the fortunes of war had brought respite for Britain from the bombing - there were still many raids, but the ferocity and frequency were much reduced. It was decided to bring the girls of the Central Foundation School back from Ely to their London home. The parents felt they could no longer do without the presence of their daughters, now that the worst of the danger was passed, so at the end of the summer term, the School went back. There was a Farewell Party for the people of Ely on 7 July, at the Ely High School, with party games, races, refreshments and then speeches. Miss Menzies thanked everyone who had made the sojourn in Ely so good and in her return speech, Dr. Tilly, Head of the High School, said she could not believe that four years had passed but she felt that they had been years of enrichment. Speeches were also made by the Billeting Officer and the Dean of the Cathedral, who said that the girls would be missed in the town, then "Auld Lang Syne" was sung, there were cheers, and the evening closed with the National Anthem. Over the next few days, some senior girls stayed in Ely to help with the mammoth task of packing up then assisting with the loading onto removal vans and by mid-July they were all gone from their temporary home.

From that mid-point of July 1943 thoughts of the civilian population began to turn towards the problem of defeating the Germans when we were an island and the enemy occupied most of the continent of Europe. This country was host to almost a million-and-a-half non-British troops, mostly American GIs, and there was curiosity as to what exactly they might be doing, both when and where. It dawned gradually that there would have to be an invasion somehow, somewhere, but there was not a hint as to where this would take place. But the build up of troops and equipment, over time, could not fail to be noticed and the workers in the factories were aware that they were producing more and more and more.

D-Day, 6 June 1944, was the day the Allies really took the war to Hitler, invading his European stronghold along the coast of Normandy. Young we may have been, but memories of the newspaper pictures of the Armada, and of the different tone of voice of the newsreaders, are very vivid. We sensed that 'things were getting better'. We also noticed other odd happenings.

John Taylor

Just before the war a dual carriageway bypass had been built to connect the Birmingham Road to the London Road, in Coventry. Down both sides of this road was a cycle track and, like many boys, I enjoyed cycling from one end to the other as fast as I could. In the months leading up to D-Day the central reservation and then the two central lanes were gradually filled with tanks and other military vehicles. Quite suddenly these vehicles disappeared and within days we were told of the landings in Normandy! Again, with newspaper wall charts we followed the progress of the liberation of Europe. At the same time we were similarly following the progress of the Russians and the push in Italy.

Peter Rex

The only wartime death I am aware of is that of Yannick Gummerson who attended St. Brendan's College from 1939–42 and who "tutored" my reading skills in primary school. His name was placed on the school Honours Board as he was killed in the war. My mother was convinced it was at Dunkirk but that is impossible - from his age it must have been one of the other raids, possibly Dieppe, but more likely the invasion on D-Day.

Christina Watt

We noticed the rumbling in early June 1944. Someone said it was from the not-very-far-away Great North Road (A1), where convoys were passing almost all of the time. The conclusion was that something major was happening somewhere. After the news of the invasion the rumblings rapidly reached a crescendo then subsided to "normal" levels after a few days. Obviously the convoys were transporting men and military supplies to the South Coast.

Gwen Pritchitt

Dad's youngest brother was in the Merchant Navy. He has the dubious honour of being the first military person to be court-martialled after the D-Day landings! His ship was one of those scuttled to form the Mulberry Harbour. He and his mates heard that the Royal Navy personnel had been given barrels of rum for their efforts - the Merchant sailors, nothing! So they all went out to steal some - and Jack got caught. I went to France with his daughter fairly recently and she showed me the house where his trial took place - while the bombs dropped all around. He was found guilty and spent a couple of months in prison in England.

The facts of D-Day are very well known and there is no need to rehearse them further apart from those few recollections. To us, the children and young people at home in Britain, what happened next was far more immediate, memorable and life-threatening, because what happened next were the V-weapons. These were "Vergeltung" weapons - retaliation weapons - the retaliation being revenge for the massive bombing offensive on German cities.

There were two of these V-weapons that became operational, the petrol-driven V1 flying bombs, the "Doodlebugs", prototype Cruise Missiles, then the V2s, the world's first operational ballistic missiles, rockets powered by a specially-developed fuel and totally silent in operation.

The Doodlebug (or Buzz Bomb, the other popular name) was a small pilotless aircraft of a very rudimentary design. The cylindrical body was packed with 2000-lbs of explosive; there was a jet engine mounted above the fuselage at the rear, and two pairs of truncated, blunt-ended wings. The nose was conical and tapered, with a very small propeller that operated an air log when the missile was either out of fuel or over target causing it to glide or shallow dive to earth. In the earliest models, the engine would cut out, giving a very audible warning of its impending fall, allowing people to take cover, but this was less immediately noticeable with later models. Detonation caused massive damage. There was very strict security in the reporting of detonations in order to deny knowledge of where they had landed to the enemy, but misinformation was put about in the hope that it would get back, that the missiles were considerably overshooting their targets, to effect a reduction in their preset range to ensure they fell well short of Central London. This campaign was successful as the missiles started falling on SE London making Croydon the most-hit town. The missiles flew at about 3000ft. They had a top speed of 410mph at launch, which was from a rail, a metal ramp, using a kind of catapult for the initial momentum to hurl it along the rail and into the air, after which the pulse jet engine took over. It sounded like a powerful, slightly malfunctioning motorbike engine. The speed dropped quite considerably by the time the Doodlebug arrived over England and as the guidance system was by gyroscopes, it was soon deduced that it should be possible to tip the bomb over and cause it to crash and detonate in relatively unpopulated locations.

John Buckingham

It was almost entertaining to watch the V1s. They flew very slowly by the time they reached London so I stood and watched them, only taking cover when the engine cut out. When I spotted a doodlebug I would follow its flight, blowing a whistle when the engine cut and the neighbours knew then that they had to get into the shelter. They came to rely on me with this service!

On the flight path to London, watchers could witness the courage of R.A.F Fighter Command again. The maximum speed of any individual Spitfire depended on what "Mark" it was, (i.e. where it came in the rolling development of the machine) but would be somewhere between 370 - 460mph, somewhat faster than the speed of the Doodlebug by then. The pilots would fly alongside the missile, in the same direction, then would nudge it gently below one wing; this would turn it over, sending the on-board gyroscopes into a frenzy and, out of control it would crash onto (hopefully) heathland or open fields. Of the 10,500 V1s launched against London between 13th June 1944 and 29th March 1945, 4000 were destroyed in this manner or by shooting them down by those self-same Fighters.

David Elcome

Sanderstead lay directly in the path of the Doodlebugs as they flew from the near-Continent to London - the suburb was part of what became known as Doodlebug Alley. Many missiles passed directly over our house. They were stubby-winged, with a primitive jet-like engine fixed above the rear of the cylindrical bomb. Their name probably came from the characteristic but menacing engine-drone that pulsated and buzzed as it passed overhead. Far more terrifying, however, was the splutter of the engine as its fuel ran out, followed by several seconds of total silence and then a dull 'crump' as the bomb exploded.

One afternoon we heard the increasingly throaty whirr of an approaching doodlebug. Suddenly it cut out. My baby sister was strapped into her high chair in the kitchen and I will never forget my mother's desperate attempts to release her. I just made it into the shelter as the blast from the bomb, which had landed in Hook Hill only 200 yards away, blew in the french-windows of our living room. Sister, mum and high chair had been wrestled to the floor and we were all extremely lucky to escape with no more than a few scratches and a pile of shattered glass. From the ceiling on the landing the square trap-door cover to the loft had been blown out and had crashed to the bottom of the stairs. Large amounts of soot had been shaken down the chimney!

On another occasion I was playing with a friend in his garden. It was a delightfully sunny spring day with white puffy cumulus clouds. Once again we heard the sinister drone of an in-coming flying bomb, but this one was accompanied by the sound of a pursuing fighter. Glinting in the sunlight and perhaps three-quarters of a mile away, they could not have been more than a few hundred feet up. Soon the clatter of guns was heard and the doodlebug exploded in mid-air. Wildly we danced and cheered as the Spitfire flew directly overhead in a low victory-roll. We could even see the pilot in his cockpit as his aircraft rotated! I remember for tea that day we had strawberries from the garden!

Muriel Gent

We returned to London and back to school again, and London food plus snoek and whalemeat. Night after night and daytime too, we had raids, Doodlebugs and Rockets. Several CFS pupils were killed. The only shelters we had at school were those used in the First World War raids, but they were not safe enough to use. We worked in bricked-up classrooms.

Sylvia Bunce

I remember the fear we all felt at home when the doodlebugs went over and suddenly stopped and we would all wonder where the bomb would fall. I do recall one of them falling on the Elmers End Bus Depot, although I can't remember when it was exactly. The flames could be seen for miles.

(On the evening of 18 July 1944, a doodlebug flew in through the open doors of the Elmers End Bus Depot (SE London/NW Kent border). The firewatcher on the roof stayed at his post to give warning of the approach of the bomb and died outright in the explosion. In that one incident sixteen people died and thirty-nine were injured.)

Ann Gamêt

In talking with my Uncle Allen, who was a young man during the war, he recalled the Bus Garage incident.

"Now, we were down the road, Churchfields Road, and I was at work. A doodlebug came along, it was just gliding along the top of the rooftops and just skimmed the roofs of all those houses, coming from the south, and it went straight into the entrance like that, "Woomf!". All the buses it wrecked set everything alight and killed all the people. It was a state that was, you know!"

Frank Bunce

The war went on and we moved back to Battersea and continued to rush to the shelters, sometimes seeing the doodlebugs pass over, listening for their engines to stop and waiting for the explosion. Also listening to the ack-ack guns trying to shoot down the bombers or flying bombs, then rushing out of the shelters at the end of the raid to look for still-hot shrapnel from the shells. I was a bit more fearful after being bombed-out once, walking back from school, hoping that my house would still be there.

Ruth Hixson

Wherever you were, air-raids were possible. As the war continued, rockets were developed. The first ones, V1s, were nicknamed Doodlebugs. You heard them coming until the engine stopped - where would it land? - that was the most frightening part. The wailing siren would give warning and you made for the nearest shelter. I didn't like it if I was out-of-doors. The public shelters smelt stale and stuffy because some people had virtually set up home in them.

Bob Jackson

A doodlebug fell on the block of flats next to us so we had to go and live with relatives in Downham (SE London) until the flats were made habitable again.

Gloria Morgan

The worst phase of the war was when flying bombs, or 'doodlebugs' were coming over nightly. These self-propelled, pilotless missiles were preset to fly a certain distance and when they reached their target the engine cut out and they crash landed and exploded. I can remember the characteristic drone of the engine and when that sound stopped, holding my breath and counting. If you counted to thirty you were safe. A few moments later, if it was near, there would be a muffled thud and if it was very near, a tremor passed through the ground. Next day, there would be another gap in a familiar row of houses that I passed on my way to school.

John Gamêt

During 1943 raids became spasmodic and we were able to move about more freely. In 1944, I took the entrance examination for Whitgift Middle School, Northend Croydon, without incident. But the day after, a flying bomb landed in the school grounds! This was the start of the V1 flying bomb blitz. In order to deter these pilotless aircraft a network of barrage balloons was deployed along the South Downs to 'protect' London. I frequently saw these flying bombs, or doodlebugs as they became known due to the doodling sound of their engines, flying straight through this barrier. As they came over in ever increasing numbers, it was decided that we should leave 'buzz bomb alley' as it was known and we were evacuated to Nottingham for safety. I returned in late September to attend school, which opened on the 18th. Later that year I was lying in the shelter in the lounge during a raid that had been on for some time when the 'All Clear' signals sounded except for the one covering our area. My mother told me I could come out as the 'All Clear' had gone, but I said ours hadn't when there was an almighty crash. The French windows appeared to jump into the centre of the room and back again in an instant. A flying bomb had landed in an oak tree above a nearby air-raid shelter. As a result it had exploded in the air which was most fortunate as, had it landed on the shelter, it would have killed the local doctor's wife and daughters.

Anyone inside a house within fifty yards of a doodlebug explosion was likely to be buried as the house crashed down on them due to the sheer force of the explosion and blast.

Jean Parrott

My sister was born in January 1944, just as the flying bombs began coming over, in fact her arrival was greeted with the firing of an anti aircraft gun sited right beside the Stone Park Maternity Hospital and which my mother blamed for causing Vivien to suffer with eczema as a baby. There must have been some rumours about the "buzz bombs" as dad said that was what it must be the first time we heard one. The silence as the engine cut out was always particularly ominous while waiting for it to explode. The nearest actually went into a house at the top of Wickham Chase, up the hill.

Diana Scott

My mother tried to make life seem as normal as possible during the time of the flying bombs and on my twelfth birthday in the midst of the doodlebugs, I had a party. My mother insisted that we limited it to five children as that was all we could fit into the shelter which was situated in the back room. We had tea and played and dived into the shelter when the doodlebugs got ominously near.

After one particularly bad incident, my father decided it was time for mother and I to leave for Gerrards Cross again. It was just as well this decision was made as a few weeks later, our house in Cherry Tree Walk was demolished when a flying bomb landed in our back garden. Fortunately my father was not there as it was in the afternoon, but a neighbour was killed. The stairs under which we were all advised to shelter landed in the front garden!

Linda Zerk

For the first time in the war, Mother got the "wind up"! These sneaky un-manned flying bombs were very scary. We got to know the sound of their engines and were taught that if one cut out over our heads we were to throw ourselves flat on the ground. The bombs were filled with the right amount of fuel to reach London and when this ran out the doodlebug would fall out of the sky and explode. This was very 'hit and miss' and some fell south of London. This was the time that our parents decided that we should go and stay with Uncle Gilbert and Auntie Phyllis at Great Barford, near Bedford.

Jean Runciman

The Normandy landings on D-Day marked a turning-point in the liberation of Western Europe, but a very sinister development occurred a few days later on 12th June 1944. The first V1 flying bomb (called the doodlebug by the British) was launched from Germany, followed by a concentrated bombardment with these terrible weapons on London and the south-east. No warning of their approach could be given, suffice it to say that we got used to taking shelter wherever we could if we heard one coming over and that the Beckenham area was badly affected.

Ann Gamêt

While we were in Leeds our home in Beckenham was requisitioned so all our possessions were moved to my Nan's house in Penge. She was told by my uncle that when the sirens sounded she should go under the stairs for safety.

One night the sirens went and she hid under the stairs. She was writing a letter to my father when a doodlebug fell in the garden next door, burying her under the rubble. They found her alive and took her to hospital where my father was able to get to see her. He came back to Leeds so upset, saying she was black and blue all over. She died shortly after. The worst part was that had she stayed in bed she would have been unhurt as only the side of the house was demolished! Uncle never forgave himself.

Doodlebugs could be and frequently were launched from Heinkel bombers over the sea, but such launching meant that sometimes they were spectacularly off course.

Christina Watt

We did have one of these doodlebugs over our Yorkshire village; memory says during the late evening, but a friend from there recalls daytime. It was quiet when suddenly we heard a motorbike engine which got nearer and nearer. Everyone froze and held their breath. There was no shelter anywhere near - the closest was at the school, nearly a mile away. The motorbike, by then very loud indeed, passed overhead and got quieter. I don't recall if we heard it cut out or not, but next day we learnt it had landed on open ground, creating a massive crater and killing an unfortunate cow which was just in the wrong place. The doodlebug had to have been launched from a plane, in the wrong direction; there would not have been enough fuel to reach Doncaster from the near Continent.

The last V1 landed in Suffolk on 29 March 1945. There were 6,000 fatalities attributed to the V1 weapon.

The second terror weapon was the V2, the world's first ballistic-missile rocket. Development of this started in 1932. The eventual weapon had a powerful warhead with huge destructive power, weighed more than 12 tons and carried 2,200 lbs. of Amatol High Explosive. It was 47ft. high with a diameter at the base of 10ft. Its range was over 200 miles. It was powered by a liquid fuel, a mix of alcohol and liquid oxygen which increased its range. The V2 launched by its own power on a vertical trajectory; 35 seconds after lift-off it would be six miles up and travelling at twice the speed of sound. In flight it was steered by a series of rudders and vanes. There was only a small fuel supply which was gone after 54 seconds' flight so it hurtled onward and downward under its own momentum at a speed approaching 3600 mph, about four times the speed of sound when it hit the ground. Impact came approximately 5 minutes after launch.

Each rocket cost about £12,000 to build and launch (at that time, a colossal sum); a total of 517 fell on London and 537 in the Home Counties, East Anglia and South East England. Each caused an average of 2.61 deaths and 6.18 serious injuries, while tens of thousands of buildings were destroyed or severely damaged. The last V2 rocket landed in the early evening of March 27th 1945, between the back gardens of two houses in Orpington, Kent; one person was killed and 55 injured.

The weapon could launch from underground bases or from mobile launchers. Underground bases were colossal concrete strongholds which rapidly attracted the attention of Allied Intelligence authorities through their agents in occupied territories. Massive bombing raids against them ensued, causing considerable damage and delay. One such raid killed one of the inventors and perhaps more importantly, all the current development updates and new plans were incinerated in the conflagration. Mobile launch consequently became the norm, from stations of several vehicles which could be easily camouflaged and could be moved to another site before any retaliatory air attack.

The weapon was so powerful that the 1-ton warhead could raze to the ground a small street of 30 terraced houses, while the blast was such that the windows of houses a mile away could be and were blown out.

When the first ones hit London there was an attempt at a cover up - the government was appalled at what was assumed to be the likely reaction of a scared and fed-up public to learning it was on the receiving end of bombardment with an undiscriminating blockbuster like this when there was absolutely no means either of warning of an attack or protection against that attack. It was therefore put about that gas mains were being hit and were exploding. Initially this was quite plausible. Because the rocket came down at such tremendous speed, the whole descent was completely silent; it hit and exploded, whereupon the sound and noise of the down-draught of the flight arrived and added to the confusion. It might easily have been a gas main - but the public soon discounted this, reasoning that there could not possibly be as many gas mains as that being blown up yet domestic pressure being maintained, and there was acceptance of the concept of yet another terror weapon. Perversely the V2 in some ways was preferred to the V1, as with the rocket, if you heard it, it had missed you; if it had hit you, you would not have heard it at all so where was the point in taking shelter 'just in case'? Whereas with the doodlebug you had the awful wait after the engine cut out to see if it would fall near to you.

Jill Jones

My most vivid memory is of early 1945, when a V2 hit the Midland Bank sports ground near New Beckenham Station. My mum threw herself on top of me (I actually remember that feeling) and all the windows blew in. The next thing I remember is my aunt careering down our unmade road on her bike, having heard the news at Burroughs Wellcome where she was working. (Mum told me later that she herself was pregnant with my brother at this time.)

Jean Runciman

On 7th September 1944 the first V2 weapon, the rocket, was launched. These weapons gave no warning and were silent, so there was no hope of taking shelter. One of them fell near my school, Marian Vian, on the night of 11th/12th March 1945, leaving a wing unusable - a great blessing that it happened when the school was closed. We had to use private homes for lessons, a teacher taking different groups of children each day and setting them work to do on the other days. We thought it great fun!

Diana Scott

The flying bombs were followed by the V2 rockets and school was delayed opening on one occasion when a rocket dropped near it causing some damage. I did not find the rockets as terrifying as the flying bombs, as if you heard a rocket you were alive, but there was the agonising space between the sound of the flying bomb cutting out and the explosion.

Jean Parrott

The rockets (V2s) I did not mind as you never heard them coming, just the final explosion by which time you knew you were not affected. The nearest of these fell somewhere in Eden Park I believe, killing two cows and a chicken!

Jill Thomas

We came back again after our short evacuation to avoid the buzz bomb attacks, but then the rockets started and they were worse as you didn't get a warning. Once again my mother took us back to the country till things became calmer, towards the end of the war and we came home again.

(There was a third V weapon - a monstrous gun which would have been built into the cliffs along the Channel coast. This gun was huge enough to be able to fire a massive shell aimed directly at London and would have had the power and velocity to complete the distance. One strongpoint for the weapon was apparently constructed, but the gun was never fired. At the end of the war, the emplacement was sealed up.)

Perhaps inevitably, this bombardment with V-weapons led to the third evacuation from the London area. People got as far away from the high explosive as they could. Yorkshire was a favoured destination. The writer's aunt and two young cousins came to the cottage in the Yorkshire mining village and stayed there until the end of war in Europe. But Ely also came into its own again as a place of refuge, despite the profusion of airfields and army camps which might well have been targets of the weapons!

Leslie Oakey

The evacuees were now arriving again in Ely in some force. They were the victims of the flying bomb onslaught and many had lost their homes and all their possessions. Once again the old arguments about the accommodation of these unfortunates raised its head and the Billeting Officer was hard put to find suitable families to take them in. This debate raged fiercely right throughout the war and rankled deeply afterwards.

Molly Oakley

I was evacuated to Doncaster with my sister in 1944 to an aunt but we returned home about nine months later with a slight northern accent which didn't please our parents.

Linda Zerk

As the Doodlebug attack got under way, our parents decided we should go and stay with our Uncle and Aunt at Great Barford, near Bedford.

What a wonderful summer! Auntie Phil went down to stay at our house in Beckenham as she really wanted to see a Doodlebug! Roy and Sheila had a beautiful rocking horse, homing pigeons, a see-saw, a dinghy with a sail on the River Great Ouse, and the most wonderful train set. We used to go out early in the morning and pick mushrooms then had them for breakfast with bacon and eggs. On most days we would wander down to the river and swim and sail the boat. One day Roy put me in a rubber inner tube and pushed me off to float along and I couldn't get out! There was a farm next door and a drain under the main road which we would crawl into and have adventures. Uncle Gilbert was the local GP and had his surgery in the end of the house and we had to keep quiet. Roy was a few years older than me and I thought he was wonderful!

Gloria Morgan

When the flying bombs and rockets got too bad the family decided it would be prudent for us to leave London. Not my dad, unfortunately. He was needed at work and on fire watch duty, so he stayed behind and came to visit us when he could. This was not an official 'evacuation' but a private arrangement to go and stay with Nan's brother in Norfolk.

Uncle Alfred, mum's uncle, was a hoary old man, a farm labourer who lived in a small house in Mulbarton, a village six or seven miles south-west of Norwich. The central feature of the village was 'the common', an extended village green, with the church on one corner, a pub opposite, another on the next corner and the duck pond on the fourth.

I have no idea what mum and nan did all day. I imagine it was difficult for them, cooped up in the tiny house. It must have been a squeeze to fit four extra people in. There was a once-weekly bus service into Norwich but, for the most part, once in Mulbarton that was where you stayed.

There was no main street as such. The houses spread around the common or down the side roads leading from it. There was one shop where my brother and I spent our sweet ration. We attended the village school. There were two big, draughty rooms, my brother with the older children in one and me, with the little ones, in the other.

Somewhere around there must have been an American airbase as periodically one or two GIs would turn up in the village. It was from them I received my first taste of chewing gum. The American drawl was difficult to understand but not nearly as hard for my brother and me as the local 'Norfik' accent. To begin with we found the village children incomprehensible. I expect we were just as outlandish to them.

David Elcome

Several houses in Sanderstead were destroyed by flying bombs. I recall the extraordinary sight of the open sides or ends of houses where walls had been blown away and the rubble and broken furniture left. London's suburbs were becoming too dangerous for us, especially after one or two of the V2 rockets had landed not far away in Purley Oaks Road. Arrangements were made for mother, sister and I to stay on a farm near Totnes in Devon. It was all fixed up by my godfather, who was head teacher of a special school that had been evacuated from London to a large Devon manor house. I remember little of the journey other than a huge and impressive engine and milling crowds of people at Paddington Station. Also that we were assisted by a porter when he recognised that he shared our rather unusual surname. In my mind I have clear pictures of scenes around the farm and I recall some visiting farmhands who, I was told in a loud whisper, 'were prisoners-of-war.' In the summer there was a plague of caterpillars that devoured a whole field of cabbages and reduced to lace the leaves on the garden nasturtiums!

Jill Whalley

We were evacuated, my mother, brother and myself, to Norfolk for a few months and I have very happy memories of being on a farm, run by a Mrs. Ritchie. We arrived with our cases and a large fruit cake baked by my mother and settled into our new surroundings. We helped feed the heifers and chickens and roamed all over the fields. We had to collect milk from the next farm every morning and on one occasion the farmer lifted me up and sat me on top of a very large horse, which put me off horses for the rest of my life! Mrs. Ritchie was a very kindly woman and showed me how to collect rose petals to make into perfume - we sat on her front doorstep in the evening doing this but I seem to remember that it smelt dreadful. There were also Land Army girls staying with her and they had to pass through our bedroom late at night to reach their own room.

One day my brother and I were exploring the fields nearby and came across a deep ditch dug at the boundary of Mrs. Ritchie's land, continuing into the next field. We set off along the ditch, the sides of which were higher than us, and after a short while came across a group of men, one standing on top of the ditch with a rifle and others working with spades extending the ditch. At the sight of the man with the rifle I turned on my heels and ran back to the house, but my brother stayed out of curiosity and was given sweets by some of the men. It turned out that they were German prisoners of war making drainage ditches, with an English guard in charge. It was all very exciting to us. We certainly enjoyed ourselves there.

Jennifer Bedford

The move in 1944 with my mother and brother to Devon was undertaken, my mother always said, because of weariness of coping alone with two small children, living as we did on the outskirts of a city that was heavily bombed. A bomb landed in the field opposite our house, probably precipitating the need to get away. We stayed in Holsworthy three months until things had eased. The journey was a novel experience. We were used to travelling by bus but a train was an adventure, even more so the escalators in London. Also my grandfather was a Publican then and going from a three-bed 1930s house to large premises like a 'pub' was different! Somewhere there was a glass-covered passage with shadows in the glass, which may have been between the private and public part of the establishment and we children would run screaming under the shadows to outrun the 'ghost' or was it 'Germans', I can't remember.

The misinformation about the doodlebugs' accuracy obviously got back to the German authorities as the missiles fell more and more in the area of Croydon/Beckenham/Penge, so when the V2s also came along it was felt expedient to evacuate many of the children and young people.

(The following accounts are taken from the magazine of the Beckenham County School for Girls where they were published only with initials to identify the author.)

Going on Evacuation. "C.C."

After a fortnight of V1 alerts Mother decided that my sister Pattie, brother Alan and I should be evacuated, so at eight o'clock in the morning of July 8th, with thirty others we boarded a special bus. I was put in charge of half-a-dozen children ranging in age from three to nine, all too excited for many tears. Nobody knew our destination but rumours favoured Scotland.

The bus took us to Marylebone Station. We sat about on our luggage until a train appeared. There were now about 400 children on the platform. We all boarded and while I was ushering my small party aboard I saw my last "doodle". The horrid thing rattled and snorted its way across London, and then its engine cut out. Hastily I pushed and dragged six terrified children onto the train. I had just slammed the door and ducked when a surprisingly inadequate bang was heard. Really, it was most disappointing!

We settled into the compartment and proceeded to let London know that we didn't care by singing, whistling and humming "Roll out the Barrel" and other favourites.

The train started to cheers and the strains of "There'll always be an England". All the way through London stations and suburbs, railway personnel waved and encouraged us, and we responded by singing "We don't know where we're going until we get there", and we didn't, but we got to Doncaster and there we stayed for nine months, out of the range of sirens and flying bombs.

A New Experience. "P.C."

Through the war, we entered a new world - one humming with activity, deep under the earth; such was our impression of a coal-mine. Having been shown over the pit-head and equipped with tin hat, lamp and stick, we came to the cage and stepped in - down, down, now up we seemed to be going, but in reality only sank to lower depths. At last we came to rest; then in single file we started on our long trek to the coal face, along a concrete-walled passage.

It was a long walk, with the roof gradually lowering and the ground increasingly uneven. The guide called constantly to encourage us to keep up. Then we came to the coal-face. We scrambled along on the conveyor belt; black faces of colliers, grinning, peered at us from every nook and cranny. We mounted a truck and eventually staggered back to the shaft to sink gratefully on to the hard comfort of a rope-hauled tram. A joy-ride followed, down tunnel after tunnel, with the constant fear of having our heads knocked off by a low concrete roof beam. An injured man was lifted aboard; we returned to the shaft and joined some hefty colliers on the upward-bound cage.

As we rode home in the bus the rain poured down on the outer world but never had the fields looked so green and pleasant as they did that evening, from the streaming windows of the bus.

The Story of our Evacuation. "E.D."

My twin sister and I were bombed out of Beckenham in January 1945, and were evacuated to Bugbrooke, Northants, for four months. There, we attended a county school on the outskirts of town, a mixed school, evacuated from London and in requisitioned premises. There was no sports ground nor facilities for science or art, so these were taken at another school.

In the winter we went tobogganing on some steep hills about three miles away from Bugbrooke, and then when the weather improved we went picnicking by a river. One day we were very surprised to see a small snake wriggle slowly through the grass and raise his head to look at us.

The countryside was beautiful but the calmness and loveliness of it all was broken by the continual hum of Dakotas taking military supplies to France and Germany.

We all went swimming quite often, for there was an open-air as well as an indoor swimming bath in Northampton. There was also a park, a museum and an aviary, as well as swings and other apparatus being among its attractions.

Although we had a very happy time at Northampton, we were extremely pleased when VE-Day came and we were able to return to Beckenham.

Pamela Wellsted

The doodlebugs started after I had been home in Beckenham only a short while and eventually a large group of us from School were evacuated to Doncaster. We travelled up by train along with hundreds of other children. On arrival we were allocated to a family, where we were billeted in twos. Rosemary and I were whisked off by coach to Conanby, just outside Conisbrough, where we were warmly welcomed by a lovely couple, their adopted daughter Nancy and son-in-law Arthur. We were very happy to be with such a lovely family. Short-lived however, as three days later Miss Rabson, our French teacher, came to say that we were too far away to be able to travel to Wath-on-Dearne Grammar School daily so we were re-billetted with a widow in Wath-on-Dearne, where Rosemary and I had to bath together once a week to save water! Our original hosts were so sorry to see us leave that they said we must spend all our holidays with them, which we did. I am not sure how long the evacuation lasted but after the war we kept in touch with Nancy and Arthur and nearly every year since we have visited each other, either locally or in Yorkshire to this day. A wonderful tribute to their great kindness.

CHAPTER 15

VICTORY, DEFEAT AND HOMECOMING

The terror/revenge attacks with the V-weapons ended on 27 and 29 March 1945. That campaign against Britain, as far as the children were concerned, obliterated most other memories; nine months of being the guinea-pigs for the effectiveness of the world's first cruise and ballistic missiles does tend to push any other recollections of the time into the background, even if, like the writer, you had the good fortune not to be living in the target areas! During this time, the war against Hitler in Northern Europe had seen the liberation of Paris, the advance of the armies across Belgium and southern and eastern Holland to the boundaries of Germany, the setback of Operation Market Garden (Arnhem) and Hitler's last stand, the Ardennes Offensive. By April, Germany was surrounded by the Allies, and the end of the war was just weeks away, a fact apparent to everyone, seemingly, save Hitler and his coterie of toadies, ensconced in their Berlin bunker.

As the bombardment of Britain finally petered out, and victory beckoned, so in Germany the onslaught intensified, bringing relentlessly closer the inevitability of defeat and occupation, twin companions to the relief of no-more-war. Taking the war to Hitler had started in late 1943 with the bombing raids on German industrial cities; D-Day and the following eleven months in Germany in some ways mirrored the time of the Battle of Britain and the Blitz in these islands.

Geseke Clark

During the night of 24/25th July 1943 Hamburg had the first of a series of very heavy air-raids. My sister Hilke describes the night in her diary:

"Daddy was in Pomerania to fetch Geseke. There was no man in the house. Mami put on Daddy's helmet and went upstairs to look whether the house was on fire. Everywhere there was glass, even in the baby's cradle. Next morning it was dark as if it were 4 o'clock. The whole morning it did not clear. There was no light or gas."

When my father and I arrived the following day, I had one night at home. Next morning my parents decided that, apart from my father, we should all leave Hamburg. More serious air-raids were expected and there was chaos in the city. My mother soon packed the most urgent things for us, in small bags or little rucksacks which we could carry ourselves, three pieces of luggage each. At 6.00pm we went to the Moorweide (a sort of common) where lorries were waiting to take people out of the city. Our hope to stay together became impossible. Hilke, my eldest sister, was the first to go - without so much as a goodbye. She went south to a farm where she had been staying before the summer holidays. My mother and the baby went to Thuringen to an aunt, Dora. Our mother's help, Klara (sixteen), my younger sister and I, got on a lorry and were taken to the nearest functioning railway station. Every train was absolutely packed. Eventually we managed to get on a train full of soldiers, where I slept on a soldier's lap and after two nights and two days we arrived at Dorow, back in Pomerania. The von der Linde family welcomed the three of us and more children from Berlin. A private teacher was engaged, Frau Smuda, who taught the five of us quite well, but she was a firm believer in the Nazi-regime and would have reported any comments against Hitler to the authorities. Eighteen months passed with only one holiday with my family, a summer in the Luneburger Heide (south of Hamburg).

In January 1945, however, it was no longer safe in Pomerania. The Russians moved fast and were near Schneidemuhl. So Meike, the teacher and I joined a family from East Prussia and fled West in two big trucks drawn by horses, with carpets as roofs above us. At night, farmers of big estates welcomed us and gave us food. The roads were icy and the horses often slipped so progress was slow. When crossing the frozen River Oder, we had to put both pairs of horses in front of one truck. At that point the Russians were only five kilometres away from us. By February we were in Mecklenburg. From there I wrote a card home saying that I was safe but, as I was still on the move, they should not write for my birthday. I was eleven then.

In February 1945 I arrived home in Hamburg, with Meike and the teacher. My parents invited the rest of the von der Linde family to come, which they eventually did. Arrangements were made for me to go to a boarding school near the Baltic Sea. I stayed there for only two months. The end of the war was obvious to everyone. The Allied troops crossed the Rhine and still Hitler did not surrender. At school on the Baltic Sea I saw how one pupil after another was fetched by her father and I wrote a card home asking to be collected too, but my parents thought that Hamburg might become a place of street fighting and felt I was safer at school. I had a card from mother saying "I wanted to bake a cake for you but we had no gas. Every time we have an air-raid, I am glad that you are not here". My parents could not know that Hamburg would not be fought over because the mayor, Kaufman, surrendered the city against Hitler's orders, thereby risking his life. Nor could they have known that our house, though very near the centre of Hamburg, would not be destroyed, although 75% of all homes were.

In May 1945 when the war was over, of the three daughters who were evacuated, I was the only one back home. The Director of the school had brought all of us back to Hamburg. When British troops marched into Hamburg I wanted to look out of the window, but my mother, who liked the English and whose father was born in London, was not happy about me doing this and pulled me gently away.

Geseke was in north Germany, in the area which later became the British Zone, but she had escaped from the East, later the Russian Zone which subsequently became the Soviet satellite country of East Germany.

Anna Piper's home town of Winnenden was basically agricultural with light industry, so escaped much of the bombing.

Anna Piper

Winnenden is located 22km. east of Stuttgart in southern Germany. Stuttgart is surrounded by hills and is primarily given over to vineyards. Its geographical location in a hollow gave it, in the mornings, a cover of mist/haze, which helped to conceal it from aerial photographic reconnaissance, so bombing there started much later than in the rest of Germany. One morning, though, the inhabitants awoke to a liberal sprinkling of leaflets in the streets and gardens saying "Stuttgart im Loch - wir finden Dich doch" (Stuttgart in the hollow - but we have still found you).

That was the start of air-raids on a regular basis in our area. We children were fascinated by the first night raids. Imagine a dark sky, then you hear a quiet droning getting louder and louder, a formation of dark shapes appears over the horizon. A few moments later the sky lights up with markers which looked to us like Christmas trees, an eerily beautiful sight. It was the first time in my life I had seen anything like it. But then pandemonium broke out, explosions could be seen and heard, even though we were 20kms from them. Within a short time we were forcibly returned to our cellars. Needless to say, that was the first and only time we were officially allowed to watch.

One of the largest psychiatric hospitals in Germany was located in Winnenden. Some members of the extended family worked there in various capacities. Buses with opaque windows started coming past our house. When we asked, we were told that patients were being taken for holidays or were being transferred. After a while, suspicions were aroused when they were not returned; we personally knew quite a few of them who were allowed out, some of them were actually employed in the community. We learned nothing of their ultimate fate until the last days of the war.

The Last Lap-

In February/March 1945, the Front moved nearer to us. German troops were being billetted in our area. And at this time bombers were over flying us with few signs of any German defence. Our school, just a few hundred metres from our home, closed to become a first aid post. The medical personnel would come to us in their breaks to listen to the radio news. Then one night they were gone. All we heard was transport vehicles, but that was nothing unusual. By early April the withdrawal of the German army was under way and had reached Winnenden. Troops were primarily on foot and had their possessions on bikes, prams or little handcarts, all presumably requisitioned or simply found. It was a very sad spectacle with few weapons in evidence. Spare parts had run out and vehicles, including tanks, had simply to be abandoned.

At this time, young men born in 1929/30 were told to report for conscription at a nearby military post. These were boys of fifteen and sixteen. A friend was one of the unlucky ones to be conscripted then. They were given a few grenades and not much else. A Home Guard member was in charge, and my friend had to hide by the side of the road to stop Allied tanks. He ended up as a P.o.W with quite a late release date. The Front had really arrived. Shortly after this, the Americans and the French both reached the Neckar, our closest major river. Our town was between these forces and became a last defence position. Bombers and low flying aircraft seemed to be continuously above us.

We were now afraid that the pitiful defence efforts were going to lead to more severe attacks on the area. We were under attack by American troops; the town was shelled because the powers-that-be had decided to dig in and offer resistance with defending troops of Hitler Youth and the home guard who between them had next-to-no weapons and little ammunition.

About the time of Hitler's birthday (20th April) the attack started in earnest, primarily shelling. The Americans thought large German forces were still based there. Winnenden was saved by Herr Schwab, a refugee himself, who led a delegation of townspeople under a White Flag to surrender.

Shelling stopped while it was still dark, in eerie silence and we were occupied on the night of 20th/21st April, an Occupation which took place without fighting. We went to the basement window, which opened into a grid-covered well in the pavement, used for deliveries. The top of the window was a few inches above pavement level. We were able to peek out. In the dawn light we saw shadowy figures proceeding in a low crouching position, guns held at a forward angle, single file in the gutters; they appeared apprehensive, looked scared. This went on for some time; we were frightened to move or make any noise. These were the first coloured people we had actually seen in the flesh; as the light improved it became clear that the invasion troops consisted mainly of coloured men. The officers were almost exclusively white.

With morning came silence. Girls and women were kept out of sight. Nobody knew what to expect. Within a day, doors were knocked on by small groups of the invasion forces, sometimes with an interpreter, other times without, but the message was clear - to get out of our homes, they were needed for the Occupiers.

We were not called on immediately; it was strawberry time when our turn arrived. We were having a celebration; Mutti had made a cake with strawberries, decorated with strawberry foam and more fruit. The Occupiers burst in, telling us, thirty minutes to collect our essentials and get out. We were prepared but the officer wanted to confiscate the cake. Mutti got really upset and refused to part with it. He produced handfuls of money, chewing gum, chocolate in exchange - nothing worked. Mutti carried off her prize. In retrospect, we were very lucky that things did not get nasty!

We moved into the barn behind the house with neighbours. Blankets, curtains and sheets gave some privacy for sleeping. Cooking and eating was communal. After a few days of this, friends who had a wine shop invited us to stay there. They were living in the shop, now closed for business. The window was boarded up so their two children and I slept there. We thought it great fun. My grandmother and the rest of the family had to move into the cellars.

The next vivid memory (probably after the National surrender) is moving back into our home. It was heart-breaking; most things were wrecked, the smell horrendous, the condition of everything, from floor to ceiling, indescribable. Surprisingly, much of the furniture could be salvaged and is still in use today. The linen, some of it my great-grandmother's, was salvageable. The lavatories had been grossly misused, some were blocked and overflowing. Normality took a long time to return.

Back at home, the ordeal by V-weapons ceased and the end of the war approached. Allied troops had crossed into Germany and were racing to Berlin, where the Fuhrer and the Party high command were holed up in a vast bunker, Hitler apparently in denial about the parlousness of the situation. Many individual German towns and cities had disobeyed central orders to hold out, and had surrendered to the oncoming armies. At last Hitler was made to understand, so married his long-term mistress then committed suicide on 30 April 1945. From that point, it was a question of surrender terms - presented as unconditional or face prolongation of the conflict - which were agreed and signed so that 8 May could be celebrated by all the Allies as VE Day.

There had been a lack of campaign news for a few days and a growing sense of something being about to happen; some military personnel were saying that the war was over but there had been no notification, then on 7 May came an odd announcement from the Board of Trade, that until the end of May cotton bunting could be bought without coupons as long as it was red, white and blue and cost no more than one shilling and threepence (6p) a square yard. The only possible reason for this would be to celebrate victory, the nation deduced, but international politics delayed the official announcement. The Allies had decided there would be simultaneous announcements in all three capitals and the Russians complicated things by warily insisting on ratification of the surrender and terms from Berlin before they would go ahead. So there was the strange situation of the German broadcast announcing defeat being picked up by the BBC and that news broadcast here before ever there was any official statement of victory. People started to celebrate - and the announcement came at 7.40pm that there would be an official announcement by the Prime Minister at three o'clock the next day, Tuesday May 8th. Because of that, the day would be treated as a holiday, Victory in Europe Day, with another holiday on the Wednesday.

It felt almost flat. The writer asked her mother if daddy would be coming home tomorrow as the war was over and being told no, went to bed and to sleep!

On 8 May, however, there was a national party. Virtually every community, no matter how small or how large, managed to celebrate appropriately. The biggest and best was in London but there were street parties everywhere which started off for the children and were taken over by the adults in the evening - often with the children still there! People sang and danced, they climbed lamp-posts, lit bonfires, burnt Hitler in effigy, let off fireworks, drank whatever was available, from beer to cocoa and left the curtains open so that there was light everywhere again. They enjoyed themselves.

Linda Zerk

The lights came on. VE day! To celebrate we went to London and had a cruise down the Thames and saw the lights come on all over the city; there were fireworks as well! It was a memorable night but I was somewhat confused and can remember asking my parents what it meant that the war was over. I thought war was for always.

Jill Thomas

Most vividly I remember the victory celebration. My father took us to central London for the VE Parade and I can remember being almost totally swept off my feet in the crowds - in fact my feet left the ground more than once as we got caught up in the rejoicing crowds, mostly of young men and women in uniform. It was only my father holding tightly onto me that prevented me being crushed and I remember the fear as well as the excitement of the occasion. I still have a fear of being in closely packed crowds to this day. I thought all the dancing in the streets and the laughter and gaiety was wonderful and it was my first experience of sheer happiness. I loved seeing the fireworks but did not like the bangs as it was too much like gunshots and the sound of bombs dropping. I also remember the street party we had with a long table down the middle of the road with all the children sitting round it and the mothers bringing out cakes and jellies and all sorts of treats we had not had for a long time. It was a wonderful feeling.

John Taylor

Finally the war ended. We had two street parties, one for the end of the war in Europe and then one for the end of the war against Japan. Trestle tables appeared from garages and I helped to set them up. Food appeared on the tables, jellies, blancmanges, cakes and sandwiches. As if by magic tea, lemonade and beer also appeared and record players gave us music to dance to. There were even some fireworks, I remember lighting a rocket in a bottle. And of course, we built bonfires and even burnt an effigy of Hitler. The blackout curtains came down and streetlights started to flicker to life and I felt some relief that the war was over. I'm afraid it gave me a lingering dislike and distrust of Germans which took many years to disappear and my hatred for the Japanese is something I still have to cope with at times.

Pat Fulmer

In the spring of 1945 mum and I were able to move back into our own house, in time for the celebrations of VE Day, when all of the children in my neighbourhood were allowed to hang out of their bedroom windows and call to each other until well after dark. Then a day or so later we had a big bonfire party in my street and it was quite magical to see all the lights after living in a dark world for so long.

Ann Dix

My aunt lived in London and had a flat in Oxford Street. I watched the Victory Parade from the pavement there and have vivid memories of a policeman lifting me up, and then my aunt poking a rather large boy scout in the back with the end of her Union Jack and pushing me to the front. The King and Queen and the two Princesses were in an open carriage and I was very impressed with the Greek Army in their uniforms that looked like ballet tutus. That night we went to the Embankment and watched a wonderful firework display. The day before, my aunt had driven me down The Mall and pointed out "The Saluting Base". I hadn't a clue what she meant until I saw the newspaper photographs. I still have the programme of events of that day.

John Gamêt

Victory in Europe was declared, which we celebrated with a street party and a large bonfire, so hot it burnt a hole in the road!

Janet Ellison

I remember the celebrations on Worthing sea front on VE Night. A firework burnt a hole in someone's coat and mother decided the crowds were a bit wild and unsafe, so took me home. Much to my disappointment!

Jill Whalley

On VE Day we celebrated with family members and when it was dark we walked round the streets to see the Christmas lights which people had put up. This was a magical experience for us as we had lived with the blackout for as long as we could remember.

David Elcome

Suddenly the war was over. On VE Day I was staying at my uncle's house near Tottenham, with my cousin and paternal grandparents. There was a huge street party. Stretched down the middle of the road was a long line of tables covered in white cloths. There was colourful bunting. In spite of rationing there seemed to be piles of sandwiches, plenty of jelly and lemonade. Afterwards I was just getting ready for bed when my cousin (a little older than me) rushed in and dragged me back to the street in my pyjamas and dressing gown. All the children were being given a shilling!

My father returned from the War with all his possessions packed in a kitbag, including a beautiful model he had made for me of a Typhoon fighter, one of the planes he had been working on in India. Every time she saw this 'strange man', my sister screamed loudly.

Anne Gordon

There were wonderful community celebrations in the Rec (recreation ground) in Village Way for both VE Day and VJ Day. Everyone was dancing and singing 'Roll Out the Barrel'!

Virginia Watkinson

The end of the war brought celebrations in the largest garden in the area which happened to be that of my mother's friend Cissie. There was a Punch and Judy show, more food than we'd seen in a while and a shortage of men. I wore a big bow in my hair.

Maureen Jordan

I remember VE Day very vividly. We were extremely excited. We travelled up to London by train and walked from Charing Cross station to Trafalgar Square and here, even by fairly early in the morning, there were throngs and throngs of people. More and more joined the crowds and we had to be careful not to get separated. At 3.00pm, Churchill broadcast from 10 Downing Street, relayed to Whitehall through loudspeakers, which we heard in Trafalgar Square. Word went round that the place to be was Buckingham Palace as the Royal Family would make an appearance on the balcony. The crowds then pushed towards The Mall and everyone was swept along in a frenzy. My mother became hysterical; father tried in vain to calm her. This was the first inkling we had of her impending nervous breakdown...the war, the sirens, the anxieties just became too much for her. She was ill for several years afterwards. We arrived at the Memorial outside Buckingham Palace and I remember being hoisted up just to the immediate left of it and having a good view of all the Royal Family. Later on I recall the street parties, the long trestle tables along the centre of our road and everyone contributing to the event.

Ruth Hixson

The momentous memory has to be that of going to London on VE Day and joining the crowds that thronged down The Mall towards Buckingham Palace. It seemed that we went through gates, which I much later realised was Admiralty Arch, then continued down a wide drive with a garden beside it, St. James' Park. There were hundreds of people, all shouting "We want the King". A kind gentleman lifted me onto his shoulders so I had a grandstand view and joined in the shouting and cheers as the Royal Family came onto the balcony and waved to us. Afterwards we walked up Birdcage Walk to Trafalgar Square where we had a photo taken beside one of the fountains.

Our road held a street party. There were tables down the middle of the road, laden with food. The houses were decorated with bunting and at some stage the road was cleared, for the grown-ups danced to songs like "I'll be your sweetheart" and "The White Cliffs of Dover".

Christina Watt

To celebrate victory there was a Fancy Dress parade through the village. Most of the children took part. It was a long, hot walk and for some reason finished up in a field behind "The Schoolboy" pub. I have a vague memory of a children's party there but no more than that. In the evening there was a big concert for the adults on that same field.

Margaret Mould

Mum, dad and I went on the train to Charing Cross, walked down The Mall and a strapping sailor lifted me onto his shoulders to see the King and Queen! Maybe that's when I decided I was going to marry a sailor, which I did!

Peter Rex

At last the tide turned and eventually the war ended. I remember VE Day which locally seemed to be an excuse for dancing and singing in the streets and getting drunk. My most vivid memory is of passing a pub and someone shouting "Let's pull all the women's knickers down!" but I have no idea whether or not they did!

June Thomsitt

My sister and I were invited to the street party in Blandford Road, Beckenham (our grandparents' house) to celebrate VE Day. Long tables were assembled in the street and we stuffed ourselves with jelly, cakes and lemonade. For my grandparents this was still a time of anxiety as one of my uncles had been captured by the Japanese in Singapore and had not yet returned home.

Gwen Pritchitt

VE and the relief of the adults was obvious. We peeled the film off the windows, and uncles and aunts returned. There were banners over the High Street in Hayes saying - The Biggest Event Since Mafeking - and we all went up to the large open space on the edge of the common where there was a parade and dancing to a band. My sister and I thought it great fun to trot about on all fours when they announced a foxtrot! BUT why was everyone so happy when my dad was still not coming home? Dad's diary tells how, in Burma, they all gathered in the centre of the camp to hear Churchill's speech on the victory in Europe. He praised the valour of the troops who had won the victory and they could hear the cheers of the people, but were stunned because there was no mention of those still fighting a dreadful war out east! The troops listened to the bulletin in silence and just turned heel and went back to their tents in silence - apart from one loud "It bloody stinks!"

The war against Japan continued for another three months. Conditions were awful, in equatorial jungle, the heat, the insect life, and the fear of the enemy whose reputation for merciless cruelty was well-deserved. Japan would not - could not - surrender. The situation of stalemate conflict could have continued for years. The decision was taken by President Truman to use the atomic bomb. Surrender came after the explosion of the second one.

Maureen Jordan

I was in Downpatrick, Co. Down, visiting relatives on VJ Day and I remember it vividly. The war against Japan hadn't impinged on me until then. The horror of the atomic bomb then became the stuff of nightmares and remained with me during the Cold War period. August 9th was my birthday; it was also the day when the Americans dropped one of the two atom bombs on Japan. We celebrated my birthday and we celebrated the end of the war but at that time we couldn't comprehend the devastation or the terrible impact for years to come on the health of millions of survivors.

Gloria Morgan

I remember exactly where I was on VJ Day in August 1945. It was in the middle of the school holidays and I was enjoying one of my special treats, a day out with my dad to the Science Museum in South Kensington. When we left, late in the afternoon, the newspaper placards were proclaiming 'Victory in Japan' - the war was finally over! Dad bought us ice creams to celebrate.

Peter Rex

VJ Day came in August, with a bonfire and fireworks. Unfortunately the organisers were remarkably clumsy. A Roman Candle tied to some railings (not taken for scrap salvage) slipped its fastenings and fired into the box containing the rest of the fireworks which promptly exploded, sending detonations everywhere. One rocket came horizontally across the road in my direction but fortunately missed by a wide margin.

Margaret Haynes

On VJ Day there was a large bonfire on the village green. It seemed as though there were big crowds there, it was very exciting and there were fireworks.

Jean Runciman

After VJ Day there were many street parties and celebrations. But with the ending of the war the hoped-for immediate improvement in our living conditions did not materialize. It seemed strange not to have an enemy any longer, but wonderful not to expect to be bombed! Amazingly, food rationing continued until June 1954.

Gwen Pritchitt

Eventually dad did come home. He had been in the Signals, so never in the front line, usually following later, establishing communications. He had enjoyed touring round Sri Lanka on a motorbike. He said the worst thing was that he had endless exotic fruit and plenty of food – while he worried about us with all the rationing back home.

But, even though the war had ended, the horror continued.

Ann Dix

I remember the day my father came home from the war; I was told to listen for the sound of his boots coming along the road! Dad went back to work two days after returning home to Ely. He and his unit had been sent to Norway for a month to help them recover from being one of the first units into Belsen Concentration Camp. Dad had been an ambulance driver and never spoke of Belsen but after he died in 1989, mother showed me the set of photographs presented to each soldier, of the Camp and how they found it. I was horrified.

Peter Rex

The last event I can recall came shortly after the war was over. An exhibition came to Bristol (and went to many other towns and cities), which I went to see. It revealed the horrors of the Concentration Camps using full wall sized photographs of the conditions discovered in them, identifying some of the Camp Commandants, including the 'Butcher of Belsen' and his lampshades made of human skin.

Anna Piper

It was only after the war was ended that we found out the fate of the psychiatric patients from Winnenden. They had all been gassed.

[The Nazi Concentration Camp system was extensive and for most of the war, highly secret. The camps, although possibly built relatively near towns, were concealed by trees or the topography generally, or were well beyond the range of the Allies' reconnaissance aircraft. Their purpose was punishment - but the 'crimes' that were punished were along the lines of being Jewish; being Jewish and owning property/a business; being mentally ill; being racially non-Aryan; being homosexual; falling foul of National Socialist dogma; being a persistent escaper from P.o.W. camps - and the punishment meted out was extreme; dehumanisation and slow starvation, slave-labour toil until the person dropped dead, gassing in mass "showers", lethal injection, or shooting. Corpses were cremated almost immediately after execution. The Winnenden patients suffered this fate. Any camp visited today screams silent despair to the world; generally the huts have been demolished (there was endemic major disease in them) but the outline of their location remains, and all the adjuncts of punishment are there, shooting gallery or "showers", crematorium ovens, but over all, the appalled silence in which not even the birds sing, is the silent testimony of and to the brutalisation of humanity, epitomised for those of us who saw them by the photos of that exhibition.]

With the advent of peace came the homecoming. Germany was divided into four administrative zones, American, British, French and Russian, with papers being demanded by each of the Allies for entry to or exit from that zone. To obtain the necessary papers, each German citizen needed a settled address. Much of the population was away from its native area - military service or the 'evacuation' of children to safer areas accounted for much of this displacement, then there were refugees streaming from the East away from Russian domination, persons who had been enslaved for forced labour by the Nazis, now free, the military, many of whom disposed of their uniforms and tried to get back "home". The country was devastated from saturation bombing and the effects of shelling as the Front advanced. It was a nightmare.

Geseke Clark

My older sister, Hilke, then sixteen, tried to make her way from the southernmost part of Germany, near Lake Constance, where she had been at boarding school, up to the north. Germany was divided into four zones and she needed a Zonenpass, but could not get one because she had no official residence. She survived by working on farms, but the work was very hard and she was often exhausted and homesick. Repeatedly, she tried to get the Zonenpass, which often kept her away from the farm and her work for hours, which the farmer did not like. In the end, she left, and hitchhiked or travelled as a stowaway on trains. For days, she had a bad rash and skin trouble, but finally, having started the trip in May 1945, she arrived safe and sound in Hamburg on August 5th.

My younger sister Brigitte was in the Russian Zone. After many attempts to bring her back home had failed, my parents finally contacted an old aunt, Dora, in Eisenach. She, at nearly eighty, with her sixty year old daughter, decided to cross the 'green frontier' by night, taking Brigitte with them. At that time, the frontiers between East and West, especially in the woods, were not as well guarded as they were later with watchtowers, dogs and barbed wire. I will never forget the joy of my family when, in November 1945, Brigitte finally returned home.

Anna Piper

Gradually normality returned. We still had shortages, coupons, a black market, movement restrictions, but for us children, life seemed pretty normal again. We started receiving mail from my uncle, who had been taken prisoner by the British forces and worked as a P.o.W. on a farm in Lincolnshire. He started sending us comics and teaching us English. We really looked forward to his letters. My mother's brother turned up one night on a battered bicycle, having made his way from northern France, out of a French detention.

During that time I was again taken to my paternal grandmother's. Mutti said she wanted to try to see her sister and travelling was still very difficult. Six days later, Mutti came to collect me and took me home. There were three of the ambulance crew, who had come to our house in their breaks to listen to the radio, when they were posted in the town. Mutti had somehow managed to spring them from their prison camp in the French occupied zone.

Those English children evacuated overseas were coming home.

Margaret Wood

On the 8th May 1945, when the news came through that the war had ended, I know I burst into tears. I was in my final year at school, studying hard for my final exams in December. So once the exams were written I was ready to go home. I left Cape Town on a gorgeous, hot summer's day sailing home on the "Carnavon Castle". As we sailed north, crossing the equator into the northern hemisphere, the days became colder. By the time we reached Southampton docks, it was the middle of an English winter - very cold, a grey sky, foggy and drizzling. We were shivering!

It was wonderful to see mum and dad again. They didn't seem to have changed very much but they had the shock of meeting a grown-up 17 year old daughter - a vast difference from the little 11 year old girl evacuee to whom they said goodbye in 1940.

In America, the possibility of Louise and Blanche Lawson going home to England was raised in 1943, after the defeat of the Germans in North Africa and the capitulation of Mussolini's Italian forces. The discussion continued into and through 1944, but with the war very much continuing, the practicalities of obtaining civilian places on Transatlantic shipping remained daunting. 'Aunt Nancy' had suggested that the girls' mother should come to collect them and have a three month stay to assess her daughters and their schools in the American setting. Blanche knew early in 1945 that their mother would be coming later that year but Louise was not told until March and was getting excited at the prospect. On 3rd June 1945 there was a phone call from Montreal; their mother was there to take them home. Louise spoke to a very precise English voice with very mixed emotions and when the call finished, went to her room for a quiet weep. The next day, Sunday, they met mother at Philadelphia station. There was no instant recognition but everything started to come back after a few minutes. Mother met many of her daughters' friends and teachers, and family friends and was able to thank them formally for their care of the girls, who had enjoyed the American experience and benefited in many ways from it.

It was hoped a passage home would be available in July. Two parcels of groceries, goods that were unavailable or in short supply, were despatched to England (this was the permissible amount that could be sent). They were all realising that the readjustment would be difficult; the girls were older and very attached to their American family while their own English one had become more distant. Neither were they looking forward to the rigours of an English school.

Cunard then informed them that a passage would be available on the 8th August, on the SS Nieuw Amsterdam, of the Holland-America Line but most recently a troopship, leaving New York, Hoboken Pier, on 20th August, expected port of arrival, Southampton. Then the sailing was delayed for three days. There was last minute shopping, packing, last goodbyes; it was daunting and heart-wrenching. The nine days at sea allowed for a period of adjustment. This time, there was little or no sea-sickness.

The Solent was entered in the early morning. Breakfast was hurried, the final things were put into the suitcases and they went on deck. Louise recognised her father easily, but not her brother who was now an eight year old boy, not a three year old toddler.

Two small cars, for which petrol had been hoarded, took them back to Plymouth. Lunch had to be taken at a Southampton cafe - macaroni cheese and cabbage, followed by lumpy macaroni pudding - but they were assured that the food was not normally this bad!

Home in Plymouth they were in time for High Tea (meat and vegetables or salad; bread and butter; cakes or in Devon, scones with clotted cream). This meal was the result of hoarded rations being eaten in one sitting but it made up for that dreadful lunch.

Blanche and Louise rushed around recognising things they remembered and noticing the changes. Much was the same; there were few changes partly because things had had to last for the duration of the war, but now all the children would have rooms to themselves; there was no longer a live-in maid, so the room at the back over the kitchen became Louise's. She took no time in putting up the ornaments brought back to remind herself of America.

On Thursday 21 June 1945 all remaining evacuee children left Ely and district to return to London. After nearly six years, there were far fewer children to return than there were that arrived on the day of evacuation. As pupils had reached school leaving age they had returned to London to find employment then in turn to be conscripted into the forces, and there had been no significant recruitment of others to replace them. Numbers in all divisions of the Jews Free School had dwindled quite rapidly, so that by May 1941 it had been feasible for the entire school to move into Hereward Hall to receive their schooling. During their long stay in the locality, the pupils of the school had provided enormous pleasure and entertainment to the people of Ely with their stage productions of fairy operettas, Gilbert & Sullivan and the immensely popular Pierrot Troupe, which had given seventy-five performances during the Ely sojourn. All these entertainments had raised more than £400 for local and national charities concerned with the war effort; all work for these productions had been done after school hours. Initially, the boys' Central School had been located in Isleham and Soham and had received their education by sharing premises with Isleham School. The Parish Church had given the use of one aisle for Jewish Sabbath services and the boys had made, as a souvenir of their presence and as a token of thanks, a Chanukah Candlestick which was presented to the church.

In the sphere of educational achievement the pupils had done exceptionally well with many scholarships being awarded. One refugee boy at the age of fourteen gained the School Leaving Certificate. There was success in the sporting sphere. Relations had been excellent between the school and the foster parents, with many great attachments formed and many enduring friendships forged. In all, the school felt they had been very well looked after, but there was much sadness at parting - many of the schoolchildren could hardly remember their London home and wanted to stay with their "lady" in Ely. Many of them were invited to spend the summer holidays in Ely and did so, maintaining the connection.

The return to London also marked the retirement of the headmistress, Miss Samuels, so the school really did return to the beginning of a new era.

It was felt that the town would miss them as much as they would miss the town, for so many of them a formative influence in their young lives. On leaving, the school presented a piano to The Chantry, then a children's home, and the long temporary presence of the JFS in Ely passed into history.

CHAPTER 16

AFTERMATH

The war was over. We had had our parties but apart from the lack of bombing raids little changed immediately. Daddy did not come home the next day. In the light of peace, the towns and cities looked wretched with hastily-erected hoardings round the bomb sites of shops and commercial buildings, and whole residential streets with large gaps where the bombs had hit. Squads of labourers, frequently Irish, were brought in to effect immediate repairs so that houses were again habitable and evacuated families could return home.

June Thomsitt
When we had moved to Wales all the furniture had gone into storage. The storage building had been bombed so my poor parents had the job of starting to assemble their home from scratch again. The new furniture bore a special symbol - the utility mark - meaning functional rather than decorative.

Ruth Hixson
We had some Irish building workers billetted with us. They were part of a team brought over to help with war damage repairs. The black lino stuff and white canvas which had temporarily replaced broken window panes was at last replaced with glass.

And it was possible to go to the seaside for holidays again, but mines remained a potential hazard. The seas had been swept on the cessation of hostilities but "escapers" appeared for several years, along with mines from out in the ocean which had been missed and were brought in on the incoming tides.

David Elcome
In 1946 we had a holiday in East Wittering, Sussex. Much of the beach was still lined with a rusting network of scaffolding poles, part-buried in the shingle - hung with mines, a deterrent to German invasion. At the top of the beach was a rusting tank. Destined for the Normandy landings, it must have slipped from a ramp while being loaded and was abandoned on the steep shingle ridge. Young boys could climb onto its sides and squeeze through the hatch into the gun turret. The picture was a best-selling postcard for several years after the war.

One morning, while my cousin and I played on the beach, a loose mine drifted in with the waves, foundering just a few hundred yards away. There was a huge explosion as it touched the seabed and a column of sand and water was thrown high into the air. My mother and uncle rushed frantically to the beach, fearing we may have been killed by the blast.

The aftermath can sometimes be as dangerous and as terrifying as war itself.

Ruth Hixson

My aunt lived in Brighton. After the war we stayed for a few days. We were able to walk along the promenade but the beach was barricaded by great rolls of barbed wire. It was still probable that mines would be washed up.

Linda Zerk

Right at the end of the war we went to stay with relatives at Poole Harbour. We used to meet up with local kids and go swimming in the Blue Lagoon Pool. Polio had just reared its ugly head so many friends were not allowed to swim there.

Every morning a sea plane took off for America and each evening one came back at 8.00pm. We got to know the son of one of the pilots and this was the very first taste I had of bananas! We went to his party and there were bananas hidden all over the place for us to find! His father used to bring them back from America.

Some aspects of the war were missed...

Frank Bunce

I remember my reaction when the war ended. I was walking to the shops round the corner, alone, on a sunny day with a clear blue sky. A single plane flew over and I wondered if it could be a lone enemy machine, determined to fight on. I imagined it dropping a few bombs and what the reaction would be. When it flew on and away I felt slightly disappointed that nothing had happened... .

Others remained.

Pat Fulmer

I remember having nightmares about Germans and for decades afterwards the sound of planes at night frightened me.

Eventually, fathers were demobbed and returned home.

Jean Runciman

My father was finally demobbed on 28th February 1946. He came home wearing a really awful brown "demob" suit supplied by the army. The long process of getting used to his family, his work and all the shortages must have been difficult. Our house needed a great deal of structural work and decoration and a couple of "cowboys" employed by the government arrived to do the essential work. They made a frightful job of it so my father had to set to and learn the art of decorating and house-painting. The Anderson was removed. Life began to get back to normal.

Ruth Stobart

When my father returned after serving in the RAMC I greeted him by saying "you aren't my daddy. I don't know you." How that must have hurt him, but in my childish way I was being truthful and it took a long time for us to get to know each other. I was never his little Ruthie again.

Christina Watt

Dad was demobbed in late 1946. He arrived home in a terrible brown suit and wearing a pork pie hat (all army issue) which reduced mother to hysterical laughter. He had to wear the suit for a time as all his clothes, which had gone into storage with the furniture, were cremated when the depository fell victim to incendiaries. He got a job readily in Doncaster but did not want to remain in the north, so in April 1947 we moved to Rugby then quickly to London, the resumption of the nomadic life that characterised my earliest years and the later childhood of my sister and me.

Wendy Walton

We went to London and I vividly remember seeing huge bomb craters there.... I don't know why we were there or anything else much about it but I do remember the craters and going to Lyons Corner House.

Not all aspects of returning home were pleasant.

Ann Gamêt

Our house in Beckenham was requisitioned and all our possessions moved to Nan's house. When that was hit by a doodlebug many of those possessions were damaged but a considerable number of the more valuable wedding presents were looted. Such is war.

There were many adjustments to be made and for a long time there was precious little variety in the food available. Bananas appeared again, generally strictly rationed and in our village, handed over only on production of a child's ration book. We had heard so much about this marvellous fruit that the reality was frequently a let-down! The fruit was eaten when hardly beyond the green stage, or when far past its best state, and the skin posed a problem to many who thought one ate that as well, as with an apple.

There was still a shortage of meat; to increase the availability of protein foods, the government increased the import of snoek. This is one of the most infamous episodes in this country's chequered gastronomic history. Snoek is a southern hemisphere fish, at that point, obviously abundant given the quantity imported here. It was available only in tins and ration "points" had to be surrendered for it. Newspapers and magazines dutifully published recipes using it to encourage people to buy. It was revolting. It stank to high heaven and, in those pre-air freshener times, the smell lingered for ever and a day in the kitchens of the nation. The one tin the writer's mother was misguided enough to try ended up in the dustbin wrapped in multi-layers of newspaper but still we smelt it. Not even the family cat, never a fastidious eater, would touch the stuff. Then, perhaps in an effort to make it more palatable, it was smoked before canning. It remained an epic disaster. Eventually, the relevant Food Ministry had to dispose of something like a quarter of a million tons of tinned snoek stored in warehouses in Newcastle. As a nation, we obviously were never so desperate as to eat that!!

Whalemeat and snoek were the two most loathed components of our immediate post-war diet. One is simply thankful that they were not around for long, that resistance won out.

During the war, the use of a private car was almost impossible; petrol was strictly rationed and was really only available to those who needed their vehicle as an essential part of working life - such as doctors, or farmers - and then only in small quantities. Consequently, many cars were "laid up" for the duration. Many were not immediately revived afterwards. Numbers of people looked forward to being able to replace the vehicle in a short while, but no! Although production of civilian cars resumed quickly, the nation had to start repaying the American lend-lease aid so that a huge proportion of national production of everything went for export, to raise the necessary cash-flow. Reluctantly, many of those mothballs were removed and the ancient vehicles pressed back into service while their owners joined a list of hopefuls at the car dealership of their choice, eventually succeeding in obtaining a brand new car after a very long wait.

Maureen Jordan

We didn't own a car during the war years. We travelled on local buses and trains. My parents had bicycles and my mother transported me on the back of hers. Immediately after the war my father was able to obtain one of the first motor cars; it was acquired through our relatives in Northern Ireland and had a Northern Ireland number plate, SZ. It was an object of curiosity for some time in our neighbourhood.

Other aspects of life changed.

Anne Gordon

It was evident that my family was far more short of money after the war than before; but I never heard my parents particularly bemoan this. I think it was taken as read that the war was a just one and therefore it was acceptable that families had to make sacrifices. After all, my father had come home intact, when many hadn't.

Many of the economical practices encouraged during the war continued afterwards. The pig swill bins were a feature of most streets for a number of years, the contents being religiously collected daily and passed to local pig farmers, and continued until the early 1950s.

And recycling is certainly not a phenomenon of the twenty-first century. Our generation practised it during the war with almost religious zeal and still continue to do so. Cloths to clean the car are recycled towels, for example, and most of us consider wasting food to be the greatest mortal sin.

Anne Gordon

The economical habits that were drummed into us had such an impact that I still stick little bits of soap together, and would feel very uncomfortable and guilty even now if I had a bath that was deeper than five inches!

The war had many "positives" for us, its children. We saw and experienced unparalleled loathing of "the enemy" as we were blitzed and bombed, yet saw this self-same enemy in its P.o.W. state working in agriculture in normal human form, not the devil incarnate of popular mythology. So we drew our own conclusions. We developed resilience in the face of adversity and laughed long at the follies the situation threw up. We also accepted that women could do important jobs just as well as men, which carried over into adulthood.

Barbara Langridge

I do not recall any of my friends having parents in the forces but that may be because it was not talked about. My mother had a cousin in the Wrens and she stayed with us when on leave. I remember her telling me that it was an exciting time for women and at twenty-nine and a spinster it had opened doors for her. The war was a brilliant adventure. This didn't shock me but it did seem different from how my parents talked of the waste of lives in war. It is remarkable that I remember this conversation which perhaps set me on the pathway of believing in equal rights for women.

Jean Runciman

Over sixty years have passed since World War II began and it is incredible to remember we passed our formative years during that conflict. If we could choose, would we have avoided the inconveniences and deprivations? Personally, I would say not. I learned a great deal about how a common purpose can bring people together and be a force for good, and how we could enjoy ourselves in the process. I am left with a few idiosyncrasies! Nowadays, I hate to see so much wasted and thrown away (particularly food) and children so showered with toys and equipment that they become more and more discontented. Our modern society has so many problems that we would have thought inconceivable in wartime - dysfunctional families, disaffected children, crime, international terrorism, to name but a few. Perhaps we were the lucky ones.

EPILOGUE

It is almost seventy years since World War II began. For us, it shaped our lives and has influenced many aspects of our existence since. The best philosophical summary comes from:

Michael Hardy (b.1933. Denmark Hill, London)
In 1941 we went to Scotland. There are two central experiences from that time although I only became fully conscious of them when an adult.

The first concerned toys. Although I had some of my toys, I can remember looking at a red pebble I had collected and thinking that, however long I owned it that would be as nothing compared with the age of the stone. An experience of the transitory nature of things or of the time one has them. All children presumably have this experience in one form or another but it was accentuated or accelerated by the war.

The second relates to reading. The library was down the street and I read avidly, above all history or historical adventure stories, motivated by a range of things, - the locality (Stirling Castle, Mary Queen of Scots), the accent on the past in official propaganda and the feeling one was living at an important moment - the escape into another time and place which reading can give, a heightening anld a distancing of experience.

What the two elements came down to was an acceleration of childhood development. Experiences that would otherwise have been later we encountered at seven or eight. In dealing with the world around one, with the adults preoccupied, their minds engaged in coping with daily life (rationing), children found their own solutions.

They were more able to do this and to lead their own lives because at that time, children were allowed to lead their own lives, they were supposed to be children and were left to their own devices, relatively left alone and told to go out and play.

It is not easy to disentangle children's experiences during war time and attitudes to parenting, but to a considerable extent they reinforced one another. The child was physically taken care of and family life was assured, a fact of daily life; the war was another fact (new to the adults but accepted by children). Within these boundaries children absorbed what they saw and drew their own conclusions. Their experience overall was of change and reaction to it. For most children in this country it was, on the whole, a positive time.

The last word has to go to an earlier contributor:

Diana Scott

When I was twelve, the war ended and life slowly got back to normal, but the five years of war were perhaps the most memorable of my life and I am glad I lived through it.

LIST OF ILLUSTRATIONS

20 Hereward Hall, Ely; Wartime base of the J.F.S. © Christina Rex

21 Margaret Mould, age 5, in her grandparents' garden, 1942. © Margaret Mould

22 In Kilbirnie, Ayrshire, late 1940. Christina, Irene, Wendy Watt,
Grandma Mary B. Watt at back. © Christina Rex

23 Ruth Stobart, parents & brother. © Ruth Stobart

24 Helmi Spitze with her mother, 1940. © Helmi Spitze

25 Inner pages, Joan Hardy's father's Pay Book. © Joan Hardy

26 Goldman sisters, evacuated to Ely, with the daughter of the host family,
Renee Goldman, Maureen Goldman & Pamela Blakeman, Pearl Goldman.
© Pamela Blakeman

27 Linda Zerk & Jennifer with their home help/nanny, just
conscripted as a bus conductress. © Linda Zerk

28 Joan Hardy with her father. © Joan Hardy

29 A picture of the red stool Christmas present to Anna Piper. © Christina Rex

30 Jennifer Bedford's red striped dress; woollen bonnet & baby blanket
made from "other fabrics". © Christina Rex

31 Glenda Lindsay & sister Valerie with mother and family dog, c1942/43
© Glenda Lindsay

32 Mrs Ethel Smith, Gwen (now Pritchitt), Valerie. © Gwen Pritchitt

33 Gwen Pritchitt with doll "Daddy Soldier", elder sister Valerie, Oct.1943
© Gwen Pritchitt

34 Monette Meulet's trek to Aubusson. Picture realised by Nancy Voak from
a rough sketch by Monette Meulet. © Monette Meulet & Nancy Voak

35 Monette Meulet's round trip journey, Montauban - Aubusson - Montauban.
Map created by Christina Rex. Author's Collection

36 Anna Piper, held by her father and wearing his formal Wehrmacht cap. 1940
© Anna Piper

37 Christina Watt, clutching her beloved Grumpy, November 1939. © Christina Rex

38 Salute for a dead comrade, Egypt 1944. © Jean Runciman

39 Jean Runciman's father Charles V. Woodward, Royal Corps of Signals, near Cairo.
© Jean Runciman

40 Valerie Bragg with her parents. Her father committed suicide 4/9/1939.
© Valerie Bragg

41 C.F.S. girls working in school garden in Ely. Marie Sternlight, Peggy Skepelhorn,
Winnie Noble. © Muriel Gent

42 Prime Minister Churchill & Harold Macmillan in Beckenham c1943.
Anne Gordon third little girl on right. © Anne Gordon

43 Joy King's "Victory" Street Party, S.E. London, 1945. © Joy King

44 June Thomsitt with her parents, brother and younger sister, in Wales
before 1945. © June Thomsitt

45 Ely Market Square: Club Hotel sign and entry lane, right. (Originally
published 1906). © Ann Dix

79 Three soldiers. (Gwen Pritchitt's father, centre.) © Gwen Pritchitt
80 Jennifer Bedford, American serviceman's wife and her friend, early 1944
     © Jennifer Bedford
81 June Thomsitt (l), younger sister (r) and a friend, Wales, pre 1945. © June Thomsitt
82 Wendy Watt sitting on the front garden wall, W.Yorks. c1943. © Christina Rex
83 Margaret Mould on holiday at Bournemouth 1944. Note Coastal Defences!
     © Margaret Mould

RECOMMENDED FURTHER READING

These publications, selected from the writer's own library, are a purely personal recommendation of a few titles giving a wider perception of the children's war through the broader civilian war perspective. For each recommendation here, the interested reader will find several others on the shelves of the library or a good bookshop, to take the subject much further.

Adams, Dennis A. *Exodus to Ely*. 2001. Published privately, obtainable Ely Museum.
   A brief survey of the evacuation of Jews from the East End of London to Ely in 1939, and their sojourn in the small cathedral city and environs.
Briggs, Susan. *Keep Smiling Through*. Weidenfeld & Nicholson 1975.
   A survey of everyday wartime life compiled from contemporary sources.
Brown, Mike. *A Child's War*. Sutton 2000.
   A description of wartime daily life from the child's point of view, illustrated from contemporary sources; contemporary first person anecdotes.
Brown, Mike. *Evacuees*. Sutton, 2000.
   Factual narrative with contemporary eyewitness accounts.
Clark, Geseke, ed. *Hilke's Diary*. Tempus Publishing 2008.
   The rivetting wartime diary of a young girl growing up in Germany during the Second World War, essential reading.
Croall, Jonathan. *Don't you Know There's a War On?* Hutchinson 1988/Sutton 2005.
   Several lengthy essays/interviews surveying events on the Home Front by those who were there.
Gardner, Juliet. *The Children's War*. Portrait, with the Imperial War Museum, 2005.
   Produced to accompany the I.W.M exhibition of the same name.
Jordan, Marie. *A Wartime Childhood*. Ely Museum, 2001
   The recollections of a little girl living near Ely throughout the war.
Compilation *Make Do and Mend*, Michael O'Mara Books, 2007.
   Reproductions of Official World War II 'Make Do and Mend' leaflets, essential reading and in parts now hilarious.

Milbourn, Louise. *A Very Different War*. Privately Printed 2004.

The story of an evacuee sent to America during the Second World War.

Miller, Russell with Miller, Renate. *10 Days in May*. Michael Joseph 1995.

The lead up to VE Day or to the inevitability of defeat. Eye-witness stories from Allied and German sources.

Minns, Raynes. *Bombers and Mash*. Virago 1999.

A survey of the Domestic Front, 1939–45, with emphasis on cooking!

Mortimer, Gavin. *The Longest Night, 10 - 11 May 1941*. Weidenfeld & Nicholson 2005

Eye-witness accounts of the devastating last night of the London Blitz.

Oakey, Leslie. *Ely Goes to War*. Published by LJO for the Trustees of Ely Museum, 1995.

A survey of the war as it affected the small cathedral city of Ely.

(Pitkin) *Britain in the Blitz*. Pitkin Guide. Jarrold, 2003.

Thumbnail sketches of defining moments of World War II.

Waller J. & Vaughan-Rees M. Blitz, *The Civilian War 1940-45*. Macdonald Optima 1990.

Survey of all the blitzed cities, much first-person eye-witness narrative.